Rape at the Opera

MUSIC AND SOCIAL JUSTICE

Series Editors: William Cheng and Andrew Dell'Antonio

From Plato to Public Enemy, people have debated the relationship between music and justice—rarely arriving at much consensus over the art form's ethics and aesthetics, uses and abuses, virtues and vices. So what roles can music and musicians play in agendas of justice? And what should musicians and music scholars do if—during moments of upheaval, complacency, ennui— music ends up seemingly drained of its beauty, power, and even relevance?

Created by editors William Cheng and Andrew Dell'Antonio, this endeavor welcomes projects that shine new light on familiar subjects such as protest songs, humanitarian artists, war and peace, community formation, cultural diplomacy, globalization, and political resistance. Simultaneously, the series invites authors to critique and expand on what qualifies as justice—or, for that matter, music—in the first place.

TITLES IN THE SERIES

Improvising Across Abilities: Pauline Oliveros and the Adaptive Use Musical Instrument
The AUMI Editorial Collective

Rape at the Opera: Staging Sexual Violence
Margaret Cormier

Jamming the Classroom: Musical Improvisation and Pedagogical Practice
Ajay Heble and Jesse Stewart

On Music Theory, and Making Music More Welcoming for Everyone
Philip Ewell

For the Culture: Hip-Hop and the Fight for Social Justice
Lakeyta M. Bonnette-Bailey and Adolphus G. Belk, Jr., Editors

Sonorous Worlds: Musical Enchantment in Venezuela
Yana Stainova

Singing Out: GALA Choruses and Social Change
Heather MacLachlan

Performing Commemoration: Musical Reenactment and the Politics of Trauma
Annegret Fauser and Michael A. Figueroa, Editors

Sounding Dissent: Rebel Songs, Resistance, and Irish Republicanism
Stephen R. Millar

Rape at the Opera

STAGING

SEXUAL

VIOLENCE

Margaret Cormier

University of Michigan Press
Ann Arbor

For questions or permissions, please contact um.press.perms@umich.edu

Published in the United States of America by the
University of Michigan Press
Manufactured in the United States of America
Printed on acid-free paper
First published January 2024

A CIP catalog record for this book is available from the British Library.

Library of Congress Cataloging-in-Publication Data

Names: Cormier, Margaret, author.
Title: Rape at the opera : staging sexual violence / Margaret Cormier.
Other titles: Music and social justice.
Description: Ann Arbor : University of Michigan Press, [2024] | Series: Music and
    social justice | Includes bibliographical references and index.
Identifiers: LCCN 2023028643 | ISBN 9780472076291 (hardcover) |
    ISBN 9780472056293 (paperback) | ISBN 9780472903634 (ebook other)
Subjects: LCSH: Rape in opera. | Opera—Dramaturgy—History. | Opera—
    Production and direction—History. | Opera—Social aspects—History—
    21st century. | Opera—Political aspects—History—21st century.
Classification: LCC ML1700 .C69 2024 | DDC 782.1—dc23/eng/20230705
LC record available at https://lccn.loc.gov/2023028643

DOI: https://doi.org/10.3998/mpub.12324662

The University of Michigan Press's open access publishing program is made possible thanks to additional funding from the University of Michigan Office of the Provost and the generous support of contributing libraries.

Cover photograph: Salome's struggle against her attackers in *Salome*, directed by Atom Egoyan. Photograph © Michael Cooper, reprinted by permission.

Contents

Digital materials related to this title can be found on
the Fulcrum platform via the following citable URL:
https://doi.org/10.3998/mpub.12324662

Illustrations

Acknowledgments

I must begin by thanking Lloyd "Chip" Whitesell who advised me in what began as a seminar paper about Egoyan's *Salome* and grew into the dissertation that provided the groundwork for this book. I am extremely grateful for his mentorship, guidance, and friendship. I was fortunate to conduct a lot of this research at McGill University with the support of its faculty and students. I could not have completed this book without the support, advice, and encouragement of Sara Cohen, William Cheng, and Andrew Dell'Antonio at the University of Michigan Press. I am grateful to my reviewers, whose astute insights strengthened this work in a number of ways, and to Kevin Rennells, Cheryl Bowman, and Paula Durbin-Westby, for their contributions and support.

I am indebted to a number of opera company archives for sharing materials with me. Thank you to: Birthe Joergensen and the Canadian Opera Company; Isabel Kopf and the Komische Oper Berlin; Jane Fowler, Antonia Channer, and the Royal Opera House; Damien Kennedy and the English National Opera; Christoph Dittmann and the Aalto-Musiktheater; Holger Engelhardt and the Oper Frankfurt; Zach Bruman and Opera Atelier; as well as Stephanie Schulze, Christian Schröder, and Oliver Binder. I am especially grateful to Atom Egoyan and to Tilman Knabe for their help and encouragement, and for sharing video and print materials from their productions with me. It has been a great thrill to have their support.

Finally, thank you to my parents, whose unwavering support made this and any other undertaking feel in reach. And thank you to Dylan, who has read this work more carefully and more times than anyone, and who makes our home a safe and warm place to do this work.

I acknowledge the Social Sciences and Humanities Research Council for their support of some of this research. Research from chapter 4 also appears in Margaret Cormier, "Production as Criticism: Staging Wartime Rape in the Opera Canon," *Cambridge Opera Journal*, https://doi.org/10.1017/S0954586723000125, © Margaret Cormier, 2023, published by Cambridge University Press, reproduced with permission.

Introduction

In May 2018, I was in the audience of director Stephen Lawless's production of Donizetti's *Anna Bolena* at the Canadian Opera Company. Originally staged at the Met, Lawless's production was simple and effective, and it highlighted the stunning performance of Sondra Radvanovsky as the titular queen. The action takes place while Anna (Anne Boleyn) is married to Enrico (Henry VIII) but preoccupied with the memory of her first love, Riccardo (Henry Percy). In the third scene of Act 1, Riccardo finds Anna in her chambers and tells her he still loves her. Anna tells him to leave and asks that he not come to see her again. At this moment in the libretto, Riccardo draws his sword and attempts to kill himself. But in Lawless's production, after Riccardo sings "Let this be my answer to your oath," he pins Anna to her bed by her wrists and attempts to rape her until her screams alert a page who had been hiding nearby.[1] I was alarmed by this unexpected twist in the production, though there was no noticeable reaction from the audience en masse. I found myself suddenly perceiving Riccardo and his relationship with Anna completely differently. Would Lawless continue to explore this dark side of Riccardo's obsession throughout the rest of the opera? Would Anna's continuing love for Riccardo be represented differently in light of this attack? But there was no clear follow-through of this story line. This moment stood alone. Perhaps, I was left thinking, we were simply meant to excuse the attempted rape as a sign of Riccardo's uncontrollable desire for Anna.

Rape at the Opera is about the phenomenon of staging sexual violence in operas of the canon in the twenty-first century. The casual interpolation of rape into operas where there was no rape before is widespread. Since I began this research, friends and family members have contacted me regularly after attending productions of canonic operas across Europe and North America, commenting that since speaking to me, they are noticing subtle (and not so subtle) sexual violence everywhere. Contemporary approaches to staging sexual violence in opera are diverse and evaluating the potential for good and for ill in any one representation is necessarily subjective. Yet opera houses are filled with survivors and perpetrators of sexual assault—in the audience, on the stage, and in the wings—and in this context, it is crucial that we think carefully about how to approach depictions of sexual violence ethically. Where some directors explicitly respond to contemporary dialogues about sexual violence, others utilize sexual violence as a sure-fire way to titillate, to shock, and to generate press for a new production. *Rape at the Opera* highlights the dynamism of contemporary opera practice with regard to sexual violence in the canon, asking how opera practitioners represent sexual violence on today's opera stages, what work these representations do in our cultural moment, and how we productively conceive of the responsibilities of opera creators and spectators when it comes to representing sexual violence.

My point of departure for this book is the discomfort I felt sitting in the audience of *Anna Bolena* and so many other opera stagings throughout my experience as a singer, researcher, and lover of the opera canon. Ellie Hisama has suggested the value that can come from approaching music analysis from a place of repulsion as opposed to the more common entry point of enjoyment. Her critical-affective analysis of the music of John Zorn engages her feelings of being objectified, devalued, and disrespected by his representations of Asian women.[2] My own analytical approach to the staged productions in this book builds outward from my experiences of unease with the way sexual violence is treated (or, in many cases, not treated) in performances of canonic operas. Over the years, I have spoken to many women and gender-queer friends who have shared my feeling of being alienated by productions of and discourse about opera when it comes to sexual violence. I hope that one of the results of sharing my critical perspective on the works in this book is that some readers may see some of their own experiences of discomfort reflected in mine. I invite all readers, and especially those with perspectives that have been historically unrecognized and unaccounted for in opera criticism and production, to reflect on and take seriously their own experiences with this art form.

Opera's Sexual Violence Problem

While this book is about representations of sexual violence onstage, I must acknowledge from the outset that sexual violence is also disturbingly commonplace in the opera industry. Longstanding problems with specific powerful men in the industry and with the culture of opera and classical music more generally came to popular attention in a new way in the wake of the #MeToo movement. Tarana Burke began using the phrase "me too" online in 2006 as an activist refrain about the prevalence of sexual violence in our society. In 2017, a number of high-profile allegations of abuse and harassment against the producer Harvey Weinstein spurred an online movement in which survivors of sexual violence shared their stories with #MeToo. This movement brought sexual violence out of the shadows and highlighted the immense scale of our society's problem with misogynistic violence. As more survivors came forward with their stories, more alleged sexual abusers faced criminal charges or social consequences as a result of public accusations.

The Metropolitan Opera's dismissal of conductor and long-time music director James Levine in 2018 and allegations against opera star Plácido Domingo are only the highest-profile examples of a much greater reckoning with sexual abuse and harassment within the operatic community around this time.[3] In the opera industry, singers can be particularly vulnerable to predation and abuse by their superiors and mentors given the stark power differential in rehearsal rooms and teachers' studios. The present study does not engage with the experience of singers negotiating sexual violence onstage and offstage, but this is a vital area for further inquiry. The absence of the performer's perspective here serves my focus on the cultural work representations of sexual violence do in the world. Yet engagement with the experiences and points of view of more opera practitioners will no doubt enrich continuing work on the politics of operatic production.

On the stage, sexual violence pervades the performance canon. Consider the ten most-performed operas worldwide from the 2018–2019 season: *La Traviata, Die Zauberflöte, La Bohème, Carmen, Tosca, Madama Butterfly, Il barbiere di Siviglia, Rigoletto, Don Giovanni,* and *Le nozze di Figaro.*[4] Half of these operas blatantly feature sexual violence or the threat of sexual violence in their libretti: *Die Zauberflöte, Tosca,* and *Don Giovanni* contain attempted rapes; in *Rigoletto,* the Duke's "seduction" of Gilda offstage can be readily understood as an act of violence; and the central conflict of *Le nozze di Figaro* is that the Count wants to have sexual intercourse with Susanna against her will. Even in the other half of the list, sexual violence is often implicit: the intimacy between Pinkerton and Cio-Cio San in *Madama Butterfly* can readily be interpreted as nonconsensual given her youth and his dishonesty; the plot of *Il barbiere di Siviglia* centers around the threat of a forced marriage; and *Carmen* ends with an act of intimate partner violence.

The sexual violence in the plots of these operas tends to be downplayed in the way they are taught and staged. I majored in voice performance during my undergraduate degree and was introduced to several of these works in the context of learning the soprano roles. I sang Zerlina, and I remember agreeing with my teachers and peers that the duet this young peasant bride-to-be sings with the aristocratic Don Giovanni works best if she has already decided to have sex with him before telling him "no" over and over. I sang Susanna, and we talked about how much more interesting the drama in *Le nozze di Figaro* is if the young maid Susanna is attracted to the Count who wants to have sex with her on the night of her marriage to another man. Insisting that these men are irresistible and the women around them harbor secret passions for them softens the sharp edges of these stories. As long as these women want it, and as long as we are all sure that they do (practically as a matter of faith), then it's not rape. I didn't think these operas were about sexual violence; sure, the women say no, but we know that they don't mean it. These interpretations, especially of *Don Giovanni,* were so pervasive and so consistent that for years it never occurred to me to interpret these operas or these characters any differently. And beyond that, these interpretations of the story didn't bother me. I was a politically progressive young woman who proudly identified with feminism, and I still didn't see the narratives of force and nonconsent at the center of my favorite operas.

It is an act of reparation, then, recognizing the sexual violence that I once ignored, to name this book *Rape at the Opera.* Calling what the Duke does to Gilda a seduction and calling Don Giovanni a womanizer is part of the problem.[5] "Rape" is a powerful word and a word that I understand is difficult for some readers. But I am troubled by the idea that using the word rape to say, for instance, "The Count plans to rape Susanna on her wedding night," is more shocking to some opera lovers than the plot point to which it refers. I believe that naming sexual violence and its perpetrators in this context is powerful in part because it highlights this disconnect. Many operatic rapes and attempted rapes happen in the shadows just offstage. My hope is that by using this language and by writing this book, I can spotlight something many fans, scholars, and practitioners of opera might rather not think about at all.

While the sexual violence of the canon is routinely understated and obscured by innuendo and ambiguity, acts of sexual violence are mainstays of contemporary opera performance practice, especially in the school of *Regietheater.* Frequently evoked as a castigation, the terms *Regietheater* and *Regieoper* (director's theater or director's opera) refer to the modern practice of granting freedom to the director to alter or disregard stage directions and indications about mise-en-scène in the texts they stage. *Regietheater* productions break with traditional interpretations of a work, frequently in a provocative manner, in the service of speaking to a modern audience and drawing parallels to modern ideas. Axel Englund argues that all *Regietheater* can be understood in terms of perversion because it flagrantly disregards the ideal of fidelity to works of the canon typically treated with reverence.[6] But although *Regietheater* is characterized by its rejection of norms regarding staging canonic operas, in practice, it has developed its own set of tropes; Englund writes at length about the pervasiveness of iconography of fetishism and BDSM, for example. Sex and violence are mainstays of the *Regietheater* aesthetic, typically represented with onstage nudity and gore.[7] Popular criticism of *Regietheater* productions typically argues that including sex and violence in canonic operas is inappropriate and a clear violation of the meaning of the operas. This is a limited interpretation. While it is true that many of the onstage representations of sex and violence that *Regietheater* productions may feature are not indicated in the stage directions, these themes are rarely as foreign to the operas as conservative critics make them out to be. As Englund notes, "opera has been scandalizing audiences for centuries through its lack of proper sexual morals."[8] I believe that *Regietheater* representations of sex and violence offend so many audiences not because they are foreign to the operas of the canon, but because they reveal something uncomfortable about that canon.

Sexual violence is central to the opera canon, despite its chronic omission from opera history, criticism, and pedagogy. Teachers, critics, scholars, and fans are frequently ignorant to the sexual violence that pervades so many of these stories. Yet at the same time, productions of canonic operas routinely feature acts of sexual violence, some of which are included in the operas' libretti and many of which are not. In the wider culture of opera in North America and Europe, sexual violence feels somehow invisible and flagrant at the same time. It lies just beneath the surface, and its position there is guarded by opera scholars and practitioners who do not see or will not acknowledge it, and by opera critics who vehemently reject its inclusion in staging and production. Given this curious ambivalence, I am interested in the specific ways sexual violence is staged in modern productions of canonic operas. The operas of the performance canon that make up the core repertory of most opera houses are at least one hundred years old. There are some notable exceptions, to be sure, but most of the opera that a typical opera-goer sees comes from a relatively short period circa 1780 to 1920 (roughly Mozart to Puccini). But when these works are staged today, regardless of their age, they are put into conversation with the cultures in which they are performed and the individuals who perform and receive them. I conceive of opera production and reception fundamentally as public discourse. Opera directors, designers, and singers are beholden not only to the composers' and librettists' written texts, but also, vitally, to contemporary producers, audiences, and critics. There are often vast social and political discrepancies between the culture in which a canonic opera was written and our own. It is up to opera performers and producers to make the practical decisions about how and whether to address this tension in the way they put these works onstage. When it comes to sexual violence, these negotiations between an opera's content and contemporary ideals become especially consequential.

Opera in Production

When I address the latent (and not so latent) sexual violence and misogyny present in the libretti of many beloved operas, I walk on well-tread ground. There is a rich history of scholarship on violence against women in opera extending back to Catherine Clément's landmark book, *Opera, or the Undoing of Women*.[9] And recent years have seen the expansion of this work specifically in regards to sexual violence in opera.[10] I continue this work here, taking up the project of resistance by critiquing the way operatic sexual violence is staged in the twenty-first century and the influence these representations have on our understandings of canonic operas and of sexual violence in our own culture. Naomi André calls this kind of approach, which is sensitive to the present-day relevance of historical works, an "engaged musicology."[11]

In general, serious consideration of operatic production and staging lags behind score-based studies of opera. Roger Parker has noted that "the musicological establishment has tended to be indifferent or even hostile to the visual aspect of musical drama."[12] But opera is a performed art form and overlooking production and staging results in a necessarily incomplete understanding of how these works convey meaning to their audiences.[13] The tension that can arise in meaning between an opera's score and its performance is a central issue in studies of operatic production, and it necessitates careful use of language around the operatic text. I will make the distinction throughout this book between an opera's "written text" and its "performance text." Following David Levin, I adopt Roland Barthes's distinction between texts and works, and conceive of operas as the former.[14] Whereas a work is a "fragment of substance," a text "is experienced only in an activity of production."[15] Texts are irreducibly plural, containing multiple meanings, interpretations, and possibilities.[16] Levin distinguishes what he calls the "opera text," comprising the score, libretto, and stage directions, from the "performance text."[17] I prefer "written text" to "opera text" because I believe that the category "opera" exists in performance just as much (indeed, more) than it exists on the page.

Feminist Spectatorship

The production analyses in this book center a critical feminist spectator—namely me—who may not be the intended addressee of many of these productions.[18] Mine is an alternative perspective on opera as much because of my feminist political alignment as my gender identity as a woman.[19] While neither of these traits are uncommon among opera scholars or the opera-going public, neither are well accounted for in the ways we discuss, produce, and respond to opera overall. Clément famously shared such a feminist, women-centered perspective by criticizing opera's reliance on the suffering and death of women.[20] Though her book made waves in the opera world, the general tone with which we continue to teach and promote operas about the murder and abuse of women indicates that this perspective is still not accounted for. When I see sexual violence onstage at the opera, more often than not, I feel consciously that I am reacting incorrectly—more specifically, that I do not feel the way the production wants me to feel. In some cases, amid signals that what is happening onstage is funny or romantic, I feel alienated in my sense of revulsion at what I recognize as sexual violence. In other cases, where rape is presented explicitly, what I suspect is meant to trigger somber reflection on the harsh realities of our world instead makes me feel unsafe in my skin.

My positionality as an opera critic engages not only my experiences as a woman but my ethical and political priorities. The analysis and evaluation of the productions in this book are grounded in an ethics of care and draw from trauma studies, legal discourse, and feminist perspectives on sexual violence. I conceive of rape as fundamentally an act of power and domination that is carried out through sex and sexuality. In general, not nearly enough is made of rape's violence and its political motivations of power and control. Instead, sexual violence is often excused as an excess or misplacement of passion and lust. This is true in public discourse and media responses to real rape cases, but it plays out in the way rape is represented in opera as well. In publicity materials and popular media surrounding productions of *Don Giovanni*, for instance, the titular Don is frequently described as a "ladies' man,"[21] but this label (along with "womanizer" or "Lothario") represents Giovanni's nonconsensual conquest of the women in the opera as having everything to do with his sexual charisma and downplays or ignores the violence that he relies on throughout the action. Along with the ineradicable violence of rape, my analysis depends on the seriousness of rape and its consequences to victims. I argue that these consequences can extend to fictional representations of rape insofar as they pose risks to survivors of sexual assault and contribute to public discourse about sexual violence. The following case study is an illustrative example of the way operatic production works as public discourse and establishes the stakes of staging sexual violence in the twenty-first century.

Care Ethics

In 2015, the Royal Opera House (ROH) premiered a new production of Rossini's *Guillaume Tell* directed by Damiano Michieletto. Before opening night, a number of industry professionals and friends of the company attended the dress rehearsal and were the first to see Michieletto's staging. During the ballet scene in the third act, a Swiss woman was stripped and sexually assaulted by a group of Austrian soldiers while the audience uncharacteristically shouted and booed. Opera singer Catharine Woodward (Catharine Rogers at the time) was in the audience of the open dress rehearsal, and she submitted a customer service form on the ROH website after the performance. She wrote that she was in "tears of shock" during the ballet scene, which she found to be "the worst kind of gratuitous," and advised that "at the very least . . . the performance should come with a strong warning, as I have many friends I would love to take to the opera, who have been the victims of sexual violence, I would never forgive myself if I subjected them to what I saw on Friday."[22] ROH General Director Kasper Holten responded to Woodward directly in an email, which she reproduced on her blog. He also wrote an open letter addressing Woodward and others who were upset, which was published on music journalist and provocateur Norman Lebrecht's classical music gossip blog, Slipped Disc. In his response, Holten defends the production for representing "the reality of warfare," but he also apologizes "for [the ROH] not issuing a strong and clear enough warning." He reflects that audience members "should be able to make an informed choice about what they want to see or not, and if an audience member does not want to be exposed to sexual violence, it should be their choice."[23]

Woodward focuses her argument on the risks that representations of rape pose to survivors of sexual violence. In her blog post, she cites an article reporting that approximately one in two women in Britain have been physically or sexually assaulted.[24] In his first response to Woodward's letter, Holten writes that given the opera's topic of war and oppression, "it is important that we do not only allow [Rossini's] opera to become harmless entertainment today."[25] Holten uses the language of harm in a figurative way here—he wants audiences to be made uncomfortable so that they will think critically about the opera's politics—but Woodward is calling attention to real psychological and physiological harm when she talks about her fear for survivors of sexual assault who will attend this production. Woodward is referring to a kind of retraumatization in which post-traumatic stress reactions can be triggered or exacerbated by stressors that are not necessarily traumatic in and of themselves. These stressors can include reminders of the original traumatic experience like, in this example, a staged representation of a sexual assault. Holten writes in his Slipped Disc letter that although the scene was meant to be upsetting, he had "no intention to disturb people in the way Catharine describes."[26]

Woodward's and Holten's different uses of language of harm in relation to viewing a representation of sexual violence amount to a misunderstanding about the stakes at play. Holten seems initially reluctant to issue a specific warning about the sexual violence in *Tell* because he believes that the scene should be shocking and should make audience members uncomfortable in service of the director's commentary on the reality of war and war crimes. Woodward, on the other hand, is not advocating for herself in her discomfort but for sexual violence survivors who may be living with PTSD. Her position echoes a foundational idea of modern psychiatry, that "trauma is qualitatively different from stress and results in lasting biological change."[27] When Woodward asks Holten to warn audiences about the explicit display of sexual violence in this production, she is not worried about discomfort. Rather, she is trying to make space for survivors of sexual violence to make an informed decision about their capacity to engage with this production in a way that does not threaten their psychological and physiological wellbeing.

Behind these two different understandings of harm, I also recognize two different moral frameworks. In her landmark 1982 book *In a Different Voice*, Carol Gilligan proposes a dichotomy between a conception of morality as justice, concerned with rights and rules, and a conception of morality as care, concerned with responsibility and relationships.[28] Gilligan argues that the ethic of justice, which had been characterized by psychologists as the most mature human morality, values masculine qualities of autonomy and rationality.[29] She identifies an alternate morality, an ethic of care, which she suggests may be just as mature in other ways. The distinction between an ethic of justice and an ethic of care is perceptible in Holten and Woodward's exchange. Holten's engagement with the question of what the ROH owes its audience is based on a concept of rights when he offers to include a stronger content warning so that audience members can choose whether they are exposed to sexual violence or not. This measure does not really respond to Woodward's complaint. She says that "at the very least" the production should come with a stronger warning, but her focus is on the effect that the production will have on survivors of sexual violence. She is not asking for justice, but for care. She is asking ROH leadership to take responsibility for her experience and the experiences of the women in her life who stand to be hurt by this production, but she does not suggest it is their obligation to do so.

Care as an ethical framework has been dismissed by some critics as too narrow and personal to be taken seriously as a type of moral thinking on a large scale.[30] Care is often relegated to private life, the home, and interpersonal relationships, in part due to its association with women. This need not be the case, though. Joan Tronto argues that although Gilligan conceives of the ethic of care almost entirely in terms of personal relationships, individuals also have connections to larger units such as their communities.[31] By Tronto's account, "caring seems to involve taking the concerns and needs of the other as the basis for action."[32] This expanded notion of care reaches beyond private life and relationships into the social and political spheres. It is this larger, political orientation toward care that Catharine Woodward invokes when she objects to Michieletto's *Guillaume Tell*. While she begins with the realm of the private—her friends whom she does not wish to expose to the rape scene—she quickly extends this care framework to her community by citing statistics about the percentage of women in Britain who have been victimized by sexual violence. In her initial message to the ROH, Woodward invites Holten to better understand others by sharing her experience as a woman viewing this production and by exhorting him to imagine, as she has, the needs of women who have survived sexual and physical violence. She is asking him to care insofar as caring, according to Tronto, involves recognizing and attending to the needs of others. Holten accepted this invitation to care by revisiting the staging of the ballet scene. Upon being alerted to the effect this scene had on Woodward (among other audience members who complained), he modified the scene with the needs of the other—specifically women in the ROH audience—in mind.

Throughout *Rape at the Opera*, I propose a model of evaluating operatic performances that holds care for the audience in mind. Theater scholar James Thompson has begun to work toward applying an ethic of care in the context of community-based and applied forms of theater. While Thompson's primary focus is on relational practices between artists, his conception of an aesthetic of care has wider implications. I am particularly interested in Thompson's brief discussion of the relationship with the audience, where he advocates for a move beyond a suspicious posture to one where the experiences and reactions of the spectator are not assumed.[33] This suspicious posture is seen clearly in the way that the creators of *Regietheater* productions typically engage their audiences. The desire to shock and disrupt an audience into productive discomfort takes for granted many assumptions about the members of that audience. In the example of the ROH *Guillaume Tell*, Michieletto and Holten are concerned with jolting complacent opera fans out of their revery and forcing them to contemplate the horrors of war. But as Woodward points out, this approach ignores all those audience members with an intimate, personal knowledge of violence and sexual assault who might be hurt by this content. Thompson argues that "caring for an audience means thinking hard about their experiences and needs. This is not to say they should witness insipid unchallenging presentations, but an event should model a caring insight into the different conditions of engagement."[34] Evaluating the extent to which a production models a caring insight, per Thompson, will obviously be an imprecise practice. I do not wish to get mired in arguments about intentionality. Instead, in the analyses that follow, I am looking for a balance between the shock of representing sexual violence onstage and what those representations accomplish in the narratives of the operas. From time to time, the voices of directors figure into my analysis, especially when they reveal choices made with real or imagined audience reactions in mind. Similarly, I engage the voices of critics and other audience members to take the proverbial temperature of the live reaction to productions (especially those I could not attend in person).

• • •

Rape at the Opera focuses on the performance texts of a number of operatic productions over twenty years of practice that feature representations of sexual violence. I do not judge the productions I study as merely acceptable or unacceptable approaches to challenging material. Rather, I highlight the diversity of approaches to and reception of staged acts of sexual violence in the twenty-first century. My analysis of the representations of sexual violence in this book focuses on the wellbeing of audience members and the health of the social body, foregrounding the experiences of those individuals who are most likely to be put at risk by careless depictions of sexual violence, especially survivors of sexual assault.

My case studies represent an array of operas from German, Italian, and French traditions from the eighteenth to the early twentieth century. Some of the operas in this book are here because the written texts feature sexual violence in relatively explicit ways that can be amplified or obscured in performance, especially the two Mozart selections, *Don Giovanni* and *Die Entführung aus dem Serail*. The other operas do not necessarily thematize sexual violence in their written texts. In some cases, sexual violence may be implied and made explicit in performance (*Salome*, *Turandot*, *Guillaume Tell*), and in others it is absent from the written texts and embedded in the operas only due to the agency of directors (*Un ballo in maschera*, *La forza del destino*). There are a couple of notable absences that might stand out to readers familiar with this topic: Benjamin Britten's *The Rape of Lucretia* and Carlisle Floyd's *Susannah*. Unlike any of the operas in this book, these two operas are *about* rape. They tell the stories of the violent rapes of innocent young women whose lives are destroyed as a result of their assaults.[35] The ways that these rapes are represented on opera stages is certainly important and politically charged. Regardless of the particulars of the stagings, however, the written texts of these two operas take for granted the fact that rape is a serious and violent crime that does lasting damage to its victims. This approach to rape is unusual in the opera canon. Much more common is the burying, obscuring, and glossing over of rape seen in productions of and discourse around operas that include or thematize rape but are not about rape. It is this latter category that I am predominantly interested in for the sake of this book because it encompasses such a large percentage of the operas currently being performed. Sexual violence is particularly insidious in those operas where it lurks just below the surface or where it is added in production. In the *Anna Bolena* production with which I opened this book, the intrusion of sexual violence into the scene between Anna and Riccardo, and the almost offhanded nature of its inclusion, was an unsettling reminder of the omnipresence of sexual violence in our culture. Similarly, in the operas I discuss in this book, I am interested in the way sexual violence emerges from or intrudes into operas that do not set out to comment on it.

The four body chapters of *Rape at the Opera* each focus on the analysis of discrete constellations of operatic performances. Individually, each chapter works as a case study for some of the concerns and challenges of staging sexual violence in the twenty-first century. Together, they model a multifaceted analytical approach that moves between concerns located within the fictional world of the opera and those located without. Over the course of these chapters, I establish five critical axes for evaluating representations of sexual violence on the opera stage: (1) the agency of the characters who are victims of sexual violence, (2) rape myths and stereotypes, (3) depictions of sexual violence in and as performance, (4) the risks and limits of using sexual violence as a tool of critique, and (5) sexual violence as a metaphor for other atrocities. The analytical approach of my chapter structure is additive; each subsequent chapter introduces one or two new axes of analysis while continuing to apply those established in previous chapters.

I start, in chapter 1, with the opera that begins many conversations about opera and sexual violence: Mozart's *Don Giovanni*. I analyze key moments from six productions of *Don Giovanni* between 2002 and 2019 from the perspective of a viewer versed in twenty-first century feminist politics. I introduce the first two axes of analysis for this book: the agency of the women who are victimized by sexual violence, and the relationship between onstage depictions of sexual violence and twenty-first-century rape myths and stereotypes. Although the opera's plot is propelled by two acts of attempted rape, the precise nature of these acts and what they mean have been interpreted and reinterpreted by critics, scholars, and performers for centuries. I focus on the representation of the three women, Donna Anna, Donna Elvira, and Zerlina, considered through three lenses central to contemporary feminist thought on the topic: consent, trauma, and believing victims. The approaches to *Don Giovanni* taken by these six productions inform the way their audiences understand the characters and story of the opera, but they also contribute to the culture in which they are performed and received. Ultimately, I argue that thinking through how sexual violence is represented in this opera is not just an issue of dramatic and aesthetic quality, but of social responsibility.

In chapter 2, I turn to a trend in recent productions of Strauss's *Salome* that sees directors using stage action during the Dance of the Seven Veils to position Salome as a victim of sexual abuse committed by her stepfather, Herod. I analyze the Salome-as-rape-victim trope and evaluate the ways in which sexual violence in these productions shapes perceptions of Salome's character and complicates the element of erotic spectacle at the center of the opera's plot. This chapter introduces a third axis of analysis through its exploration of the problems with representing sexual violence in the context of performance—both Salome's dance as a performance within the world of the opera and *Salome* itself as a performance for opera-goers. I introduce a collection of fourteen *Salome* productions between 2008 and 2018, all of which use the Dance of the Seven Veils as an opportunity to introduce sexual abuse to the opera's action or as a vehicle for disclosing a past sexual abuse. Staging a rape in this scene encourages the audience to view Salome's abuse as an erotic spectacle, and representing Salome as a rape victim serves to explain her violent desire for Jochanaan and strips her of much of her power and agency in the story. Some of these interpretations of Salome as a victim can humanize her and encourage an audience to sympathize with her in a new way, but they also qualify and pathologize every choice she makes in the opera. The most successful productions according to my framework are those that find ways to grant new agency to Salome's character in light of the agency she loses when her violence toward Jochanaan is pathologized—specifically, those that stage acts of retribution not included in the opera's written text.

In chapter 3, I introduce my fourth critical axis for analysis that considers the limits and risks of criticizing problematic elements of canonic operas through production. I contrast the different approaches to the violence in the written text in two productions of Mozart's *Die Entführung aus dem Serail*: Calixto Bieito's infamous 2004 production for the Komische Oper Berlin and Wajdi Mouawad's 2016 production co-commissioned by Opéra Lyon and the Canadian Opera Company. Bieito's *Entführung* takes seriously and amplifies the threats of violence and torture that litter the opera's libretto. The resulting production stages multiple rapes and murders of sex workers. Mouawad takes a different approach to the themes of violence and non-consent in *Entführung*, attempting to neutralize them almost entirely by means of an ambitious reconceptualization of the narrative aimed at a reparative representation of the Turkish characters. These productions both offer pointed critiques of some element of *Die Entführung*'s content, but both have only limited success. Bieito's production uses its excruciating depictions of graphic violence to highlight the violence already pervasive in the opera, but he perpetuates some of the harm of the opera even as he critiques it by objectifying women's bodies in his staging. Mouawad humanizes the Turkish men in the opera, but in so doing, he asks us to ignore or to forgive their threats of violence including specific references to torture and rape. Through comparison of these productions, I demonstrate—perhaps counterintuitively—that the choice *not* to represent sexual violence onstage is not necessarily preferable from a feminist ethical standpoint.

Chapter 4 draws together all the axes of analysis introduced in the previous chapters and adds one more that considers the hazards of employing sexual violence as a metaphor for other forms of violence. I analyze four productions of four different operas which are all set by their directors at wartime and feature explicit representations of sexual violence not included in the operas' libretti. Damiano Michieletto's 2015 *Guillaume Tell* for the Royal Opera House is set in a twentieth-century war zone inspired by a number of real-world conflicts including the Balkan crisis; Tobias Kratzer's 2019 production of Verdi's *La forza del destino* for Oper Frankfurt sets the third act during the War in Vietnam; Tilman Knabe's 2007 production of Puccini's *Turandot* for the Aalto Theater Essen takes place in a contemporary authoritarian state; and Calixto Bieito's 2000 production of Verdi's *Un ballo in maschera* for the Gran Teatre del Liceu is set in a contemporary police state. These wartime opera productions survey some of the most prominent ways in which the metaphorical weight of wartime rape can be harnessed to raise the stakes of stories about political strife. However, employing rape as a stand in for other kinds of violence dilutes the interpersonal meanings of rape for individual victims.

Together, my production analyses sketch a picture of the complexity and plurality of the creative undertaking and spectatorial response associated with opera and sexual violence today. They also reveal central problems inherent to representing sexual violence onstage. My conclusion reflects on the potential of production to change the way we interact with the opera canon and the stories we tell when we perform these works. *Regietheater* can be a powerful tool in the service of creating opera in a way that is responsive and responsible to its public, provided it can mitigate the risks of representing sexual violence and other charged themes. I close this book with recommendations for the improvement of this powerful resource: first, by making space for more diverse voices in direction and production, and second, by centering both care for audiences and care for performers through practices of intimacy direction.

Rape at the Opera reframes the primary responsibility of opera critics and creators as being not to opera composers and librettists (many of whom are long dead) but to the public. In the best cases, staging sexual violence can allow for nuanced commentary on the subject in our cultural moment and can open up space for new understandings of familiar stories and characters. But the risks of staging sexual violence are ever present. Ultimately, through my analysis of sexual violence, I want to open up a new chapter of opera criticism that takes the ethical and the political as central and not peripheral to the enterprise of staging and production.

One

Staging Rape Myths in *Don Giovanni*

Don Giovanni is a fraught subject in conversations about opera and sexual violence. On its surface, the story of *Don Giovanni* is very simple: Giovanni has sex with as many women as he can, even when they don't want to, and he is punished for his misdeeds. Yet this opera has had a rich history of interpretation that has resisted its categorization as a simple morality tale. Don Giovanni has been at various times a hero of the Enlightenment, an embodiment of the will, and a cunning sexual predator. And the written text of *Don Giovanni*, especially the richness of its music, has the capacity to support a diversity of interpretations effectively. This characteristic of the work elevates the role that staging plays in its interpretation. The written text of *Don Giovanni* is replete with ambiguity which may be accentuated or (at least partially) resolved in performance.

Over the years, *Don Giovanni* has no doubt lost some historical meanings as it has acquired new ones. Audiences today may be less sensitive to references to Commedia del'Arte archetypes and they may be less likely to interpret Giovanni as a Romantic hero. Different elements of the story and different interpretations begin to come to the fore when we approach *Don Giovanni* in light of our current cultural values and experiences. In this chapter, I focus on the way twenty-first century productions of *Don Giovanni* interact with contemporary rhetoric around sexual violence. On the question of sexual violence in *Don Giovanni*, the representation of Giovanni himself certainly matters; staging choices can make him more or less sympathetic and more or less desirable to the audience. But I am particularly interested in the way the women in the opera are represented in production. I find that the way Donna Anna, Donna Elvira, and Zerlina respond to Don Giovanni to be a powerful indicator of a production's take on the nature of his crimes. A focus on the women also centers a feminist perspective on the opera's story, which I believe is vital to understanding this work in the twenty-first century.[1]

I have seen a lot of productions of *Don Giovanni*. For many years, it was my favorite opera and I sought out video recordings wherever I could find them. It is a favorite work not just of professional opera houses but of amateur groups and university opera programs as well. The six productions I analyze here are not representative of productions of this opera in the twenty-first century in general. I have chosen them in order to paint as broad a picture as I can about the diversity of contemporary performance practice for this opera. Different productions here have different relationships with the written text. Some of these stagings are more radical and interventionist, featuring different settings and stage action than Mozart and Da Ponte indicated, and others are more conservative. There is no single typical production of *Don Giovanni* of course, but there are patterns and tropes that I have grown quite sensitive to after viewing dozens of productions of this opera.

The following six productions span seventeen years of practice. Calixto Bieito's 2002 production for the Gran Teatre del Liceu breaks the most with the written text of the opera. It is set in Barcelona's abandoned Olympic village circa 2000, and the class distinction between the characters is collapsed; they all drink, smoke, do drugs, and have sex throughout the course of the action. Francesca Zambello's 2008 production for the Royal Opera House is much more traditional, representing a chic, minimalist seventeenth-century setting in its costume and set design.[2] Jonathan Kent's 2010 production for the Glyndebourne Festival is another modern-dress production, though this setting is less specific than Bieito's and the costuming maintains the sense of class difference between the peasants and the aristocracy. Jean-François Sivadier's 2017 production for Festival d'Aix-en-Provence highlights the timelessness of the story with minimalist costuming and set pieces that resist any particular setting. Rufus Norris's 2010 production for the English National Opera also appears to be set in roughly the modern day and, like Bieito, Norris adds significant stage action not present in the opera's written text. Finally, Marshall Pynkoski's 2019 production for Opera Atelier is set in the seventeenth century and features period dance and gesture. My analysis focuses on six scenes that exemplify the way these productions represent the women of the opera as victims of abuse. My focus is on the stage action, which is variable among all of these productions. Close readings of the selected scenes are particularly sensitive to two analytical axes: the agency of the characters who are victims of sexual violence, and the interaction of the stage action with twenty-first-century rape myths and stereotypes. A table in the appendix includes general notes on the directors' approaches to help keep the productions straight throughout this chapter.

The amount of agency asserted by the women in *Don Giovanni* is highly variable among the different productions surveyed here. In the opera's written text, Donna Anna, Donna Elvira, and Zerlina all make choices and take actions to influence the story around them: Anna seeks revenge for her father's murder, Elvira warns the other women about Giovanni's true nature, and Zerlina repairs her relationship with her fiancé. But the impact these actions actually have on the world of the opera is largely determined by the staging. Some of these directors accentuate the ways in which the women are powerless by representing them as injured and traumatized and highlighting how much stronger the men around them are. Others give the women opportunities—sometimes beyond what is afforded them in the written text—to assert themselves and to connect and communicate with one another. The question of consent is especially central to the representation of agency in this opera. A director's choices can inform the ways and the extent to which we believe these women are capable of giving consent to men who wield incredible power over them physically, socially, and financially.

The representations of sexual violence in these productions of *Don Giovanni* are in dialogue with contemporary beliefs and narratives about rape. I am particularly interested in the ways that these productions alternately challenge or reinforce rape myths. Rape myths are common, prejudicial beliefs about sexual violence that serve to excuse perpetrators and discredit victims. Prominent examples that come up in this chapter include the ideas that women routinely lie about rape for revenge and that women secretly want to be raped. The common parlance of calling these ideas myths can lead to some confusion. It is not controversial, for instance, that some women have lied about sexual assault or have said no to a sexual encounter when they meant yes. But when media representation amplifies anti-victim stereotypes about sexual violence, public perception can become skewed and real-life victims are put in the position of having their own stories doubted based on their resemblance to the stereotype.[3] In the context of opera, choices about how fictional sexual violence plays out are entirely at the discretion of the creative team behind the production. It is worth thinking about how these productions as cultural texts interact with popular ideas and conceptions about sexual violence.

At the intersection of the axes of agency and rape myths is the question of trauma associated with sexual violence. One rape myth common to news coverage of sexual violence is the idea that rape is just sex and does not need to be taken seriously as a violent crime.[4] In reality, sexual violence is the type of trauma associated with the highest conditional risk for development of post-traumatic stress disorder.[5] These productions vary greatly in their representations of trauma in the characters of Donna Anna, Donna Elvira, and Zerlina. In some cases, depicting the trauma responses in these women leads to a nuanced exploration of the relationship between trauma and agency in the aftermath of sexual violence. In other cases, the absence or careless depiction of trauma suggests that rape and attempted rape are inconveniences from which women can easily move on. Onstage, realistic representations of trauma can shape an audience's understanding and move their sympathies. The way that a production of *Don Giovanni* represents the suffering of the women is closely related to how seriously it takes Giovanni's crimes.

Act 1, Scene 1

The first two scenes I analyze concern the noblewoman Donna Anna and her encounter with Don Giovanni that spurs the opera into motion. *Don Giovanni* opens with Leporello standing guard outside a house while Don Giovanni, his master, is inside with a woman. Donna Anna and Don Giovanni enter the stage in a flurry of action: Anna clutches at Giovanni, crying for help and vowing not to let him escape, while Giovanni insists that she will never discover his identity. Typically, we do not see what happened between the pair inside the house. Instead, we infer what happened inside based on the way Donna Anna and Don Giovanni interact during this scene, which varies fairly significantly in these productions.

Costuming and staging of this scene typically makes it immediately clear that Don Giovanni's villainy offstage had to do with an unwanted sexual advance. In nearly all these productions, Donna Anna appears in sleepwear or underclothes with her hair loose, indicating that Giovanni, who is masked, has interrupted her in a vulnerable, private moment. Of the five productions that stage this fight between Anna and Giovanni, four depict Giovanni kissing or groping Anna throughout the encounter so that we see at least some of the sexual violence we imagine happened offstage.[6] More often than not, Anna's attempts to control Giovanni's movements—either to stop him from escaping, or to stop him from kissing and touching her body—are ineffective. She is typically depicted as physically much weaker than Giovanni, and her attempts to injure or restrain him prove futile. Sivadier's Anna stands out as an exception here as she is more than a match for Giovanni physically. She is only bested when Leporello joins in the fight to pull her away from his master. On one hand, it is satisfying to see Donna Anna portrayed in this exceptional case as strong and capable of defending herself. But I am also sensitive to rape myths about the ways that women are supposed to resist being raped. A popular misconception about rape has long been that women should be able to fight off their would-be rapists, and if they do not, it is because they did not really want to.[7]

Despite similarities in stage action, the tone across these productions varies widely in this scene. Kent's staging teases comedy out of Anna and Giovanni's fight; Giovanni scales down the wall from Anna's window with Leporello's comically ineffectual assistance. At the other end of this spectrum is Norris's production wherein, during the overture, we see Giovanni rape a woman onstage assisted by Leporello and a group of other men who act as his accomplices.[8] After the rape, Giovanni proceeds directly to Donna Anna's house before the overture concludes. We see him enter her room and grab her. The set rotates the pair out of view as Donna Anna struggles to escape. In this context, the comedy is entirely sapped from Leporello's "Notte e giorno faticar"; now, while Leporello complains about standing guard for his master, we already know what is going on inside. The comic music becomes ironic and Leporello's line "Forced to stand here as a sentry while he's trying to force an entry" takes on a heinous double meaning.[9] Norris amplifies the discord between the comic tone of Leporello's music and the reality of this scene further by punctuating Leporello's singing with offstage sounds from the struggle. In the brief silence between the end of the overture and the beginning of the first scene, and in two more moments of silence between musical phrases, we hear screams and sounds of exertion from Anna, a loud slap, and finally Giovanni howling in pain just before Anna chases him onstage.

While the overall character of this scene and its approach to the onstage violence differs among these productions, the stagings by Kent, Norris, Sivadier, and Zambello all evoke a classic stereotype of what an attempted rape looks like: a disguised assailant who is unknown to—or at least, unrecognized by—the victim, and a victim who violently attempts to fight him off.[10] We know that this stereotype of a stranger attacking women at random with the intent to violently rape them represents only a tiny fraction of sexual assaults, and that in reality, women are much more likely to be raped by intimate partners, family members, or acquaintances.[11] While stranger-rape is relatively uncommon in reality, it is overrepresented in the media.[12] The prevalence of this trope reinforces the idea that rape is a problem of individual bad men knowingly committing crimes and downplays the cultural conditions that support rape. But not all approaches to staging this scene follow this stereotypical rape script.

The productions by Pynkoski and Bieito stage this scene differently, working to various degrees against the libretto to implicate Anna as Giovanni's sexual partner rather than as a potential rape victim. Bieito's *Don Giovanni* goes furthest, representing Donna Anna as fully engaged in intimate contact with Don Giovanni in the first scene. This production opens with Leporello on the hood of a car that is bouncing on its suspension as the silhouettes of two figures jostle around inside. Don Giovanni and Donna Anna emerge from the car for their entrance, fastening and adjusting their clothes. Anna follows Giovanni around the stage, embracing him, groping his buttocks, and reaching into his pants. He lifts her onto the hood of the car, stands between her legs, and begins unfastening his pants again when the Commendatore enters and Anna runs away. Giovanni does not wear a mask or anything resembling a disguise. Anna's text in this scene, in which she calls for help and swears she will die before letting Giovanni escape, is played humorously. She delivers her words coyly to him as they stroll around the stage and share a beer. The singers, Wojtek Drabowicz and Regina Schörg, play their parts convincingly; Schörg delivers her musical lines with gracefulness and ease, deemphasizing the breathlessness and desperation that typically characterize Donna Anna's musical lines in this scene. Although I find no evidence in the opera's written text to suggest a desire for Don Giovanni on Donna Anna's part, Bieito's approach to this scene is entertaining and the performances are convincing. From the beginning, we know that this will be a different Don Giovanni story than the one Mozart and Da Ponte tell.

Pynkoski's 2019 staging of *Don Giovanni* exists between the two extremes above and represents a troubling trend I have encountered in a number of productions spanning from some of the earliest video recordings of the opera to the present. These Annas are not embroiled in a conflict with a predator in this opening scene, but a conflict within themselves; they desire Giovanni against their better judgment. In Pynkoski's production, the scene begins by following the opera's written text closely. Giovanni runs onstage with Anna in pursuit, calling for help and attempting to stop him from leaving. As the scene continues, Anna begins to respond differently to Giovanni's aggression. When he grabs her, there are moments when she stops struggling and her body language seems to betray a moment of relishing his touch. Finally, Giovanni and Anna are face to face and he is holding her wrists behind her back. He kisses her neck, and she tilts her head to the side as if to give him

Fig. 1. Donna Anna (Regina Schörg) embraces Don Giovanni (Wojtek Drabowicz) as Leporello (Kwangchul Youn) looks on. *Don Giovanni*, directed by Calixto Bieito. (Photograph © Toni Bofill, reprinted by permission.)

better access. He releases her wrists and the pair slowly move a few steps apart. The music changes, signifying the entrance of the Commendatore, but the other characters have not yet noticed him. This musical change instead seems to signify a change in Anna. She runs to Giovanni and puts her arms around him. They embrace and kiss until they notice the Commendatore, then Anna flees. At first, when Anna stops fighting Giovanni, it is possible to read this not as desire but a survival instinct. Perhaps upon witnessing how easily he can overpower her, she realizes it is futile to resist and is trying to minimize injury. This is not an uncommon reaction to sexual assault.[13] But just before she sees her father, Anna runs to Giovanni even after he appears to have let her go. And as they kiss, she lays her hand tenderly on the side of his face and wraps one leg partly around his hips. Soprano Meghan Lindsay's portrayal shows more signs of ecstasy than fear when in close proximity to Giovanni, even in moments when he cannot see her face. This staging *could* have shown us a pragmatic victim trying to mitigate harm to herself, but it does not. The reading that fits better is that despite the fact that this man has snuck into her bedroom and tricked her into intimacy, she still wants him. This representation depends on the particularly pernicious rape myths that some women want to be raped, and that when women say no to sex, they might really mean yes.[14] Even as Anna cries for help and calls Giovanni a betrayer and a villain, Pynkoski, like many directors before and after him, shows us an Anna whose body language is at odds with what she says. Pynkoski's Anna says no, but based on the staging of the scene, she means yes.

In the productions in which Anna fights with Giovanni, especially when he tries to kiss and touch her in explicitly sexual ways that she rebuffs, her nonconsent is crystal clear in her body language as well as in the words she sings. Bieito transforms this scene up to the entrance of the Commendatore entirely, so that what we are witnessing is not the moment after an attempted rape, but rather a cheeky post-coital game between intimate partners. Pynkoski shows us a Donna Anna who is attracted to the masked man who has invaded her privacy. This Anna is not fighting Giovanni as much as she is fighting herself. We might infer that she is torn between the requirements of her position as a woman of class betrothed to a good man and her base desires. While her words still convey nonconsent, her actions tell a different story, and so Giovanni's aggression takes on a different meaning.

"Don Ottavio, son morta! . . . Or sai chi l'onore"

In his piece on *Don Giovanni* and rape culture, Richard Will cuts to the heart of the problem with making the women, especially Donna Anna, complicit sexual partners for Giovanni: "If consenting women cleanse the story of rape, they also introduce one of the most familiar and debasing stereotypes of rape culture, lying women."[15] In the fourth scene of Act 1, Donna Anna recognizes Don Giovanni as her attacker and her father's murderer. In her recitative "Don Ottavio, son morta!" Donna Anna tells her story. She says Don Giovanni entered her room late at night, disguising his identity: "Silently he approached me and tried to embrace me. I tried to free myself, but he held me tighter. I cried out, but no one came. With one hand he covered my mouth, and with the other he held me so tight that I thought I was lost."[16] She describes how she ultimately freed herself and pursued her attacker as he attempted to flee. At the conclusion of her story, she moves into her rage aria, "Or sai chi l'onore," in which she asks Ottavio to avenge her father's murder. The staging of "Don Ottavio, son morta! . . . Or sai chi l'onore" shapes our understanding of what happened between Anna and Giovanni before the events of the opera, and it indicates a production's point of view about Anna's character.

The majority of the productions I survey here approach staging this scene in almost identical ways. This typical Donna Anna, dressed in elaborate mourning attire, performs her grief and rage to the audience or the camera. She rarely looks at Ottavio, to whom her words are addressed, and instead gazes into the middle distance with her pained expression clearly directed toward the viewer. This scene is obviously a serious one, but Donna Anna's seriousness in most of these productions is so exaggerated that it calls attention to itself as performance. There is contention among Mozart scholars about how the opera seria style should be viewed in his comic operas generally, and *Don Giovanni*'s already complicated relationship with genre amplifies the discord.[17] Donna Anna's highly stylized performance reflects the highly stylized aria she sings, but regardless of the original or intended meaning of Anna's opera seria attributes in the context of *Don Giovanni*, when modern-day stagings emphasize the distance between Donna Anna's pathos and her comic surroundings, Anna's extreme emotion can feel absurd to an audience, especially to those who may not be sensitive to the nuances of this opera's relationship to genre. The trappings of conventional nobility can make it difficult for audience members to identify with Anna and, as a result, empathize with her. In sum, this approach to the scene in which Anna discloses her abuse feels outdated in light of contemporary victim-centered discourses about sexual violence. Given recent discourse about making space for victims to tell their stories, we might rethink the way that we stage Donna Anna telling hers.

In the written text of the opera, Don Ottavio believes Donna Anna when she tells him her story. But from the audience's perspective, the director can choose to make Anna's story a lie. For Bieito and Pynkoski, who both represent Anna as at least partially complicit in the opening scene of the opera, the story Anna tells in "Don Ottavio, son morta!" is not strictly true. In Bieito's production, Donna Anna is the willing intimate partner of an un-disguised Don Giovanni in the back seat of his car. When Donna Anna next encounters Don Giovanni, she and Don Ottavio ask for his help to find her father's killer. Anna and Giovanni surreptitiously exchange glances and gestures in this scene that Ottavio is oblivious to, confirming that in this production Anna and Giovanni are having a secret affair. Donna Elvira enters and warns Anna and Ottavio not to trust Giovanni. As Giovanni tells the couple that Elvira is troubled, he embraces Elvira, and Anna looks furious. Giovanni and Elvira exit together and Giovanni blows a furtive, taunting kiss at Anna. Anna, livid, turns to Ottavio and begins her recitative "Don Ottavio, son morta!" In this production, the entirety of the story she tells about Giovanni sneaking into her bedroom is a concoction; we know she is lying to Ottavio because we saw what really happened. Anna's delivery of this lie features a number of exaggerated, dramatic flourishes that stand out in the otherwise highly realistic style of acting in this production. She performs false trauma to convince Ottavio of the lie she is telling him. In context, this lie appears to be an act of revenge on Don Giovanni for fraternizing with Elvira; Donna Anna feels betrayed by her lover, and so she tells her betrothed that he tried to rape her.

The version of Donna Anna's story in this production, considered in isolation, is not without value. The exaggerated, theatrical performance that Anna gives in this number is an interesting way of resolving the tension between Anna's high opera seria style and the more comic elements of the opera by making the former self-consciously parodic within the drama of the scene. But Bieito's production does not exist in a vacuum, and reading his *Don Giovanni* in its larger context complicates my perception of his interpretation of the story. It has been well established that Donna Anna has not been treated generously in the reception history of *Don Giovanni*, with critics frequently reducing her to a "repressed hypocrite, vengeful harpy, or humorless ice princess."[18] Additionally, critics and directors have often suggested that Donna Anna may harbor a secret, burning desire for Don Giovanni.[19] Bieito hyperbolizes this reading of Anna in his seedy, contemporary setting, but the basic interpretation of her character is not new. Believing that Anna desires Don Giovanni necessitates interpreting the words she sings in the opera through a skeptical lens. In Bieito's version of events, Anna's secret desire has become an explicit sexual relationship, and skepticism about the story she tells Ottavio is now utter disbelief.

In addition to the context of the opera's reception history, there is the context of twenty-first century sexual politics, into which Bieito's production has been received since its premiere in the early 2000s. The rape myth that women routinely lie about sexual violence is a relatively complex one. Concrete numbers about the percentage of false rape allegations are incredibly difficult to measure as rape cases are often difficult to investigate and prosecute and many remain unsolved for lack of evidence. Accusations deemed "unfounded" often bolster the numbers of false accusations even though this classification refers more to an unavailability of proof than to any evidence or perception that the alleged victim has been dishonest. Despite the methodological challenges, the question of the prevalence of false accusations of rape is a hotly contested issue with high stakes for rape victims. There is a troubling and persistent disparity between researchers, who estimate very low rates of false allegations, and front-line criminal justice professionals, who insist a great number of rape accusations are false.[20] The nuances of this issue have been somewhat flattened in popular rhetoric about "believing victims," but this rallying cry has its place as a reminder that when listening to accusations of rape, as with accusations of any crime, the best practice is to assume an alleged victim is telling the truth until their report is contradicted by some other evidence.[21] "Believing victims" is a response to a culture in which stories about women who wantonly lie about rape are overrepresented. When women accuse powerful men of sexual misconduct, we hear again and again that they are doing it for attention or out of spite. Rosalind Gill has argued that the prevalence of the stereotype of women crying rape for revenge or for attention has led to a situation where "it would not be an exaggeration to say that all rape claims are viewed through this sceptical lens—which constitutes a major barrier to women reporting sexual attacks, since many fear, quite rationally, that they will not be believed."[22]

Bieito's Donna Anna invents a story about rape and falsely accuses Don Giovanni because she is angry. The rape accusation allows Anna to tell Ottavio that it was Giovanni who killed her father without admitting that it was her affair that motivated the confrontation. She convincingly accuses Giovanni of both the crime he committed against her father, which she had been covering up, and an invented crime against herself. When she asks Ottavio to seek vengeance for her, her father's murder and the concocted rape are merely excuses—she really wants to see Giovanni punished for being unfaithful to her. This is a shrewdly calculated lie told by a jilted lover as punishment. This kind of false allegation is exceptionally rare in reality, but dominant in the kinds of stories we tell about rape.[23]

In Pynkoski's production, Donna Anna's account in "Don Ottavio, son morta!" is not a complete fabrication as it is in Bieito's, but we have reason to suspect it may be an edited version of the truth. We did not see what happened in Donna Anna's room before the opening scene of the opera, and it is certainly possible that Anna's account for Ottavio is accurate and that she only omits the very ending, when we saw her embrace and kiss Giovanni seemingly of her own volition. But this kiss plants a seed of doubt. A viewer of this production might legitimately wonder whether Anna and Giovanni's encounter offstage involved more intimacy than she lets on. Is the kiss we see onstage the first time Anna has given into her inconvenient desire or only the latest? Nevertheless, Giovanni conceals his identity from Anna and she calls for help all throughout this first scene. The desire and pleasure we see Anna experience does not excuse what still appears to be an attempted rape. But in the context of a fictional representation of an act of sexual violence,

Pynkoski's choice to depict Anna experiencing illicit pleasure perpetuates the idea that sexual assault is titillating even when victims say that it is not. And, like Bieito's production, it asks us how we really know that we can believe women when they make accusations of sexual assault.

While it is uncommon for women to lie about being sexually assaulted, incidents of sexual violence are traumatic events, and trauma has a powerful effect on memory. Research on trauma and memory has been increasingly visible in recent years, in particular as a way of illuminating some of the problems with the way we investigate and prosecute rape cases.[24] During a traumatic incident, stress hormones have two distinct effects on the way that memory is encoded: while early moments of the traumatic event are super-encoded as "flashbulb" memories, an extended traumatic experience can temporarily impair the hippocampus leading to minimal encoding and fragmentary memories.[25] A charitable interpretation of the disjunction between the scene we see played out at the opera's opening and the one Donna Anna recounts in Pynkoski's production might view the moment at which she recognizes that the man in her bedroom is not Ottavio as a vividly encoded memory at the beginning of a traumatic experience, and everything thereafter as fragmentary. Perhaps the details of the ways in which she played along and the length of time spent in his arms are lost to her. This certainly could be an interesting way to represent this storyline in a production of *Don Giovanni* informed by our improved understanding of trauma and memory. For a reading like this to be readily legible to an audience, though, it would take some more work from the staging than we see here.

Sivadier's production stages trauma in "Don Ottavio, son morta!" more successfully. In the first scene of Act 1 in this production, Donna Anna is a fierce adversary to Don Giovanni. At one point, she incapacitates Giovanni by holding his arm behind his back in a wrestling lock. She intercepts a knife that Leporello was trying to give to his master and attacks Giovanni with it. Giovanni disarms her just before the Commendatore enters. When recounting the attack to Ottavio, she appears more terrified than angry. Eleonora Buratto's vocal performance through "Don Ottavio, son morta!" communicates Donna Anna's sense of panic. She incorporates a wide palette of vocal colors, over-accentuates some consonants, and takes audible, gasping breaths at the musical pauses. The effect is quite different from other interpretations of this scene, which can feel a little stuffy and false. Whereas most of the Annas in these productions confidently perform their fury and horror for the audience, Sivadier's Anna hides her face in her hands and clings to Ottavio for support. As she gets into the details of the attack, she demonstrates on

Ottavio what Giovanni did to her, holding her hand over his mouth from behind. She reaches into his pocket and removes his knife, which she clutches as she continues her story. Ottavio has his back to her, and she crosses to him, handling the knife, while she recounts following Giovanni out into the street. When she says she became the assailant rather than the victim, she points the knife at Ottavio's back. When she recalls Giovanni killing her father, she raises the knife over her head to strike. At the last moment, Ottavio turns around to face Anna and she staggers back, dropping the weapon.

This is a compelling representation that evokes something real about trauma. Cathy Caruth writes that "trauma is the confrontation with an event that, in its unexpectedness or horror, cannot be placed within the schemes of prior knowledge . . . and thus continually returns, in its exactness, at a later time. Not having been fully integrated as it occurred, the event cannot become . . . 'narrative memory' that is integrated into a completed story of the past."[26] When Donna Anna is called upon to recount the traumatic event of her attempted rape, she is unable to intellectualize it. She cannot simply narrate it as something that happened in the past. Rather, she relives it vividly, to the point that she loses her grip on reality. When she wields the knife in this scene, we see her revert to her state of mind from the opening scene with Giovanni. When Ottavio turns and she sees his face, she crashes back into the present and drops the knife. This representation aligns with a common understanding of flashbacks associated with post-traumatic stress. Sivadier's production makes Anna much more sympathetic in this scene. Because her pain and fear are represented in a way that reflects what we know about trauma and the psyche, Sivadier's Anna appears more human to us.

Norris's production represents yet another element of the potential trauma responses to sexual assault in Donna Anna. As in Sivadier's production, Norris's Anna reenacts elements of her encounter with Giovanni while she recounts it to Don Ottavio. At first, she embraces Ottavio as if for comfort and support, but as the story becomes violent, she twists his wrist causing him to drop to his knees in pain. She shoves him down onto his back and grabs him roughly by the lapels as she recounts how she fought Giovanni. In Sivadier's staging, Anna loses herself in the narration of her trauma and seems shocked at the end to see Ottavio there instead of Giovanni, but I see Anna's violence toward Ottavio differently here. Norris's Anna struggles throughout the entire production to be physical with her fiancé after her assault. It is not uncommon for survivors of sexual violence to experience changes in their attitude toward sex and sexuality. A lack of satisfaction and pleasure in sexual activities is especially common in the first year after an assault.[27] At the beginning of "Don Ottavio, son morta!" Anna accepts Ottavio's embrace, but he quickly becomes a stand-in for her attacker. After her aria, she kisses Ottavio for a long time before hastily backing away from him and running offstage.

Anna's ambivalence toward intimate contact with Ottavio continues through the rest of Norris's production. In the scene before her second-act aria, "Non mi dir, bell'idol mio," Ottavio tries to comfort Anna and straddles her while she lies on the stage. At first, Anna seems to be enjoying the intimacy, but as Ottavio moves his hand from her back to her breasts, she throws him off. Her text in this scene expresses her inability to think about marriage while she is still mourning her father, but in this staging, it is difficult not to see her negative reaction as a consequence of Ottavio's attempt at physical intimacy as much as, or at least in conjunction with, his desire to talk about marriage. When Ottavio tells her she is cruel to put him off, she slaps him across the face but then almost immediately embraces him. We never get to see how Anna and Ottavio interacted before her assault, but based on Ottavio's shock and sadness each time she rebuffs him, we can assume that there was tenderness and intimacy that she is struggling to recover. She appears to desire closeness, but whenever Ottavio tries to initiate intimate contact, it triggers a powerful negative response. In the final ensemble of the opera, Ottavio offers Anna a bunch of heart-shaped balloons that symbolized his love for her earlier in the production, and she walks away from him. They sing the rest of the finale from opposite ends of the stage with the rest of the cast between them. Critics of Donna Anna in the written text have often used her frigid response to Ottavio's affections and their looming marriage as evidence of her alleged desire for Don Giovanni, but Norris's representation of Anna as traumatized by her assault humanizes her and encourages sympathy for her plight even as she rejects Ottavio.[28]

"Alfin siam liberati . . . Là ci darem la mano"

Later in Act 1, Don Giovanni happens across a wedding party for the peasants Zerlina and Masetto, and we get to see his famed approach to seduction for the first time in the opera. Giovanni gets Zerlina alone, and in their recitative and duet, "Alfin siam liberati . . . Là ci darem la mano," he invites her to return to his villa with him where they will be married. Zerlina refuses Giovanni's advances at first, but ultimately accepts him when she repeats his invitation, "andiam," back to him at the end of the A section of the duet. Before Zerlina and Giovanni can leave together, Donna Elvira intervenes, tells Zerlina what kind of man Don Giovanni is, and sends her away.

The staging of "Là ci darem la mano" establishes the nature of Zerlina's consent in her first interaction with Don Giovanni. Unlike Anna, she is informed about who it is she is consenting to, though Giovanni has misled her in saying he wishes to marry her, which we know is almost certainly not true. In all of these productions, Zerlina ultimately agrees to leave with Don Giovanni; her consent is in the written text. The music of the final "andiam" section rollicks merrily through a rustic 6/8, and none of these directors attempt to circumvent the quaint romance of this moment. But staging choices affect how we read the nature of Zerlina's initial refusal of Giovanni: does she express true nonconsent before Don Giovanni changes her mind, or does she intend to leave with Giovanni from the start and only say no as part of a coy game of cat-and-mouse? In the productions by Bieito, Kent, Norris, Pynkoski, and Sivadier, Zerlina portrays quite minimal and often playful resistance throughout the duet and preceding recitative. These Zerlinas seem to say no as part of a seduction script, or perhaps out of curiosity to see what Giovanni might try next. By contrast, in Zambello's production, Zerlina portrays convincing reluctance and discomfort at the beginning of her time alone with Giovanni and does not respond to him positively until her "andiam." After her genuine resistance, her final capitulation is of a different nature than in the other versions of this scene. It feels like Giovanni has outsmarted her. Giovanni's tactics are also varied between these productions. For Kent, Zambello, and Sivadier, he is immensely subtle in his approach; he seems to know exactly how close he can get to Zerlina and where and when he can touch her without frightening her. By contrast, the productions by Bieito, Norris, and Pynkoski stage more sexually aggressive advances: Bieito's Giovanni undresses Zerlina without her involvement, and in Norris's and Pynkoski's productions, Giovanni startles Zerlina with an amorous embrace that she only warms to once her initial alarm wears off. The approach to staging this scene indicates if a director perceives Giovanni as a deeply attractive paramour with whom women cannot help but fall in love, a sexual predator taking advantage of a vulnerable young woman beneath his station, or perhaps both.

These different versions of Zerlina and Don Giovanni raise different issues for audiences today in light of contemporary sexual politics. When Zerlina appears to be in control of the situation throughout "Là ci darem," obviously intends to leave with Giovanni from the beginning, and plays coyly with him through the duet, we might be happy to see this young peasant girl harnessing what little power her gender and sexuality grant her. But at the same time, she enacts a potentially dangerous myth of feminine sexuality: she says no, but she means yes. This myth came up in the opening scene of the opera in those stagings that show Anna as desiring Don Giovanni even as she proclaims the opposite. In Zerlina's case, there is evidence in the libretto that she is charmed by this handsome stranger, and she does eventually agree to run away with him. Still, approaching the scene in this way reinforces the myth that women really want sex even as they say they do not. And this myth can have real consequences. In studies of college students, for instance, there tends to be a gender gap in conceptions of consent. Whereas women tend to indicate that they grant consent verbally, men are more likely to interpret consent through body language.[29] This disparity can be dangerous in cases where a woman's words and her body language are perceived as being at odds, as they are for these Zerlinas before they say "andiam."

In watching this scene today, audiences might also be more sensitive to the fact that Zerlina's ability to grant or withhold consent is affected by her class relative to Don Giovanni. Zerlina even says in the recitative before "Là ci darem" that she knows noblemen are rarely honest and sincere with women.[30] Catharine MacKinnon argued in the 1990s that consent does not actually grant women the power that the law typically attests that it does. She writes, "The law of rape presents consent as free exercise of sexual choice under conditions of equality of power without exposing the underlying structure of constraint and disparity."[31] In most of these productions, Giovanni is significantly larger and stronger than Zerlina, and when he grabs her before she has agreed, it can appear that she has little choice but to say yes. And the disparity between Zerlina as woman and Giovanni as man is further amplified by Giovanni's wealth. His offer of marriage would assure Zerlina a measure of security and privilege she would not otherwise have access to. In Pynkoski's production, Giovanni even dangles a pouch of coins in front of Zerlina just before she sings "andiam." Legal philosopher Scott Anderson advocates for defining rape as coerced sex rather than nonconsensual sex. While the focus on consent succeeds in omitting the perception that rape relies on excessive force, it "fails to capture what is distinctively problematic about rape for women."[32] Anderson argues that by reconceptualizing rape as coerced sex, we can understand that when consent is achieved through coercion by a man who "simply refuses to take 'no' for an answer," rape is not precluded.[33] He notes that "uses of force and intimidation in intimate settings rely on contextual features such as a background of male social dominance and a propensity toward violence."[34] Don Giovanni's relative size compared with Zerlina in most productions, his social status as a man and a nobleman, and his wealth create a severe imbalance of power and the contextual possibility of violence and force—which will become more than a possibility shortly. Different productions can certainly suggest different interpretations of this scene, but overall, the written text "Là ci darem" today reads less like romance and more like coercion.

Act 1 Finale

Zerlina and Don Giovanni meet again in the Act 1 finale. They dance together, then Giovanni takes Zerlina offstage, and she cries for help. The approach to this moment varies among these productions in terms of the kind and degree of force Giovanni uses to take Zerlina with him, as well as the state Zerlina is in when she reappears. In Sivadier's and Pynkoski's productions, Zerlina is an eager partner to Giovanni throughout most of the first act. These productions both significantly scale up the violence in Giovanni's treatment of Zerlina in the finale. Sivadier's Giovanni carries Zerlina offstage with the assistance of an associate while she struggles. Pynkoski's Zerlina catches sight of Leporello physically restraining Masetto, gets scared, and tries to run away, but Giovanni catches her by the hand and flings her in the opposite direction. Both stagings make it clear that despite Zerlina's previous interest in Giovanni, at this moment he is forcing her.

Kent and Norris also portray explicit force from Giovanni at this moment, and they both make it clear that Zerlina has become intoxicated. In Norris's production, one of Giovanni's henchmen delivers shot glasses to all the party guests. Upon draining their glasses, everyone but Giovanni doubles over, coughing and retching. The party immediately changes as the revelers stagger about the stage and loll against set pieces. Giovanni appears carrying Zerlina, who is barely conscious. He sets her down to dance with her, but she cannot stay upright without him. These versions of the scene evoke a familiar date-rape scenario: Zerlina is interested in Giovanni, has consented to some intimate contact in the past, and is now intoxicated. Research has established clear links between alcohol consumption and acquaintance/date rape and shown that victims are more likely to be blamed for such rapes if they are intoxicated when they occur.[35] However, despite Zerlina's intoxication, the productions by Kent and Norris are still explicit in showing Giovanni using excessive force, indicating that he knows she is unlikely to agree to sex, even while intoxicated. Kent's Giovanni binds Zerlina's wrists with his scarf before

Fig. 2. Don Giovanni (Iain Paterson) gropes Zerlina (Sarah Tynan). *Don Giovanni,*
directed by Rufus Norris.
(Photograph © Tristram Kenton, reprinted by permission.)

dragging her offstage. Norris goes further, relocating Giovanni's assault from the wings and putting it onstage. While Zerlina is leaning against Giovanni for support, he runs his hands over her body and when he touches her groin she calls for help. The set rotates the pair out of view, and when we see them again, Zerlina is attempting to crawl up the stairs away from Giovanni. At the top of the staircase, Giovanni lifts Zerlina up, bends her over the banister, and thrusts his hips against her twice as she cries out in pain.

We hear a lot about Don Giovanni's seductions of women, but in the opera, Zerlina is our only example. It says a lot about Giovanni that when his attempt to deceive Zerlina into sleeping with him in "Là ci darem" fails, his response is to force her at his next opportunity. This scene shows us what we were denied in the scene at the opera's opening with Giovanni and Anna—this time we know exactly what happened, and we can see that as attractive as Giovanni might have been to Zerlina at first, she does not want him now. This is the pivotal moment in the opera when we see Giovanni act as a predator without question, and all of the above productions are agreed on this point. All six directors make it clear that despite Zerlina's earlier enthusiasm about Giovanni, what happens next is assault. This kind of clarity is vital in this scene.

That said, Norris's choice to stage what I expect we are meant to read as a rape center stage is a contentious one. To my mind, the other stagings also make Giovanni's culpability and Zerlina's innocence undeniable, even though they locate the assault offstage. In general, I am in favor of showing as little explicit sexual violence as possible to clearly communicate sexual violence. However, when looking at this group of productions that also includes Pynkoski's representation of Don Giovanni as a hero and a delight, I am sympathetic to the impulse to overcorrect by representing explicit violence and predation. But shock is a blunt instrument. Perhaps there were opera fans in Norris's audience who would only accept this Giovanni as a predator after seeing the rape of a named character (remember, we already saw Giovanni rape an anonymous woman during the overture). For other audience members, however, explicit and unexpected depictions of rape not only have the potential to be upsetting but may also potentially trigger trauma responses for abuse survivors. While staging multiple rapes in this opera may communicate that Norris's production takes Giovanni's crimes seriously and pushes back against readings of Giovanni as heroic, doing so also risks alienating audience members who may share these goals but are sensitive to the graphic depictions that this production could have done without.

Zerlina displays no ongoing distress as a result of events of the Act 1 finale in all but one of these productions. Zerlina's unflappability in the face of Giovanni's manipulation and attempted assault can be refreshing—she is a woman who refuses to let Giovanni ruin her life—but to an audience thinking about real-world sexual violence, it can also appear to shrug off the seriousness of sexual assault as a violent crime. Giovanni tries to force himself on Zerlina and on Anna, but whereas Anna seems deeply impacted by her experience, Zerlina typically is not. Even in Norris's production, in which Giovanni appears to drug and then rape Zerlina at the party, she displays no signs of ill effects in the subsequent act of the opera.

Bieito's production alone presents a Zerlina who does not navigate the opera painlessly. Bieito portrays Zerlina and Masetto's relationship as abusive from their first scene. In the recitative before "Là ci darem," Don Giovanni tells Zerlina she can do better than Masetto. In a period production of this opera, Giovanni's dismissal of Masetto as coarse and oafish typically refers to his relatively low class. But in this production, Giovanni seems to be telling her that she deserves someone who will not batter her.[36] The seduction in "Là ci darem" loses a lot of its charm in this new context. Zerlina is afraid of Masetto, and she only concedes to Don Giovanni after he has shown her that he is armed and lets her handle the gun, which she does eagerly. After Elvira separates Zerlina and Giovanni, Zerlina returns to Masetto to smooth things over in her aria, "Batti, batti, o bel Masetto." Typically, this aria shows the control Zerlina wields over her fiancé as she easily convinces him to forgive her by facetiously offering to let him beat her. Bieito, though, takes her words literally, and instead of a cheeky manipulation, this aria now accompanies domestic abuse culminating in a sexual assault.

Bieito's Zerlina is terrified to see Giovanni in the Act 1 finale and does not want to be anywhere near him. She drinks to excess and eventually Giovanni lifts her over his shoulder and carries her offstage. Zerlina reappears bleeding heavily from the mouth and with bloodstains down the front of her wedding dress. Giovanni pulls off her blonde wig of ringlets to reveal her short brown hair underneath. If Giovanni's heightened violence serves the plot here, it is by marking Zerlina physically with the bloodstains and short hair so that the trauma she has endured thus far will not be easily forgotten through the rest of the opera. She neither changes out of the bloodied dress nor replaces her wig. Now, when she returns to Masetto again to comfort him in her second aria, "Vedrai, carino, se sei buonino," we cannot forget what she has just gone through. In Bieito's production, Zerlina's interminable cheerfulness, expressed in her words and her music, begins to look like a coping mechanism. Herman writes that "the ordinary response to atrocities is to banish them from consciousness," but that despite our efforts "atrocities . . . refuse to be buried."[37] Bieito literally marks Zerlina with her traumatic experience so we cannot ignore it even as she tries to ignore it herself.

Act 2, Scene 1

We are first introduced to Donna Elvira in Act 1, right after Don Giovanni kills the Commendatore. At that point, we learn that Elvira had been a former conquest of Giovanni's and she has come looking for him. Leporello reveals to her the truth of Giovanni's exploits with women, and she spends the rest of the first act trying to convince Zerlina, Donna Anna, and Don Ottavio that Giovanni is not to be trusted. In the first scene of Act 2, Giovanni's humiliation of Elvira continues. He devises a plan to seduce Donna Elvira's maid: in the courtyard outside Elvira's window, Giovanni and Leporello swap clothes; Giovanni hides and calls up to Elvira while Leporello gestures along; Elvira comes down, expecting a reunion; and Leporello keeps her occupied while Giovanni moves on to the maid. Elvira believes that Leporello is Don Giovanni until the end of the next scene. Elvira's interaction with Leporello-as-Giovanni is marked by tender and erotic language. Leporello plays along until he is able to extricate himself, at one point remarking as an aside, "I'm starting to enjoy this."[38]

This scene is almost always played as strictly comic. Elvira's exaggerated, voluptuous overtures coax Leporello from nervous resistance to gleeful participation. Yet in spite of its consistently comic depiction, this seduction by deception, especially in the context of this opera, is troubling.[39] What happens to Elvira in this scene is similar to what we presume has happened to Anna offstage at the beginning of the opera. As Giovanni impersonates Ottavio to be intimate with Anna, Leporello impersonates Giovanni—albeit not of his own volition—to be intimate with Elvira. But while the written text of the opera casts the previous offense as serious, the latter is farce. Bieito's production is notable for portraying the scene between Elvira and Leporello in a more serious way. His setting is an empty bar, dark and littered with refuse from the party in the Act 1 finale. Giovanni and Leporello are playing pool and are interrupted by Elvira, who is drunk. The men swap clothing, but in their contemporary street clothes, they lack the large hat and cape that typically helps to carry off the disguise in productions with period costuming. Leporello sits on the bar behind Elvira who stands between his legs, both facing out to the audience. He embraces and caresses her and wraps her in a wedding veil left over from the previous scene, further obstructing her ability to see him. Standing behind the bar, Giovanni thrusts Leporello's hips into Elvira, and in response Elvira appears to be performing or preparing to perform fellatio on Leporello beneath the veil before they are interrupted. When Leporello remarks that he is enjoying the ploy after all, he does not deliver the line to the audience but to Don Giovanni, and the two of them laugh. Elvira continues drinking throughout this scene, and her drunkenness dominates the way we understand the deception. Bieito does not ask us to suspend our disbelief when Elvira mistakes Leporello for Giovanni; he makes it clear that she does not recognize him because the men are deliberately and maliciously taking advantage of her intoxication.

In addition to making Elvira's seduction by deception more believable in a realist modern setting, Elvira's drunkenness in Bieito's production calls to mind the popular rape myth that if a victim of sexual assault is intoxicated, she bears some responsibility.[40] Particularly common is the contention that women frequently consent to sex while intoxicated and then, regretting their decisions the next mornings, "cry rape" to protect their reputations. Bieito's staging of this scene pushes back against this victim-blaming narrative by making it exceedingly clear that Giovanni and Leporello are knowingly taking advantage of Elvira, who is clearly not an equal participant in the sexual activity depicted onstage. It is clear from the staging and the body language of the singers that we are meant to recognize Elvira as much more inebriated than Giovanni or Leporello, who both seem relatively unaffected by their drinking in the Act 1 finale. Elvira is already unable to consent to intimacy with Leporello in this scene because she has been deceived about his identity. And she is also incapable of consent due to her extreme intoxication.[41] An intoxicated Elvira makes this scene more believable and highlights a real contemporary problem about alcohol-assisted sexual assault.[42] I would not suggest that all productions of *Don Giovanni* should perform this scene as the gritty examination of the relationship between alcohol, consent, and sexual abuse we see here. But Bieito's production models one way of engaging with problematic material in this opera informed by contemporary attitudes about sexual violence by sacrificing the humor of this scene.

"In quali eccessi, o Numi . . . Mi tradì"

Donna Elvira displays powerful and mercurial emotions throughout the opera. In many productions of *Don Giovanni* I have seen, Elvira's emotions are exaggerated to the point of comedy; she swings irrationally between hatred and love for Giovanni, highlighting how truly irresistible this man is.[43] These representations reinforce a misogynistic stereotype of women's irrationality and they ignore the historical context of the opera's written text; Elvira, having given herself to Giovanni and having been abandoned, may no longer be a viable wife to another man. In production, a director chooses how to portray Elvira's pursuit of Giovanni and how sympathetic an audience may find her to be.[44]

A particularly good snapshot of a production's opinion of Elvira's suffering is found in the second-act recitative and aria, "In quali eccessi, o Numi . . . Mi tradì quell'alma ingrata." After having Giovanni and Leporello's deception revealed and Giovanni's guilt in the murder of the Commendatore and assault of Masetto confirmed, Elvira is left alone onstage. She is torn between her desire for vengeance and her desire to be with Giovanni. She muses on the terrible things Giovanni has done but admits she would still forgive him.[45] Kent treats this aria as a simple expression of a tragic love. Elvira emotes sadness and anger with a straightforward high-operatic affect. Like most of the approaches to Anna's "Or sai chi l'onore" above, these opera seria snapshots do not typically strive for emotional realism. If there is a problem with this traditional approach, it is in the potential disconnect between present-day audience expectations and operatic performance traditions. In 2014, Mary Hunter noted that many of her students were approaching Mozart's operas looking for role models and were not finding them: "They had expected feminist exemplars and had gotten, basically, warnings."[46] She asks how productions of operas "might make contact with an audience that takes female 'strength' as an article of faith."[47] Feminist consciousness, especially around the issue of sexual violence, has only grown in the opera-going public since Hunter posed this question. The other productions that stage "Mi tradì" explore different depictions of women and trauma that are worth considering.

Norris's production amplifies the stakes of Elvira's choice to forgive Giovanni. Elvira shares the stage with two of Don Giovanni's henchmen, dressed at this moment in monks' robes to match Giovanni, who wore the same robes to trick Leporello in the previous scene.[48] These agents of Don Giovanni silently flank Donna Elvira as she sings, and a silent chorus of women dressed in black file onto the stage and stand around the perimeter of the set. Elvira does not react to the presence of any of these witnesses. Instead, they appear to represent her dual allegiances: to Don Giovanni and to his other victims. Elvira is clearly tormented by these ghostly figures. At one point, she collapses onto the stage, and it is the two robed men who come and set her back on her feet, foreshadowing the choice Elvira will ultimately make. Within this production's iconography, the silent figures in this scene also evoke a dichotomy of heaven and hell. Elvira's ultimate allegiance to Giovanni is not portrayed as a bad romantic decision but the triumph of evil over good in Elvira's soul. In representing Elvira's struggle as a monumental moral undertaking, this production resists portraying her as foolish.

Sivadier's production is also noteworthy in its approach to Elvira in this scene. It can be tempting to condemn Elvira for continuing to defend and forgive Giovanni. A performance of "Mi tradì" as straight tragic romance does little to combat this inclination. But Sivadier emphasizes in his Elvira a sense of confusion and even fear at her own feelings. She shares the stage with the post-coital sleeping bodies of Don Giovanni and her maid. She wakes her maid and interacts with her as she sings, holding the young woman's face in her hands in a pleading gesture. She moves to sit with Giovanni, who does not wake up as she holds his head in her lap. Her actions and body language throughout are loving and angry in equal measure, and her expression of emotional torment never wanes. She runs her hands through her hair and clutches at her scalp looking childlike, lost, disoriented. The sentiment of this aria, when staged in this way, becomes less a great romance and more the fallout of abuse. In the opera, we have seen Giovanni and Leporello mock her, gleefully share with her the truth that she is merely a name on Giovanni's list, and discredit her to the other characters. Then, in order to trick her into an intimate moment with Leporello, Giovanni professes to love her and threatens to kill himself if she will not give him another chance. Given this context, Elvira's behavior here can read as another manifestation of trauma. In her landmark text, *Trauma and Recovery*, Judith Herman notes that traumatized people sometimes dissociate the emotions caused by traumatic events from clear memories of the events themselves.[49] Elvira's wide-eyed confusion and terror here feels like proportionate emotional distress for what we have seen Giovanni put her through, but she is struggling to make the connection between that pain and Giovanni himself. Her overtures of forgiveness here read not as the steadfastness of her love but as a failure to account for Giovanni's ongoing mistreatment.

Zambello's production also emphasizes the damage Giovanni has done to Elvira during "Mi tradì." This time, Elvira's performance itself is fairly typical of stagings of this aria: she plays the tragic heroine, embracing and singing to Giovanni's hat, which he has left onstage. While she sings, Donna Anna and Zerlina enter and intervene. They gently pry the hat from her arms and comfort Elvira, their concern for her clear on their faces. They remain with her for the duration of her aria, and the three women leave together. This gesture of sympathy and support from Giovanni's other victims also highlights the fact that this is not just a tragic love aria—Elvira is wounded and confused. Anna and Zerlina model how we as spectators might appropriately respond to Elvira's actions: not with judgment but with sympathy, focusing not on her failings but on what Giovanni has put her through. Sivadier also finds an opportunity to create a sense of solidarity and mutual support among the three women, though not in "Mi tradì." After capturing the man they believed to be Don Giovanni but was in fact Leporello, Anna lies down at the front of the stage in motionless sorrow. While Don Ottavio sings a beautiful and elaborate aria about consoling and avenging her, "Il mio tesoro," Elvira and Zerlina kneel down next to Anna and slowly help her get to her feet. Ottavio's mannered performance of his love pales in comparison to the intimate moment between the three women.

In Zambello's and Sivadier's productions, Anna and Zerlina display deep empathy for Elvira's pain, having been the victims of Giovanni themselves. Feminist therapist Laura Brown pointed out in the 1990s that old definitions of trauma considered traumatic events to be those that fell outside the typical boundaries of the human experience. She finds that this definition excludes the trauma of sexual assault and domestic violence, because they occur so frequently in women's lives as to appear "normal." She advocates for a feminist analysis that draws attention to "the private, secret, insidious traumas" experienced by women in our society.[50] We know Elvira has been lied to and betrayed by a man she trusted. We know that man has gone on to mock and denigrate her and has continued to manipulate her feelings for his own gain. She believes that she is in a relationship with Don Giovanni that can still be healed. On stage today, she resembles a victim of intimate partner violence. Zambello's and Sivadier's approaches to representing Donna Elvira's experience encourage us not to see her as ridiculous but to feel for her the way Anna and Zerlina do.

. . .

Regardless of the meanings *Don Giovanni* would have held to its first audiences in Prague and Vienna, its meanings today intersect with and are mutually informative with contemporary discourse about sexual violence. Although these characters are conventional archetypes, modern audiences tend not to interact with them in that way.[51] Mary Hunter noted the disconnect she perceived between the way her students approached Mozart's characters, looking for role models, and the archetypal representations of class and gender that they found instead. The stories we tell about sexual violence, its perpetrators, and its survivors matter, and *Don Giovanni* is a story we continue to tell today in opera houses around the world. The striking twenty-first-century relevance of its plot and characters is no doubt part of what makes this opera so beloved. It also entreats producers, performers, and critics to engage with this work at least in part from their own cultural historical perspectives.

Though Kent updates the setting of his production to the 1950s, the representation of the women in the opera remains rooted in the eighteenth century. He doesn't grant his characters any additional agency in his staging choices, with one significant exception. The Glyndebourne Festival advertised this production as a rare opportunity to see the full Vienna version of the opera.[52] Notably, this means that Kent's version included the rarely seen second-act duet between Zerlina and Leporello. In this scene, Zerlina ties Leporello up and threatens to shave him without any soap. It is charming and light-hearted, but it also grants Zerlina some resolution to her arc in the opera and allows her to take some action in the plot that is not informed directly by Masetto or Don Giovanni. I would love to see more productions of *Don Giovanni* consider including this duet. I believe it could satisfy a part of what audience members like Mary Hunter's students are looking for when they seek out strong women in this opera.

In contrast to Kent's production, Zambello's is conservative in its setting, yet Zambello makes subtle but meaningful choices to engage with the women in this opera as people. Most notable is the camaraderie between the three women during Donna Elvira's aria "Mi tradì." In the written text, Elvira warns both Zerlina and Anna about who Don Giovanni really is. In Zambello's staging, it is refreshing to see Zerlina and Anna step in to comfort Elvira when she most needs their support. This moment of solidarity, while brief, adds another dimension to these characters and it encourages the audience to sympathize with Elvira.

Pynkoski's production has an interesting relationship to conventionality in this opera. The producing company, Toronto's Opera Atelier, specializes in historically informed performance and their productions are characterized by period dance and gesture. Pynkoski rebuffs the incursion of "modern psychology" into *Don Giovanni* and treats it as an opera buffa informed by Commedia dell'Arte.[53] A strictly comic presentation makes it difficult to sympathize with the women whom Don Giovanni uses because his misdeeds are so minimized. This production also cuts not only Donna Elvira's aria "Mi tradì," which was a later addition to the score, but also Donna Anna's second-act aria "Non mi dir." The women already have so few opportunities to show depth of character, and the omission of these arias impedes their ability to share their point of view. Central to Pynkoski's conception of this story is the idea that Don Giovanni "adores all women. He falls in love with the last woman to cross his field of vision, and the schtick is that all the women, in turn, find him irresistible."[54] On its own, I find this an unsatisfying explanation of the written text of *Don Giovanni*—surely Giovanni's attacks against Anna and Zerlina are about something other than (or at the very least in addition to) love. However, there is another element to Pynkoski's production that smooths over some of the logical inconsistencies of making Giovanni a comic hero. At the beginning and end of the opera, Giovanni presents himself to the audience, posing and bowing, breaking the fourth wall and setting himself up as the narrator of the story. In this context, the staging makes a lot of sense. In Giovanni's version of events, of course Anna and Zerlina really desire him even as they tell him no. Of course the women are flat representations lacking nuance. And yet as a spectator interested in ethical representation of sexual violence, this production made me uncomfortable. When Giovanni is depicted as irresistible and Anna and Zerlina both welcome his advances, the acts of sexual violence in the written text become essentially misunderstandings or bad timing. If we believe the women really want Giovanni, and their hesitancy comes solely from fears of social judgment, then his attempts to force intimacy with them can be understood as assaults not against the women but against the puritanical society that represses their natural impulses. This representation of Giovanni and his crimes does not sit well with me as a woman in a culture that routinely fails to hold men accountable for sexual violence.

Sivadier's production also frames the story of *Don Giovanni* with a degree of artifice, but within this context he does a lot to humanize and sympathize with the women. Sivadier's stage features a central raised platform on which the action of the opera takes place. Around the edges of this platform, we see the singers setting props, applying makeup, and preparing for their entrances.[55] Sivadier explains that Da Ponte's setting has no real bearing on the action, which could happen just as well anywhere over any period of time. What is important is the constant dance of emergence, disappearance, and interruption which suggests "an exposed space, an arena, a ring, a circus track, the stage of a theater."[56] On this stage, the characters appear strikingly human and complex.[57] Both Donna Anna and Donna Elvira express deep, human emotions and complex representations of trauma. Sivadier does not hesitate to add characters to the opera to support his interpretation. I discussed Elvira's maid, who appears onstage with Don Giovanni to bring greater poignancy to Elvira's heartbreak in "Mi tradì." Sivadier also gives Don Giovanni an entourage of several strapping men who assist Giovanni in carrying Zerlina offstage in the Act 1 finale and hold Masetto while Giovanni beats him up. The addition of these brawny henchmen contributes to the demystification of Giovanni's power in this production; he only overpowers Anna with Leporello's help and he only overpowers Zerlina and Masetto with the help of additional servants.

The final two productions, directed by Norris and Bieito, are by far the most violent and both include explicit representations of sexual assault onstage. The Don Giovannis in the other four productions are ambivalent figures—their brutish actions are balanced (to varying degrees) by their charm and humor. But Norris and Bieito subscribe to a different vision of Don Giovanni. Gritty, dark *Don Giovanni*s have been popular for some time now.[58] Even the Metropolitan Opera, that bastion of operatic conservatism, has experimented with gruff, violent Giovannis, especially Bryn Terfel's famous performances from 2000. But leaning into this opera's darker themes does not in itself produce more ethical representations of sexual violence and violence against women.

Norris's production represents Don Giovanni transparently as a rapist. His techniques of seduction, when he bothers with them at all, quickly give way to brute force. And like Sivadier, Norris introduces a posse of strong men who help Giovanni throughout the plot. While the representations of rape are alarmingly and upsettingly explicit, this production also commits to representing Donna Anna and Donna Elvira with sympathy and nuance. In the second act, Norris's production inverts the placement of Donna Anna's and Donna Elvira's arias and the reorganization sets up both women for more sympathetic interpretations of their characters. Anna's aria "Non mi dir" and the preceding dialogue with Ottavio happens directly after Leporello escapes and the other characters become certain that Don Giovanni killed the Commendatore (Don Ottavio's aria "Il mio tesoro" is cut). Donna Anna's rejection of Don Ottavio's advances is particularly understandable when it occurs just moments after she gets confirmation of the identity of the man who tried to rape her and murdered her father. This sequence of events makes it much easier to see why Anna is upset by Ottavio wanting to go straight back to talking about their wedding. Similarly, by moving Elvira's "Mi tradì" later in the act, between the graveyard scene and the dinner scene, we are able to more clearly see the thought process that leads Elvira to interrupt Giovanni's dinner and try once more to be with him. Norris's staging of "Mi tradì," in which Elvira is tormented by the ghostly figures of Don Giovanni's previous victims, demonstrates clearly how deeply troubled Elvira is as a result of her tryst with Giovanni. Her appearance in Giovanni's home a short time later is more clearly connected to the agony she expressed in her aria—we are encouraged to connect her desperation with the trauma she has suffered at Giovanni's hands.

Even more than Norris's production, Bieito's production is saturated with sexual violence. In addition to the scenes I have discussed here, Don Ottavio also forces himself on Donna Anna during her second-act aria. All three women are abused by the men in their lives brutally and explicitly throughout this production. The violence is as explicit as it is rampant, and it draws attention to itself. Bieito makes *Don Giovanni* a story about violence, about abusive relationships, and about predatory sexuality. In many ways, Bieito approaches *Don Giovanni* in the same way I have in this chapter, asking what the story of this opera means now. Unlike any of the other productions here, Bieito represents Leporello's deception of Elvira as serious sexual misconduct. And Bieito is the only one to represent Zerlina as experiencing trauma after the attempted rape. But while it is sympathetic to the women, Bieito's production achieves this sympathy by emphasizing their victimization. The criticism of the opera's social politics is so complete that the opera ceases to resemble itself. *Don Giovanni*, in Bieito's hands, is a scathing critique of misogyny and violence. It is also entirely joyless.

All but one of the productions in this chapter were conceived of and premiered before the #MeToo Movement came to mainstream prominence in the fall of 2017. After this watershed moment for sexual violence awareness, #MeToo rhetoric began to crop up in promotional and press materials around productions of *Don Giovanni*. In advance of Opera Atelier's 2019 production, the *Toronto Star* ran an interview with Pynkoski under the headline, "Is Don Giovanni a #MeToo Monster or an Honest Seducer?"[59] Although Pynkoski's approach to this opera was explicitly historical, the press around this production still tried to frame it in terms of contemporary politics. At the end of the *Star* article, Pynkoski makes his resistance to the interviewer's #MeToo framing clear: "I don't want to adjust any existing work of art to reflect anything that is happening socially right now. . . . We change; I don't think the work changes."[60] But some directors have been interested in seeing *Don Giovanni* change to reflect the society around it. I close this chapter with a brief look at an English production by a young director who consciously and sensitively engages with contemporary feminist politics of sexual violence.

Laura Attridge's 2018 *Don Giovanni* for the Waterperry Opera Festival in Oxfordshire lays bare the contemporary resonances Attridge and the singers found in the characters and story. Set in the present day, this production highlights a number of the issues I have raised in this chapter: the trauma of sexual violence for Anna, the psychological manipulation by a trusted partner for Elvira, and the relationship between alcohol and consent for Zerlina as a modern bride-to-be. In the epilogue after Giovanni's death, Attridge has the full ensemble onstage singing, including the singers who have portrayed Don Giovanni and the Commendatore. The full company step out of character and break the fourth wall to address the audience directly as they sing the celebratory words that evil deeds will never pay and evil men will go to hell. Attridge describes the effect she wanted:

> Rather than a triumphant celebration of the defeat of Don Giovanni, when layered on top of our realization of the story as a contemporary tale of toxic masculinity and its poisonous effect on all of those around it, the epilogue became a strong rallying cry to go away and fight the injustices still going on around us because of this kind of man—both real and allegorical. We were saying not only, "We all know this man, and men like him. Open your eyes, go out and fight, because we have to believe that goodness can win. There's no Commendatore who's going to do it for you." But also, "*We're* here, and *we* see him, and *we're* not giving up."[61]

Attridge's comments illuminate some of the kinds of thinking that can go into crafting representations of sexual violence that are victim-centered and informed by contemporary feminist politics. Increased popular awareness of the prevalence and harm of sexual violence today practically ensures that many audience members and critics will bring these ideas into the theater with them. *Don Giovanni* presents a number of problems when staged in the midst of our cultural conversations about sexual violence, and they are problems that need our attention. In the 2019/2020 season, *Don Giovanni* was the eighth most performed opera worldwide with 662 performances of 129 different productions.[62] This is an opera that is widely beloved, even by many of its harshest critics, and its continued popularity feels assured. An ethically informed approach to the production and reception of this opera entails facing the issues presented by the opera directly, through the lens of our own Zeitgeist.

Failing to think through the way sexual violence is represented in this opera is not just an issue of dramatic and aesthetic quality, but of social responsibility. It is important to ask what we hope to achieve by staging *Don Giovanni* now, and how we might best accomplish those goals when we represent this story and its characters onstage. The complexity of the question of morality in *Don Giovanni* is not a detriment to an ethically informed performance; opera practitioners can use this narrative and cast of characters to explore pressing contemporary issues around consent, trauma, and memory with nuance, guided by contemporary scholarship and discourse. I do not wish to see a reduction in the diversity of different approaches and interpretations to this opera. Rather, I hope that opera companies, directors, and their creative teams might approach this opera with a consciousness of the complexity of its relationship with rape myths and other stereotypes around sexual violence.

Don Giovanni had been an increasingly challenging opera for me even before 2017, but in the wake of #MeToo I found I struggled to stomach classic productions of the opera with swashbuckling Giovannis heroically going to their deaths. *Don Giovanni* was and is a big part of my life, as it is for so many opera scholars, practitioners, and fans. It does not feel like a historical artifact—its archetypes and its themes have always felt incredibly relevant to the world around me. In this chapter, I have modeled how different staging choices can impact interpretation of this opera in performance in regard to sexual violence, especially the agency of the women and the promulgation of or resistance to popular rape myths. A common objection to ethical criticism of this and other historical operas is that it is unfair to hold Mozart to the ethical standards of the present. But rather than framing this issue in terms of Mozart's beliefs or ethical orientation, I think we would be wiser to focus on what we want out of this work now. We can respect and appreciate Mozart's legacy while also holding ourselves to the ethical standards of the present. Instead of asking what Mozart and Da Ponte meant for *Don Giovanni* to say, I want to ask instead what we want it to say, and what we can say through it and about it in our contemporary practices of performance and reception.

Two

Salome as Victim

When Salome demands that Herod deliver her the head of John the Baptist, Herod pleads with her to reconsider. He reminds her of how kind he has always been to her, bemoaning, "I have ever loved thee . . . It may be that I have loved thee too much."[1] These words, coupled with his wife's ongoing complaints that Herod looks at Salome too much, carry a menacing implication for the relationship between stepfather and stepdaughter in Oscar Wilde's play. This sentiment has inspired a host of contemporary opera directors to interpret Richard Strauss's operatic adaptation of *Salome* as a story about incestuous sexual violence. In these productions, Herodes's leering and his lecherous desire become indicators of a sexually abusive relationship. At least thirteen productions of *Salome* in the first two decades of the twenty-first century add sexual violence to the story during the Dance of the Seven Veils to depict Salome as a survivor of sexual trauma. Presenting Salome as a rape victim shapes and delimits possible interpretations of her character and her actions in the opera.

Richard Strauss's *Salome* premiered in Dresden in 1905, just two years after Strauss saw Oscar Wilde's play performed in Berlin. Strauss used as his libretto a German translation of the play written by Hedwig Lachmann and trimmed it to size himself. Early Salome narratives come from the biblical story told in the Gospels of Matthew and Mark and from Josephus's first-century historical volume *Jewish Antiquities*. Salome is the stepdaughter of Herod Antipas, the first-century tetrarch and ruler of Galilee and Perea. According to the Gospels, Herod arrested John the Baptist, who had been publicly condemning Herod's marriage to Herodias given her previous marriage to Herod's brother. In the biblical account, Herodias bears a grudge against the Baptist, but Herod is unwilling to execute the man he believes to be holy. On Herod's birthday, Herodias's daughter (who is named Salome, according to Josephus) dances for Herod and pleases the tetrarch so much that he offers to give her any gift she desires. Herodias tells the girl to ask for the head of John the Baptist, and Herod, unwilling to break his word in front of his guests, agrees. Oscar Wilde's *Salomé* came out of a fin-de-siècle obsession with the mysterious dancing princess. He captured the Orientalism, eroticism, and scopophilia that characterized many depictions of Salome's body in contemporary art, and he also gave her something new—a powerful and deviant sexual desire. Wilde's Salome tells us definitively, "It is for mine own pleasure that I ask the head of Jokanaan in a silver charger."[2] She is not her mother's pawn and this is no whim; she desires Jokanaan for herself, and she will have him to do with as she pleases.

The Wildean Salome exerts an incredible amount of agency over the events of the story. She uses her body and her sexuality in a calculated and intentional way to force the hand of a powerful man. Although Salome uses her power to do harm, that power in itself is thrilling. Hers is a monstrous but also a revolutionary sexuality. Since the opera's premiere, the Dance of the Seven Veils has frequently been appropriated as a showcase for erotic feminine power. When *Salome* had its first American performance at the Metropolitan Opera in 1907, it was banned after opening night and the remainder of the performances were canceled, but the Dance of the Seven Veils lived on in American vaudeville, dance, film, and burlesque.[3] Indeed, Susan Glenn has argued that in the twentieth century, Salome was "an important resource for women performers and audiences, a vehicle for self-expression and sexualized assertiveness."[4]

The reception of *Salome* the opera has also been informed by psychoanalytic readings of its main character. Strauss's music for this opera belongs to a tradition of Expressionism concerned with emotional interiority.[5] Musicologist Gary Schmidgall has extended this interiority to fictional characters in Strauss's opera, understanding the music of *Salome* as a kind of compositional psychoanalysis. He argues that Strauss's music does not aim to set Wilde's stilted poetic language, but rather takes into account "the play's second, submerged level of potential musicality—the level upon which exist the poisonous melodies of sexual fixation and frustration, nervous exhaustion, and neurosis. Strauss, in short, responded to the psychological implications rather than the textual sonorities of 'Salomé.'"[6] Lawrence Kramer has similarly connected psychoanalysis to what he calls "post-Wagnerian compositional logic" in an article that likens the relationship between John the Baptist and Salome to that between Freud and his patient Dora.[7] He suggests that Salome sings to Jochanaan's head as if it is her psychoanalyst, freely associating without pause for eighteen minutes.

Given this history of reading Strauss's *Salome* via psychoanalysis in general and Freud in particular, it is perhaps not surprising that many twenty-first-century productions of the opera hang their interpretations on ideas of sexual trauma and memory. Sander Gilman suggests that in 1905 Germany, Salome would have been a simple case of hysteria for Freud: "The symptom, Salome's sadism—manifested by her desire to possess a fetish, the severed head of a man who has rejected her—had its origin in the trauma of her attempted seduction by her stepfather, Herod."[8] Compounding the opera's Freudian inheritance is the proximity of *Regietheater* itself to psychoanalytic thought. Wieland Wagner's post-World War II productions of his grandfather's operas in Bayreuth focused on the symbolic and psychological elements of the works. As the popularity of conceptual productions of canonic operas grew in the late twentieth century, directors largely continued this legacy of uncovering—more accurately, creating—an underlying psychology for their characters.

While the psychoanalytic bent of so much musicological discourse about both Strauss's Expressionism and the tradition of *Regietheater* can explain in part where this production trend of Salome-as-raped comes from, I am more interested in what this concept *does*. In particular, I am concerned about the ways the popularity of this trope might tilt popular understanding of this opera further toward trauma and victimhood to the exclusion of narratives of sexual empowerment. Salome's agency in her story changes drastically with the explicit inclusion of a sexually violent backstory. My analysis considers the ways these directors guide us to understand Salome's power differently when it is motivated by trauma and asks what opportunities Salome has in these productions to exert power over her environment. I also introduce a new axis of analysis for these productions that will continue to operate through the remainder of the book: rape in the context of performance. Here I am concerned both with the real-life performance—professional singers, dancers, and actors performing fictional acts of violence for an audience of opera-goers—and the performance that takes place within the world of the opera when Salome dances for Herodes and his guests. Framing depictions of rape as spectacles for entertainment may invite audiences to take voyeuristic pleasure from witnessing sexual violence. Among the productions in this chapter are those that alternately play into or resist this type of spectatorship.

The earliest production I have found that explicitly represents Salome as having been raped is Atom Egoyan's 1996 *Salome* for the Canadian Opera

Company (COC). In Egoyan's production, Herodes oversees Salome's gang rape during the Dance of the Seven Veils, which is framed by her childhood memories of his ever-present voyeurism. I saw this production when it was remounted in 2013, and that experience sparked many of the ideas that form the backbone of not only this chapter, but this book. The other twelve productions featuring Salome as a rape victim all fall between 2008 and 2018 and are scattered across North America and Europe. It is not feasible to cover all thirteen productions in detail. In order to analyze the ideas presented by these productions without becoming overwhelmed in the minutiae, I employ a two-pronged approach. Below, I offer an in-depth analysis of Egoyan's *Salome* from 2013 focusing on the Dance of the Seven Veils. Then, I look at the other twelve productions primarily in terms of their construction of and participation in a number of representational tropes. I highlight emergent patterns in the way these directors use sexual violence to tell the Salome story and zoom in on individual productions only insofar as they help to flesh out these tropes.

Trauma and Agency in Atom Egoyan's *Salome*

Atom Egoyan's 1996 *Salome* explores themes of trauma, sexuality, and scopophilia, which are common in much of his film work. Like all of the productions in this chapter, Salome's sexual assault is the locus of her trauma and of the main action of the opera. Salome's relationship with her stepfather links this production with Egoyan's film oeuvre, in which the theme of father-daughter incest is common. Richard Bradshaw, the COC's General Director, approached Egoyan about creating a new Salome production after seeing the director's latest film, *Exotica* (1994), in which a father loses his young daughter and becomes obsessed with a stripper with a school-girl persona. And a year after Egoyan's *Salome* debuted at the COC, he released his next film, *The Sweet Hereafter*, in which a fifteen-year-old girl is sexually abused by her father.[9]

Incest was also an important theme for second-wave feminism. In a 1977 article, Judith Herman and Lisa Hirschman situate incest in the context of patriarchal societies and argue that in such societies, including our own, the incest taboo is asymmetrical; although incest is prohibited between mothers and sons and between fathers and daughters, the latter prohibition is considered to be less serious and it is violated more frequently.[10] In the 1980s and 1990s, incest narratives took on political weight for feminists working to overcome victim-blaming narratives of sexual abuse. Father-daughter incest in particular made particularly visible the vast power differential feminists argued was inherent to sexual violence. Incest stories allowed for representations of vulnerable victims and unquestionably guilty perpetrators. Russell Banks's 1991 novel, *The Sweet Hereafter* fits into this narrative frame with its depiction of a fourteen-year-old girl in a coercive sexual relationship with her father. When Egoyan adapted Banks's novel for his 1997 film, the girl is fifteen and the relationship with her father appears to be at least somewhat consensual.[11] Egoyan said of this revision, "There was no way I could depict the incest the way it was in the book because it has become a cliché."[12]

In his production of *Salome*, Egoyan similarly represents an unusually ambivalent victim. Though in this case, Salome's ambivalence comes not from complicity in her abuse but from the extremity of her response to it. Egoyan's Salome, we surmise, gets her violent appetite from her abuse. But these themes of trauma and incest do not tell the whole story for *Salome*'s audiences; they run alongside existing and sometimes conflicting interpretations of the story. Egoyan's production, and his staging of the Dance of the Seven Veils in particular, highlights the tensions and the new meanings that can be born from the introduction of sexual violence to a familiar story. My analysis focuses on the 2013 production, in which Egoyan reworked the Dance scene. I discuss the nature of and potential motivation for these changes in due course.

The guiding logic of Egoyan's *Salome* is the politics of looking. At the center of his production is the idea of the frustrated gaze. Egoyan describes the plot of the opera thusly: "The page is infatuated with Narraboth, who does not return her gaze, and Narraboth is totally consumed with Salome, who does not return his gaze, and Salome of course is completely consumed with Jochanaan, who does not return her gaze."[13] This frustrated gazing all takes place within a culture of surveillance in which the guards carry hand-held video cameras in 1996 and 2002, and camera phones in 2013. So, Salome is being watched all the time, not only by Narraboth and the other men onstage who desire her, but also by Herodes's cameras. Egoyan describes his setting as a kind of panopticon, achieved not by architecture as in Jeremy Bentham's formulation, but by video technology. Video clips are projected on the upstage wall of the set, and we see Salome on video before we see her in person. According to David Levin, "Egoyan derives not just a theatrical effect from this gambit, but a dramaturgical focus. . . . By introducing us to a Salome beyond the space and medium of her stage presence, Egoyan prepares us for the possibility that her pathology originates in some offstage space and medium as well."[14]

This offstage locus of pathology is revealed to the audience during the Dance of the Seven Veils. As a striptease (an act of revealing) the Dance would seem a natural fit for the atmosphere Egoyan has created, yet Egoyan does not stage Salome's dance. Upon agreeing to dance for Herodes, Salome sits on a swing hanging downstage that lifts her up into the rafters. Her dress unfurls as she rises and becomes a projection screen, which fills most of the proscenium. We see a video projection of Salome as a young girl on a swing, smiling into the camera. The footage has the feeling of a home video. After a few moments (letter G in the score), the video changes to show child-Salome wearing a blindfold in the woods. She begins to walk in place, still blindfolded, holding her arms out in front of her as the forest moves past. Herodes appears onstage in front of the screen and watches the video. When Herodes leaves, child-Salome removes her blindfold. The projection is now replaced by a shadow-play ballet performed behind the screen as the orchestra begins to play a Viennese waltz (7 mm. after letter P)—the first explicit dance music in the movement. We see the silhouette of a dancer portraying Salome dance and remove her clothing. As the waltz accelerates, several more dancers appear who we later recognize as the five Jews. They encroach on dancer-Salome and the light sources behind the screen move so that the shadows of the men appear more than twice their true size. The tempo suddenly increases ("sehr schnell" at letter Y), and the men begin to toss Salome around from one to another. She fights and struggles but cannot keep them off. Eventually, one of the men forces Salome onto her back on the ground. He undresses and crouches down between her legs. At what seems to be the moment of penetration, the lights cut out, and the screen is filled with another video projection: an extreme closeup of an eye with the footage of child-Salome on the swing filling the pupil. The scrim drops to the stage revealing Salome huddled at the feet of the men who step back, adjusting and refastening their lab coats, under Herodes's watchful eye.

The addition of a rape storyline to *Salome*'s narrative serves, first and foremost, to explain the heroine's troubling, gruesome actions in the second half of the opera. In an interview for the COC in 2013, Egoyan said that he wanted to use the Dance "as a way of gaining some insight into Salome's state of mind: what leads her to this extraordinary act of violence, asking for the head of the man that she is obsessed with? So, we're thinking that there's something else going on in this family, in her background, and the music of the Dance of the Seven Veils is a way of accessing that."[15] In his program notes, Egoyan says further that he felt "a pressing need to make certain things clearer—to find some justification for Salome's horrific behav-

Fig. 3. Salome struggles against her attackers during the Dance of the Seven Veils. *Salome*, directed by Atom Egoyan.
(Photograph © Michael Cooper, reprinted by permission.)

iour."[16] A preoccupation with finding logical, comprehensible motivations for Salome's monstrosity seems to be one of the guiding aspects of all of the *Salome* productions in this chapter, and Egoyan articulates it clearly here. This interest in locating Salome's behavior in her psychology, and even manufacturing life experiences to lay the groundwork for that psychology, allows us to reimagine *Salome* as a post-Freudian pop-psychology story which has a certain modern-day appeal. But it also serves to strip Salome of her choices in a tangible way. The story becomes about what—or who—*caused* Salome to take these actions.

Salome's present-day psychological malady is implicitly attributed to childhood trauma as revealed, albeit vaguely, in the Dance of the Seven Veils. The gang rape we witness appears to take place in real time in the world of the opera. When dancer-Salome's shadow appears, she seems to be the present-day Salome we had been watching before the screen went up. She begins to dance, but she is interrupted and raped while the music plays. When the scrim drops at the end of the dance, Salome and the men are all positioned where the shadows had been projected a few moments before. Time is continuous here even as the visual mode shifts from shadow ballet back to opera. Although the rape we see takes place in the present, the remainder of the Dance of the Seven Veils sequence makes it clear that for Salome, this experience is inextricable from her childhood. Herodes's presence in the foreground as the child-Salome wanders blindfolded through the dark forest implies not only surveillance but violation, and indicates that Salome understands her rape as an extension of her experiences with her stepfather in childhood.[17] The emphasis on Salome's childhood and Herodes's violation is so great in this production that I misremembered the dance after my live attendance in 2013 and attributed the rape to Herodes with the assistance of the other men until viewing archival footage years later.

Within the framework of sexual violence and trauma, Egoyan still traces a kind of development toward agency for Salome, though not the one his audience is accustomed to seeing. His Salome begins to come to terms with her trauma through acts of blindfolding to see and unsee her world as she chooses. In the Dance of the Seven Veils, the blindfold is a metaphor for self-knowledge and Salome's ability to understand her trauma. The child-Salome wandering through the woods ties a blindfold over her eyes to begin her walk and removes it at the end just as dancer-Salome's shadow appears on the screen. The blindfold in this instance is a symbol of the unknowability of Salome's trauma. Trauma theorist Cathy Caruth defines the experience of trauma in a structure of belatedness: "Trauma is not locatable in the simple violent or original event in an individual's past, but rather in the way that its very unassimilated nature—the way it was precisely *not known* in the first instance—returns to haunt the survivor later on."[18] Salome is unable to comprehend the memory of her trauma in full. She dons the blindfold herself in a gesture of self-preservation. Then, when child-Salome removes her blindfold, there is a moment in the crossfade to the shadow-play when it feels as if she can see dancer-Salome. The act of unblindfolding implies a new sense of clarity, even an act of recovered memory. As the two Salomes briefly glimpse one another, Egoyan dramatizes a revelation for Salome about her own history—a glimpse of a truth in her past that she had been unwilling or unable to see until now.

Amid the surveillance and the power of the gaze that rules Egoyan's stage, blindfolding is also a tool of rebellion in this production. Jochanaan is blindfolded when Narraboth first leads him onto the stage to speak with Salome. The prisoner removes the blindfold but averts his eyes from Salome throughout their long exchange. Upon uttering his final rejection, he ties the blindfold back over his own eyes. As Herodes's prisoner, Jochanaan cannot control what happens to him. He is shackled and imprisoned, his movements are strictly controlled, and he is executed at a mere word from his captor. He cannot stop Salome from gazing at him, but he can choose not to return her gaze. His refusal to meet her eyes and his ultimate act of self-blinding at the end of their exchange disempower the spectacular Salome. Her power over the other men in the opera comes from her awareness and manipulation of their gaze, but she cannot exert this power over Jochanaan. This dynamic is already at play in the opera's libretto and is made explicit in Egoyan's production. Ultimately, though, Salome appropriates the power of Jochanaan's blindfold for herself. When she is delivered Jochanaan's still-blindfolded head, she uncovers its eyes and dons the blindfold herself in what Egoyan describes as "a moment of communion" with Jochanaan.[19] She kisses the head while she wears his blindfold in an act of defiance against the rules of the surveillance society in which she lives. With this kiss, she chooses to possess Jochanaan not by gazing on him, as she has been gazed upon, but on her own terms: blind. When she removes the blindfold, she holds it over her head victoriously for her final ecstatic "I have kissed thy mouth, Jochanaan" over the crashing orchestral climax.[20] Of course, Salome's command over how and what she sees at this moment cannot go unpunished in Herodes's world of surveillance and control. Herodes snatches the blindfold from her hands and strangles her with it.[21] In one sense, Salome is only ever a victim of the gaze and of her own beauty. The power she wins at the conclusion of the opera cannot alter this. What she claims is a different kind of power. It is a power over her own perception, allied with her newfound understanding of the truth of her past trauma. Although she cannot be allowed to survive to the end of the opera, Salome dies victorious in at least this one way. She dies with her eyes uncovered, having truly seen Herodes and what he has done to her.[22]

Egoyan's Salome is a complex figure. Directorial changes to the story strip away much of the power with which Wilde imbued her. By rendering her obsessive desire symptomatic of a pathology of childhood trauma, Egoyan reduces the amount of agency Salome has to make choices. But he gives her a dense, carefully spun trajectory toward self-knowledge and self-determination through the use of the blindfold. There is an unavoidable tension here between victimhood and agency. These two Salomes, the monstrous young woman who demands the head of the man who denies her and the abused child, vie for dominance, but each is tainted in light of the other.[23] How much sympathy can we conjure up for the rape victim who has a man murdered in cold blood to satisfy her lust? Salome's death at the end might be more tragic in light of her trauma, but I fear it also begins to feel inevitable. If Salome's violence was an unavoidable symptom of her pathology, does her murder become an act of mercy? Is her death the natural conclusion of her rape? In Egoyan's production, making Salome the victim of rape asks as many questions as it answers about who this woman is and how we understand the story this opera tells. Yet the idea of Salome as a rape victim has become increasingly popular since Egoyan's production premiered.

Emergent Tropes in Sex Abuse *Salomes*

The following twelve productions of *Salome*, encompassing ten years of practice in North America and Europe, all similarly disclose sexual abuse of Salome during the Dance of the Seven Veils, and in all of these instances, Herod is the perpetrator. Common themes emerge in the way Salome's agency is represented in these productions as opposed to the written text of *Salome*. In some of these productions, violent sexual backstories primarily add context for the existing plot (as is the case for Egoyan), whereas in others, the directors have significantly altered the onstage events, particularly at the opera's conclusion, to tell a different kind of story about sexual abuse. Individually, productions in this collection may be quite nuanced in their representation of Salome as a rape victim. Yet I am troubled by the implications and popularity of this trope, by which Salome's agency is frequently diminished.

Salome Does Not Dance: Salome is objectified by the constant desirous gaze of the other characters in the opera, but Linda and Michael Hutcheon and Lawrence Kramer have argued that by performing the Dance of the Seven Veils, Salome gains agency by using the power of that gaze to her own advantage.[24] In the Dance, she gets to control exactly how she is seen, and she uses the power of her own bodily spectacle to compel Herodes to give her what she desires. Mary Simonson sees Salome's dance as "modeling feminine possibility and reminding us that it is not only voice and vocality that promise to recover female character but also bodies, dance, and movement."[25] When these productions stage traumatic flashbacks or rape scenes during the Dance of the Seven Veils, the revolutionary character and potential of the Dance is compromised. In some productions, we assume that Salome does dance for the onstage audience, though we are shown something different. In others, she begins to dance only to be interrupted by Herodes and abused either in view of the audience or just offstage. Rather than watch the Dance of the Seven Veils, which Salome controls, we see her raped, or we watch involuntary flashbacks triggered by the experience of performing this dance for her abuser. We are left with Salomes that cannot control our gaze and cannot control the telling of their own stories.

Salome's Regression (Salome via Freud): Freud's influence on these interpretations of Salome is conspicuous. The generating logic for this staging concept seems to be the psychoanalytic premise that dysfunction, and especially sexual dysfunction, originates in traumatic experiences in childhood. Freud's concept of regression is of particular importance in several productions. Regression refers to a defense mechanism by which the ego responds to trauma by reverting to an earlier stage of development. On the stage, evidence of this type of psychoanalytic interpretation can be seen in productions in which Salome displays childlike mannerisms or appears in juvenile costumes that do not align with our perception of the character's age.[26] The following productions fit into this pattern and represent Salome's trauma either through a specifically psychoanalytic lens of regression or marked with childlike physicality more generally.

Alexandra Szemerédy and Magdolna Parditka's *Salome* for Theater Bonn in 2015 makes its psychoanalytic framework particularly clear. Set in the early twentieth century, this production resonates with Freud both in its time period and its pervading dream-logic. Like Egoyan, Szemerédy and Parditka conceive of the Dance of the Seven Veils as a moment of psychic dislocation for Salome. While in the world of the opera Salome performs a dance for Herodes, we in the audience are made privy to her internal experience of trauma stirred up by that dance. This production makes the split between Salome's physical and psychological selves visible by using a dance-double who looks just like Salome. The double performs a ballroom dance with a tuxedoed partner for Herodes's delight. Soprano Nicola Beller Carbone plays the other Salome in this scene—the inner Salome. She replicates the double's choreography before peeling off and sitting downstage apart from the dancing. She grows more and more visibly distraught and writhes in pain. She removes her evening gown, dons a blue-and-white sailor dress, and puts a bow in her hair. Her clothes now match those of a badly tattered baby doll that she carries around with a large red stain between its legs. The dance then gives way to what feels like a scene from Salome's dreams. She is surrounded by banquet guests and her family who present her with a large birthday cake. The chandelier above drips blood onto the white frosting. The nightmare escalates into Salome single-handedly massacring everyone present with a shard of glass. After the dance sequence, back

Fig. 4. A waiter (Rolf Broman) presents Salome (Nicola Beller Carbone), Herodes (Roman Sadnik), and Herodias (Anjara Bartz) with their own heads on platters. *Salome*, directed by Magdolna Parditka and Alexandra Szemerédy. (Photograph © Thilo Beu, reprinted by permission.)

in reality, Salome demands the head of the Baptist, but is delivered Jochanaan's decapitated body instead. In the final image of the opera, Salome, Herodes, and Herodias sit around the table with Jochanaan's headless corpse on the ground as a waiter serves the trio three heads on silver platters—their own. The lines between reality and fantasy in the action following the dance are blurred. It is unclear whether Salome's fantasy about killing everyone was more than a fantasy, and thus unclear who, if anyone, is left alive at the end of the opera. What is clear, however, is the Freudian approach we are encouraged to take to interpret dream-images concocted by a developmentally stunted victim of childhood abuse.[27]

Egoyan's production does not evoke Freudian regression as explicitly, but soprano Erika Sunnegårdh imbues her Salome with childlike gestures and body language at several moments throughout the opera.[28] The swing that lifts Salome into the rafters for the Dance of the Seven Veils is set on the stage from the beginning of the action, and Salome frequently sits on it. There is some level of childlike whimsy in being on the swing at all, which is compounded by the image we get in the Dance of Salome as a smiling child also on a swing. When Egoyan's Salome seduces Narraboth to convince him to bring Jochanaan to her, her body language is a troubling blend of coy womanly sexuality and childish pleading. She lets her robe fall around her elbows and moves around him with a studied shyness, averting her eyes and peering at him over her exposed shoulders. But she also tugs on his arm petulantly and spins herself around on the swing when he resists. Many of the traditional wiles of femininity are uncomfortably close to those displayed by children, and this becomes especially clear as Salome seductively pouts her way to exactly what she wants. Sunnegårdh also depicts Salome's fear of Herodes with childlike gestures. When Herodes makes his first entrance after Salome's conversation with Jochanaan, she abruptly sits up from the posture of prostrate ecstasy she had assumed at the end of her encounter with the Baptist and clutches her knees to her chest. She sits in this fetal huddle and holds her robe around her bare legs throughout the entirety of the following scenes until she agrees to dance for Herodes.

Three more *Salome* productions also rest on our shared cultural understanding of Freudian regression and trauma. In Matthias Kaiser's 2010 production at the Theater Ulm in Germany, Salome changes into a pleated pink overall skirt and ties her hair into pigtails with pink ribbons as Herodes dons a surgical coat and rubber gloves to stage the Dance of the Seven Veils as a perverted game of "doctor." Mariame Clément staged a Salome in 2018 at the Aalto Theater in Essen in which Salome performs the Dance of the Seven Veils wearing a pink tutu given to her by Herodes. In Clément's production, there is an implication that Herodes actively feeds Salome's regressive tendencies by treating her as a child even as she grows up, gifting her a new pink tutu every birthday. David McVicar also evokes a childlike image of Salome in his 2008 production for London's Royal Opera House, though somewhat more subtly.[29] Soprano Nadja Michael plays the part of Salome's childhood self in a series of flashbacks in place of the Dance of the Seven Veils.[30] Then in the present-day events that follow, she continues to display childlike body language, seizing Jochanaan's head from the executioner and wrapping her whole body around it on the floor.

In these productions, encumbering Salome with an explicit childhood sexual trauma serves to compromise the agency with which she desires Jochanaan and manipulates Herodes. Some of these Salomes do not seem to be making choices at all; their actions are presented as strictly symptoms of their trauma. Film theorist Mary Ann Doane describes the *femme fatale* as "an ambivalent figure because she is not the subject of power but its *carrier* (the connotations of disease are appropriate here)."[31] Similarly, in these productions, Salome's power in the opera is no longer something she consciously wields, but something she is burdened with. These Salomes are still powerful in the way they influence the action, but within these structures of trauma and pathology they cannot understand that power or wield it with real agency. Their power and their trauma are diseases caught and carried, whose effects on the world of the opera are enormous but essentially involuntary.

Salome's Electra Complex (Salome via Jung): Classic psychoanalytical readings of Salome in these productions do not end with Freud. Several among these directors draw parallels between Salome's perception of Jochanaan, the object of her lust, and Herodes, her father figure. Carl Jung's Electra complex is a gender inversion of Freud's Oedipus complex: it refers to a girl's psychosexual competition with her mother for possession of her father.[32] To be clear, none of these productions explicitly represent Salome as being sexually attracted to Herodes. And as her stepfather, it is uncertain whether Salome's psyche would recognize Herodes as a father on whom to be fixated. We do not know how old the historical daughter of Herodias was when her mother married Herod Antipas, and there are no details in any of these productions about the particular circumstances of Herod and Herodias's union. But although Salome might not be a candidate for an Electra complex reading on any Neo-Jungian psychoanalyst's couch in the real world, we can still recognize implications of psychosexual regression and fixation in the choice of some directors to equate Jochanaan with Herodes in their productions.

Daniel Slater's 2015 production for Santa Fe Opera actually represents a more by-the-book Electra complex by equating Jochanaan with Salome's birth father. Like the Szemerédy and Parditka production above, Slater's mise-en-scène nods to Freud and Jung in its early-twentieth-century setting. The Dance of the Seven Veils stages the psychoanalytic uncovering of Salome's repressed memories, including pantomimes of Herodes molesting Salome as a child. We see Salome's memories of her birth father too, whom Herodes murdered. We learn that Salome's father closely resembles Jochanaan and that Herodes held him in the same cell that now holds the Baptist. The seven veils of the Dance are veils in Salome's mind—psychic partitions behind or beneath which she has tried to conceal her trauma. As director, Slater plays psychoanalyst by constructing this scenario to diagnose the root cause of Salome's dysfunction via memory recovery. This Salome longs to possess Jochanaan as a surrogate father, and her desire is informed by psychosexual regression caused by her trauma.

Three other productions blur the lines between Jochanaan as Salome's object of desire and Jochanaan as a stand-in for her father. Slater's production implied that Salome sexually desired her birth father, while these productions imply that she sexually desires Herodes. Most explicit is Kay Metzger's 2015 production of *Salome* in Detmold, in which Salome fantasizes about Jochanaan while Herodes rapes her during the Dance. James Tolksdorf, the baritone who sings Jochanaan, appears wearing Herodes's costume in this scene. We watch him and Salome engage in a romantic prelude to lovemaking, but then he becomes violent, and as Salome struggles to get away it becomes clear that her fantasy about Jochanaan cannot sufficiently protect her from the terrifying reality of her rape by Herodes. This staging leads the audience and Salome herself to identify Herodes's violence with Jochanaan's body. In Clément's production, in which Herodes gifts Salome pink tutus symbolizing ongoing abuse, Jochanaan is equated with Herodes in terms of the psychic trauma both men inflict on her. When Jochanaan rejects Salome, we see flashbacks to memories of self-harming projected on the walls of the set. Then later, during the Dance of the Seven Veils, we learn that this behavior is how Salome has responded to Herodes's sexual abuse. The pain of Jochanaan's rejection reminds Salome of her trauma, and Jochanaan becomes a scapegoat for Herodes. A similar transference seems to be at work in Szemerédy and Parditka's Freudian dream-like *Salome*. At the opera's conclusion, we see Salome sitting next to Jochanaan's headless body but presented with Herodes's head on a platter. These productions suggest that Salome's desire for Jochanaan's head has more to do with wanting him dead as a stand-in for Herodes than sexually desiring Jochanaan or the head itself. They also complicate her desire from the outset by aligning her sexual interest in Jochanaan with sexualized feelings for her stepfather. Overall, this concept contributes to diminishing Salome's agency in these rape stories. We cannot begin to understand her desire for Jochanaan outside of the terms of her abuse in these productions.

Salome Is Denied the Head of Jochanaan: Productions of this opera can diminish Salome's agency by qualifying and pathologizing the actions she takes. Still, the agency that Salome necessarily has in the way the events of the opera unfold is significant. In the end, she gets her hands on the head of Jochanaan despite Herodes's protests. Even though she is expeditiously killed for her delinquency, her success in this endeavor is remarkable. In four productions in my collection, though, the action is changed so that Salome never holds the decapitated head of Jochanaan. In Szemerédy and Parditka's production, for instance, Salome is delivered Herodes's head instead of Jochanaan's at the opera's conclusion in a Freudian twist. Francisco Negrin directed a *Salome* at the Palau de les Arts in Valencia in 2010 in which Salome is delivered the full corpse of the Baptist, under whose head Herodes slides a silver platter with an air of mocking compliance.[33] Negrin has said that he dispensed with the delivery of the head simply because he interpreted Salome's demand as an expression meaning she wants him killed.[34] But regardless of Negrin's intent, the absence of the lone head in Salome's final soliloquy feels like an anticlimax and a failing on Salome's part because of both the ubiquity of the image of the decapitated head on the silver platter and the fervency with which Salome again and again insists she be given "den Kopf des Jochanaan."[35] Romeo Castellucci's abstract, symbolic staging for the 2018 Salzburg Festival ends in similar disappointment.[36] This Salome is delivered the head of a horse, which had symbolized the Baptist earlier in the production, and then later, Jochanaan's headless body. Salome is clearly disappointed by these deliveries; she holds the horse's head over the neck of the corpse, and later, she holds her hands over the severed neck, mimes the shape of an invisible head, and kisses an invisible mouth. Although Jochanaan is still executed in these three productions, Salome is not granted precisely what she asks for. In Negrin's and Castellucci's productions, there is some sense that Herodes or other powerful figures in the court are humoring Salome. The specifics of her request are not taken seriously and so the power of her words is diminished.

Salome Takes Revenge: Five productions see Salome through an extra-textual revenge arc. In these revenge stories, Salome's history of sexual abuse motivates her to take actions that she does not take in the opera's written text, and in many of them, she survives the opera's conclusion.[37] In Clément's production, characterized above by the pink-tutu and self-harm flashbacks, Salome uses the threat of violence to force Herodes's hand after the Dance of the Seven Veils. When Herodes issues his initial refusal, Salome holds him at gunpoint until he agrees to give her Jochanaan's head. Tatjana Gürbaca's 2009 production for Dusseldorf includes much more violence and ends in a massacre. Salome kills Herodes and every other character left onstage in the opera's final moments. Metzger's production, in which Jochanaan's body stood in for Herodes's during the rape, similarly ends in wild gunfire as Salome kills Herodes and all the men who uphold his rule. These extra-textual acts of violence grant Salome some more power in this story, and in Gürbaca's and Metzger's productions, it is quite exciting to see Salome still on her feet as the curtain falls. But these acts of violence, like the Dance of the Seven Veils,

Fig. 5. Salome (Annemarie Kremer) holds Herodes (Rainer Maria Röhr) at gunpoint. *Salome*, directed by Mariame Clément. (Photograph © Martin Kaufhold, reprinted by permission.)

are framed by these productions as symptoms of Salome's trauma. Herodes's abuse and manipulation continue to steer Salome's actions even as she threatens or takes his life. Two revenge productions, though, do more to empower their Salomes through their acts of vengeance.

First, the Salome in Guy Joosten's 2009 production for Barcelona and Brussels stands out for her capacity to leverage her past trauma to achieve her goals with Herodes. During the Dance of the Seven Veils, Salome dances briefly, taunting and teasing Herodes. Then she screens a video that exposes her stepfather's abuse in front of her mother and the assembled banquet guests. The video contains footage shot by Herodes of Salome as a child in which his hand reaches into the frame to touch his stepdaughter. Toward the end of the video, Herodes overcomes his shock and gets to his feet. He tears the projection screen down, but Salome turns the projector around into the audience. The onstage spectators stare out into the house as if watching the remainder of the film projected onto the imagined fourth wall. They react in horror to what they see, though this footage is no longer visible to the real-world audience. Unlike the Salomes in many of the productions above who have involuntary flashbacks during the Dances of the Seven Veils, this Salome chooses to reveal the past in order to shame Herodes and compel him to give her Jochanaan's head. The ending of Joosten's staging is curious, and it suggests a greater sense of triumph for Salome than is typically possible for the murdered heroine. Alone at a deserted banquet table, Salome sings her final line of music, slumps back with an expression of ecstasy, and goes limp in her chair with her eyes open but glazed over. Herodes comes back onstage, observes Salome's limp body for a moment, and then orders her death, but she still does not move and no guards appear to obey the command. At the percussive chords in the orchestra that typically accompany Salome's murder, an inexplicably recapitated Jochanaan walks onto the stage. Herodes runs away, terrified. Salome sits up in her chair suddenly and the lights go down as she and Jochanaan look at each other. I understand this ending as a kind of Liebestod for Salome; she expires having accomplished everything she desires and is united with Jochanaan in death. There is a great sense of fulfillment that comes from seeing Salome and Jochanaan share the stage in these final moments.

Ted Huffman's *Salome* for Oper Köln in 2018 stages a cathartic revenge fantasy for Salome and has been heralded in the press as a laudably feminist production. Huffman took full advantage of the backdrop of Cologne's Statehouse and created a patriarchal dystopia in a modern political setting. The columned hallway is lined with identically dressed women sitting leashed on stools. Throughout the action, we witness men leading the women offstage and then returning them to their perches while the women grow increasingly disheveled. This Dance of the Seven Veils is remarkable among this group of productions because it is actually a striptease. As Salome dances and undresses for Herodes, she exudes a power and confidence in her motives that has been largely absent from these other Salomes. As the dance progresses, the sex-slaves get riled up and join in. They fight back against the men that are holding them and dance energetically around the stage and on the banquet table. After the dance, when Herodes finally agrees to deliver Jochanaan's head to Salome, guards escort an alive and intact Jochanaan onto the stage. While Salome sings her final soliloquy, she kills Jochanaan herself by cutting his throat and then smothering him. Salome's silent confidante—an addition by Huffman—frees the sex-slaves from their bonds, and then all the women jointly kill every man onstage. Salome shoots Herodes herself, and she is alive when the curtain falls.

In Huffman's production, it is not actually made explicit whether Salome herself has been raped. She is spared the debasement of the sex-slaves, which

Fig. 6. Salome (Ingela Brimberg) after shooting Herodes (John Heuzenroeder), surrounded by freed sex slaves. *Salome*, directed by Ted Huffman. (Photograph © Paul Leclaire, reprinted by permission.)

is presumably a privilege of her class. But even though this Salome is not necessarily a victim of rape, as a woman she is still certainly a victim of this culture of extreme male dominance and sexual violence. The act of revenge here is shared by all of the women oppressed by Herodes and his patriarchal order. This Salome is the only one we have seen that remains essentially in control of herself in her dance, despite the trauma and oppression of her life. There are glimmers of her inner turmoil at moments in the Dance, but primarily we see a crafty manipulator at work. The Dance of the Seven Veils retains its status as a tool with which Salome can control Herodes's gaze and gain a tactical advantage. She executes her dance with a cool professionalism that makes its transactional character clear, while behind her we see the stirrings of rebellion in the other women. Although this Salome never has a scene with the decapitated head of the prophet, this absence is not disappointing in the same way as it is in the productions above. Huffman's Salome has different priorities from the other Salomes discussed here and from the Salome of the opera's written text. While we have no reason not to believe that her desire for Jochanaan is motivating her, the real thrust of Huffman's story is toward the violence the women wreak on their oppressors at the opera's close. The spectacle of Salome gleefully smothering the bloody and struggling Jochanaan displays an interest in vengeance more than a sexual desire for his mouth. This is a man Salome can punish, both for his own sins against her and as a scapegoat for the sins of her stepfather and his cohort.

. . .

One of the principal things that giving Salome a history of sexual abuse does is account for her actions after the Dance of the Seven Veils. I have mostly focused on how justifying Salome's actions in this way serves to qualify them and thereby to strip them of much of their power. But it is also important to recognize the ways in which this interpretive project can humanize Salome. In an article on Egoyan's production, David Levin applauds the director for "[refusing] to reproduce a conventional account of the eponymous heroine as a cunning little vixen."[38] Similarly, Caryl Clark writes that "rather than being reduced to a seductive *femme fatale* figure or hysterically decadent woman, Egoyan's Salome emerges as a youthful and sympathetic character, an adolescent who is tragically molested and abused both physically and psychologically."[39] For a female monster written by men, a project of sympathetic humanization certainly has value. I also do not mean to understate the kinds of agency that the Salomes introduced in this chapter do have. In most of these stories, Salome still exerts an incredible amount of power after the Dance of the Seven Veils. And some of these Salomes take new action not assigned to them in Wilde's or in Strauss's *Salomé/e*. Still, the introduction of a traumatic pathology muddies our view of Salome's agency.

The power differential between Salome and Herodes is already immense in *Salome*'s written text, and it is exacerbated in these productions where Herodes is Salome's rapist. This power relationship is the reason I have not hesitated to refer to Herodes's sexual abuse of Salome in this chapter as incest. Feminist analyses of father-daughter incest have focused on the power differential between a male parent and female child rather than details of genetic relation or specific sexual acts.[40] Feminist social worker Lena Dominelli defines incest as "all unwanted sexual advances that occur between individuals who are involved in relationships of trust and in which one individual is subordinate to and possibly dependent on the other."[41] Herodes is not only a parent to Salome but is also a political leader; his power over her is both patriarchal and political. The fact that Salome is able to wield any power and take any action against Herodes is exceptional. Introducing the rape backstory tempers this power extraordinarily by pathologizing Salome's motives for wanting Jochanaan's head. Further, her choice to use her body and sexuality to get what she wants from Herodes is deeply complicated by the introduction of a history of a nonconsensual sexual relationship.

The worst thing that the Salome-as-rape-victim trope does is sanitize Salome's radical femininity. Traditionally, Salome's social power comes from her adherence to a stereotypically masculine constellation of sexuality, power, and violence.[42] Her predatory sexuality is abnormal and frightening in part because she is a woman. By making Salome a victim of rape, these productions place her firmly back on the feminine side in the patriarchal order. She is made to be the receptor of sexualized violence first, so that her later forays into a violent sexuality can be explained by means of this instigating trauma. But there is a potential antidote to the tragic victimization of Salome in these productions in the revenge-fantasy trope. Many of this subgroup of productions revel in their violence in a way that reminds me of those Renaissance paintings of Judith beheading Holofernes that emphasize the brutality of the act and the power of the woman.[43] At its best, introducing a storyline about sexual violence to this opera motivates Salome into an ultimate act of triumphant, revolutionary female rage. And in the absence of a canonical opera about Judith, Salome does seem a good candidate for such directorial treatment.[44] Huffman's revenge *Salome* stands out: a grotesque exploration of deviant sexuality this production is not, but Huffman's Salome claims agency in different ways. Not only does she kill Jochanaan herself, she plots to free all the other women onstage and leads them in a massacre of the men. Huffman invokes sexual violence in his *Salome* to tell a story about radical female agency, but he tells it through the mode of violence more than the mode of sex. His Salome still manipulates Herodes during the Dance of the Seven Veils but only as a precursor to staging a bloody revolution.

Rape as Performance in the Dance of the Seven Veils

In all of these productions, the Dance of the Seven Veils is the backdrop for the images that reveal Salome's sexual abuse. These revelations of abuse are therefore necessarily in conversation with the context of the Dance as a spectacle of erotic performance. Conflating the Dance of the Seven Veils with rape has striking consequences for the way we engage with the sexual violence as spectators. An audience member familiar with *Salome* will be used to seeing a striptease take place during this scene accompanied by this music. Even an audience member unfamiliar with the story will expect a dance to take place because that is what Herodes asks for in the lead up to this scene.

Aligning images relating to sexual violence with the music of this scene in the context of a performance creates a kind of dramaturgical dissonance. Within this dissonance, there is room for a productive critical commentary on the nature of Salome's dance for Herodes, but there is also the potential to encourage a voyeuristic gaze that eroticizes sexual violence against a child.

Few of the productions above stage a sexual assault in view of the audience as a part of their revelations during the Dance of the Seven Veils. There are several assaults that occur offstage or otherwise out of sight during the Dance, though. In Clément's production, Herodes forces Salome under the banquet table with him, and she emerges looking disheveled and distraught. Negrin's Herodes similarly interrupts Salome's dance by dragging her into an adjacent room offstage. When they reemerge, he is fastening his clothing and she is clearly in pain. McVicar's Salome also follows Herodes back out onto the stage after the Dance, doubled over and wringing her hands, leaving us to guess what took place as the music played. There are many reasons for not staging a rape in these and the other productions that subscribe to the trope of Salome-as-raped. Locating the act offstage avoids a great number of practical problems that arise from performing rape, including risk to performers and audience members. It cordons off sexual assault as an unspeakable horror that can be alluded to but never made clear. But directors who do not stage the rape must sacrifice some of their control over how it will be understood. In her analysis of Mary Birnbaum's 2015 staging of *The Rape of Lucretia* for Juilliard Opera, Ellie Hisama applauds the production for leaving "no doubt as to the sincerity of Lucretia's vigorous resistance."[45] This kind of clarity is important. The tension between Wilde's sexually predatory Salome and the sexually traumatized Salomes of these productions means there is a real risk of implying Salome's culpability in her own abuse. When directors tell stories with sexual violence at their center, making strong, thoughtful choices about how to represent that violence allows them to push back against problematic social ideas and conventions.

Those productions that do stage acts of sexual violence are able to exert control over these representations, yet the context of performance and spectacle in this scene has troubling implications. The role of the gaze is central to Wilde's and to Strauss's *Salomé/e*. Salome is an object of constant visual fascination and scrutiny by the other characters and by the audience. In this context, the choice to make her rape visible—to make it a spectacle—is a fraught one. Egoyan's production thematizes surveillance and centers the politics of looking, and representing Salome's rape as an act of performance for spectators is a part of this larger project. By thematizing the gaze of the other, Egoyan makes us aware of our own voyeuristic role in the drama. Like Herodes, we peer at things we are not meant to see, looking in on Salome at her most vulnerable. But this critical awareness of our own gaze is not the only way an audience might interact with Egoyan's Dance scene. What we see is not the dance that Salome performs for Herodes in the action of the opera, but it is, in part, still a dance. The shadow-play depicting Salome's gang rape is danced throughout; the violence is precisely choreographed and highly stylized. Levin notes, "the aestheticization acts as a kind of fulcrum, allowing the horror to teeter between a mimetic performance (Salome's dance as rape) and a performative mimesis (Salome's rape as dance)."[46] But by aligning Salome's rape with erotic dance in the context of the story and then staging the rape itself as a dance, Egoyan's Dance of the Seven Veils may be seen as a beautiful spectacle for entertainment, even within Egoyan's larger critique of the gaze.

Egoyan's aestheticization of the rape in the Dance of the Seven Veils can be understood in part as a response to early criticism of the production. The most significant change between the earlier productions (1996 and 2002) and the 2013 remount was to further stylize the shadow play during the Dance, which in the earlier versions had been more graphic. With a single, motionless light source, the shadows cast were true to life and Salome's penetration and violation were more apparent to the audience. In *Theatre & Violence*, Lucy Nevitt warns that "an image of rape has such power that it can easily escape its context and come to dominate a spectator's experience of the performance."[47] This is evident in the earlier version of Egoyan's *Salome*, when the critical response to the production in 2002 centered on the rape. Egoyan told me that the audience reaction to the 2002 staging did play into his decision to soften the depiction. He said that in the earlier production the rape was "incredibly raw" and "very, very upsetting to people, maybe even more than it needed to be."[48] He understood this to be essentially a problem of calibration and felt privileged to have had the opportunity of a restaging to make adjustments. In 2013, Egoyan collaborated with shadow artist Clea Minaker to rethink this portion of the Dance. Egoyan says of the changes: "We mitigated [the graphic nature of the violation] with this new imagery. . . . We made it more lyrical, I suppose. It was less harsh. The first presentation was extremely harsh."[49] This new imagery included a carousel of ballerina figures casting shadows and flurries of leaves in the forest shots. Most apparently, the gang rape is rendered harder to see because of the motion of multiple light sources and the inclusion of the shadows of tree limbs that recall the imagery of the forest. The whole scene is more metaphorical, even somewhat veiled, and the moment of penetration is obscured.

While Egoyan and Minaker's reinterpretation of the rape in 2013 is certainly less shocking than the earlier version, I worry that this emotional distance and aesthetic softening might serve to glamorize and fetishize the violence being depicted. In the context of a performance of *Salome*, this relationship between the content and form of violent representations is further complicated by the music. The music of Strauss's Dance of the Seven Veils has been widely lambasted as kitschy, Orientalist, and uninspired. But, perhaps due to Strauss's generally high standing as a composer among musicologists, a number of scholars have searched for ways to understand these qualities of the music as an intentional dramatic choice. Lawrence Kramer has remarked that "the famous 'badness' of [the music] seems meant to guarantee both a certain power and a certain sleaziness."[50] Similarly, Robin Holloway remarks that "we all know how strangely potent cheap music can be."[51] There are a couple of dominant theories about why Strauss may have wanted this music to be "cheap" and "sleazy," and they come down to the question: Which character's point of view does this music represent?

Some critics have suggested that the music speaks to Salome's point of view and contains clues about her true character. Derrick Puffett has suggested that because the orchestra sensually "heaves and gyrates" in the Dance, Salome cannot be chaste.[52] Kramer also attributes the music to Salome, but to a deeper level of her consciousness. He understands the Dance as a form of psychoanalysis and as "the one moment in her opera when Salome, with uncontested success, translates the unspeakableness of her desire at full tilt into a body language."[53] Another camp sees the music as speaking more to Herodes's experience of the dance than Salome's. Davinia Caddy suggests we might see the Dance as a moment of repositioned subjectivity where the "heaving" and "gyrating" reflect Herodes's sexual climax rather than Salome's.[54] Holloway's colorful descriptions of Strauss's music are frequently cited as examples of the alleged musicological distaste for the music of Strauss's Dance of the Seven Veils—in particular his oft-quoted descriptor, "bargain-basement orientalism."[55] But Holloway's critique actually rests on the tension between recognizing the "badness" of the music and still being stirred by it, and this dual recognition of badness and arousal lends itself quite well to an interpretation of the music of the Dance as representing Herodes's experience. Our discomfort may be attributable in part to being made to feel allegiance with a distasteful character, his incestuous desire, and his violent point of view. These two primary interpretations of the music, as representing Salome's sexuality or Herodes's odious desire, both have merit based on the written text of the opera. But in performance, such multivalence is somewhat limited by the creative choices made by the cast and production team. And when this music scores not just a dance but an assault, the implications that the music might represent Salome's sexual desire becomes fraught.

Egoyan described the music of the Dance to me as a "very perverse soundtrack to a whole series of possible imaginings."[56] He also said: "[Herodes's] ability to extract a performative element [from Salome's] own sexuality was something that I found quite disturbing and I wanted to give us a glimpse into how that relationship might have worked."[57] So to Egoyan's understanding, the music belongs both to Salome and to Herodes. It is a self-consciously performative rendering of Salome's sexuality, endowed with layers of repressed trauma from her past sexual abuse. It speaks to both the darkness in Salome's past and the cheap sexuality demanded by her abuser. In one sense, the "flagrant . . . bump-and-grind exoticism" of the dance music is a deeply troubling accompaniment to Salome's rape.[58] But even in its softened, aestheticized 2013 form, the rape itself is still too horrifying to be rendered sexually arousing by the music. Instead, the music takes on the violence of the action. Egoyan is aware that representing violence in an aesthetic medium carries the risk that viewers may find such imagery titillating. When I asked him about his approach to this fine line between stylization and fetishization, he stopped himself mid-sentence and said, "I was going to say you have to be cautious, but you don't have to be cautious at all. I think you have to be bold, and you have to test what those balances are, and sometimes you're going to go too far."[59]

I appreciate that in Egoyan's staging the rape is not pornographic—Salome's flesh is hidden from us and the sex acts we see are not performed for realism. Yet the presence of the gaze is felt powerfully in the opera and amplified further in Egoyan's staging. And the music that underscores the images of Salome as a child and Salome being raped is music intended for and associated with a striptease. The music sexualizes the child-Salome and turns her trauma and loss of innocence into spectacle. Lucy Nevitt uses the example of Peter Brook's famous 1955 staging of *Titus Andronicus* at Stratford's Shakespeare Memorial Theatre to explore the issue of stylized violence. Lavinia appeared with highly stylized wounds symbolized by scarlet streamers coming from her wrists sand mouth. Nevitt argues that the beauty of the imagery "foregrounds the spectator's sympathy for Lavinia's plight. She is an innocent victim, and the spectator is guided to contemplate her suffering without being asked to imagine too precisely its actual manifestation on her body. . . . Brook's choice was to communicate *suffering*. The image communicates very little about brutal violence and rape."[60] In this instance, Nevitt sees the veiling of the harsh realities of Lavinia's injuries as a tactic to keep the audience trained on Lavinia's pain—to make them cry rather than to make them sick.[61] I agree that a beautiful representation of violence can evoke pity where a graphic representation would trigger some amount of spectatorial revulsion or even perverse pleasure. Yet making Lavinia's injuries beautiful also poeticizes them, and by locating her suffering in the realm of art it becomes a spectacle *to be looked at*. Suffering loses its immediacy; audience members are not bystanders of a horrible event but spectators of a tragic artwork. This kind of aestheticization mitigates outrage—but maybe we should be outraged.

Serge Bennathan's choreography for the rape ballet in Egoyan's 2013 *Dance of the Seven Veils* is beautiful but does not exclude violence. Levin says of the dance choreography, "[Salome] is whirled about overhead, and in the process, her figure remonstrates with the frantic melodramatic gestures of early twentieth-century modernist dance-theater."[62] The movement is all highly stylized, but within that framework we see dancer-Salome kicking and writhing as she is violated. Still, the beauty of this ballet gives me pause. While this kind of veiled half-seeing of the rape may prevent fetishized looking at realist depictions of nudity, blood, and sweat, I worry about the stylization itself being an act of fetishization. The projection screen separates the shadow-image of Salome's dancing feminine shape from the body of Salome we have seen onstage to this point. Singer-Salome is objectified by the gaze of the soldiers, the audience, Herodes, and his surveillance, but she is also deeply embodied. Paul Robinson and Carolyn Abbate have argued that the incredible acoustic power of women's voices in opera prevents their characters from being experienced simply as passive victims.[63] Salome's embodied power is also typically expressed through the Dance of the Seven Veils when we get to see her dance. At this moment in Egoyan's production, when we come to understand Salome as a victim, she is without her voice and her dancing body is flattened into silhouette. Griselda Pollock has argued that throughout art history, men's representations of women are typified by bodily presence and vocal absence.[64] The shift from the embodied singer-Salome to the disembodied silhouette of dancer-Salome encourages us to perceive the depiction of the assault at a distance—that is, fetishistically. And as per the performance convention of this opera, the separation between Salome's body and her shadow is amplified by the knowledge that the singer and dancer are different performers.

The scrim on which we see Salome's disembodied form, as shadow and as video, also serves to block some elements of the rape from view. As we have seen, themes of veiling and specifically of selectively blocking what is seen are part of Egoyan's overarching approach to this opera. The scrim as a veil acts in part as a demarcation of past from present. The images and events presented on the screen are removed in time from the rest of the opera. Memory preserves events imperfectly and subjectively, and the images we see projected onto the scrim are likewise blurred—emotionally evocative rather than dispassionately precise. The projections during the Dance also mark this scene as a representation and highlight its constructedness. The events and ideas we see are mediated not just through Salome's memory, but through Egoyan's, Minaker's, and Bennathan's art. The artfulness of the Dance of the Seven Veils is marked in contrast to the rest of the opera. This movement in particular requires an act of interpretation by its audience. Subjective and in some senses unknowable, this mode of representation might be seen in the context of ideas from trauma studies about the nature of trauma and memory. Cathy Caruth writes that the history a traumatic flashback tells is "a history that literally *has no place*, neither in the past, in which it was not fully experienced, nor in the present, in which its precise images and enactments are not fully understood."[65] The drastic shift in Egoyan's style for the entire flashback sequence of the Dance of the Seven Veils establishes that the images we see have a different relationship to reality than the rest of the opera. We appear to be in Salome's mind as she remembers her own childhood in a series of flashes and metaphors. The home-video footage of the child on the swing stands in stark contrast to the blindfolded girl wandering alone through the endless forest. The camera failed to capture the dark truth of Salome's childhood. Egoyan's Dance of the Seven Veils dramatizes Salome opening her eyes to the trauma in her past, but the way she comes to perceive that trauma is necessarily irrational. The artfulness of the Dance represents the impossibility for Salome to precisely report what happened to her, even within her own mind.

Put briefly, the context of performance in Egoyan's rape scene is complicated. The stylized depiction of sexual violence evokes sympathy, and it can be understood as a compelling representation of traumatic memory. But it also places Salome's striptease in troubling proximity to her rape. This representational closeness might encourage voyeuristic consumption of Salome's rape as an erotic spectacle, and it also risks equating these two events causally within the world of the opera. The choreography for the shadow ballet in both versions of this scene begins with Salome performing her striptease before she is interrupted by the men, and her movements shift from dancing qua dancing to stylized resistance to her attackers. Two rape myths identified by Rosalind Gill are pertinent to this scene: "One of the most pervasive and established beliefs about rape is that victims in some way provoke it—by their dress or conduct,"[66] and another is that "the male attacker is assumed to be full of pent-up sexual feelings, and is driven beyond normal self-control by the lust engendered by a particular woman."[67] By including Salome's performance of an erotic dance in the same shadow-play as the rape, Egoyan encourages us—intentionally or not—to understand the two events in tandem. And doing so plays into pervasive myths about rape familiar to audiences from the real world. As much as the depiction of the rape itself is unquestionably violent and nonconsensual, its proximity to Salome's striptease sets up a narrative wherein, even if we do not blame her for what happened, we can say that Salome got raped *because* . . .

Metzger's production also stages a rape during the Dance of the Seven Veils—sort of. This is the production in which Salome fantasizes about Jochanaan during the rape, so she perceives it first as a sexual encounter with the object of her desire and only later as a rape. At the beginning of the Dance, we seem to watch Salome and Jochanaan engage in consensual, romantic foreplay. James Tolksdorf, who sings Jochanaan, appears in this scene wearing Herodes's costume. As the Dance scene continues, Jochanaan/Herodes becomes more and more violent, and the spell is broken. Salome struggles to get away as Herodes, who still looks like Jochanaan, holds her down and rapes her. The rape stands out as particularly brutal and frightening after the sweet romantic play at the beginning of the encounter. As spectators, we are made to adjust the image of the rape in our own minds' eyes. We remind ourselves that the man raping Salome is not who he appears to be. Actually, he is Herodes. He is her stepfather. The act of correction required of us as spectators highlights the wrongness of the incest while we watch the horrors of the rape. To my mind, the progression from foreplay to rape in this production does not draw sex and rape closer together. Instead, it makes particularly clear how unlike sex rape is. Salome tries to hide from the reality of this scene in her fantasy, but she is unable to recast Herodes's violation as anything like the kind of union she desires with Jochanaan. Metzger's staging thus affirms the irreconcilability of sex and rape from Salome's point of view.

The only other production I have uncovered from this period of practice that both participates in the Salome-as-raped trope and stages an explicit act of sexual violence during the Dance of the Seven Veils is Silvana Schröder's 2011 *Salome* for Kiel Opera. It provides an interesting counterpoint to Egoyan's production because its approach to staging the sexual violence in this scene eschews stylization in favor of stark realism.[68] In Schröder's production, the Dance culminates in Herodes forcing Salome to perform oral sex on him onstage while a video projection shows a great dark hand pulling back seven blankets from a child-Salome's sleeping figure. Here, the sevenfold unveiling of Salome's body is transferred from the context of an exotic striptease to that of the sexualization and abuse of an unconscious child. The onstage assault is starkly realist. The placement of Salome's body between Herodes's legs means there is no need for onstage nudity, but the implication is unambiguous. It is jarring to watch an explicit real-time assault while listening to the exaggerated performance of Orientalist eroticism in Strauss's score. This discomfort can be valuable for a representation of abuse. This scene certainly lays bare the humiliating, terrifying, and painful realities of sexual violence. But depicting a sexual act so realistically also has a troubling pornographic potential, especially when allied with overtly erotic dance music as it is here.

No approach to staging Salome's rape during the Dance of the Seven Veils can avoid all of the pitfalls I have outlined here. There is not a single right way to ethically represent sexual violence, especially not in a story like this one that is not necessarily about sexual violence at all. Simply, the context of the Dance of the Seven Veils is not conducive to an ethical representation of rape. Within the story, it is an erotic performance and a moment that displays Salome's unlikely power over her own body and image. Replacing or augmenting that dance with an act of sexual violence committed against Salome both eroticizes that violence and strips Salome of her agency.

...

Wilde's and Strauss's *Salomé/e* have richly ambiguous written texts that can support a plurality of meanings. Salome can be understood in terms of feminist empowerment, as she was by so many exotic dancers in New York in the early twentieth century. To be clear, I am not suggesting that objectifying and executing men is feminist, only that as a fictional woman, Salome critiques and counterbalances traditional narratives that cast women as innocent victims and sexual objects.[69] Wilde's *Salomé* in particular has also been read by some critics as a queer figure and her obsessive desire for Jochanaan as an allegory for non-normative sexuality.[70] Some productions of Wilde's play have toyed with the idea that beneath her veils, Salome conceals a masculinity and specifically a queer masculinity.[71] Indeed, queer readings of Wilde's *Salomé* have often suggested that the antiheroine is a stand-in for Wilde himself.[72] But in addition to these potential empowering readings, both play and opera can also be understood in terms of an old antisemitic trope. Consider an 1892 review of Saint-Saëns's *Samson et Dalila* that characterized Dalila as "the Jewish woman who sells her body for the good of her country or the vengeance of her God" and compared her with Salammbo and Judith who he claims are "the same woman," three seductresses that use their sexuality to destroy men.[73] Salome trades her body to Herodes, in a sense, for vengeance, but it is her own vengeance and desire that she serves with this act.

Productions of Strauss's opera can heighten or resist the different possible interpretations of Salome. I find this to be one of the most exciting things about this written text; speculating about Salome's character and motivations allows for so many different possible stories. Egoyan's reading of *Salome* as a story about the profound effects of sexual violence on a developing sexual subject is an interesting and worthwhile contribution. The story is recast and rendered unexpectedly tragic by the choice to imagine Salome not in terms of her monstrosity but in terms of her pain. But it is a problem to take this interpretation as the truth of the matter, or even as the most convincing reading. The productions in this chapter all represent Salomes defined by the trauma of sexual violence and they do so in general to the exclusion of queer themes and critical reflection on the opera's representation of Jewishness.[74] Despite the Orientalist music of the opera's written text, the Salomes in this chapter are conspicuously white overall. The whitewashing of exotic stories when white directors want to tell stories about sexual violence is a recurring theme in this book that I will discuss in the conclusion. For now, suffice it to say that the prevalence of these productions of *Salome* as a story about the consequences of childhood sexual abuse, and the tendency of the productions to tell that story through a white racial frame, minimizes our perception of other interpretations of this story.

Egoyan told me that with his initial approach to *Salome* in 1996, he could take for granted that the COC audience was familiar with a traditional production of the opera that they had been living with through several remounts. He said:

> What I did in 1996 was a response and a dialogue I was trying to create with that more traditional production that people had seen. Now, over twenty years later, a new generation is removed from that production, and it does give me pause to think, what if someone is seeing my production of *Salome* for the first time and it's their first exposure to the piece? Is that responsible? And that's a good question.[75]

It is among my aims with this book to expand this question of responsibility. I believe that the stakes of introducing sexual violence to a work and putting it onstage are greater than those relating to spectators misapprehending a work's original or intended meanings. In *Theatre & Violence*, Nevitt writes "production decisions about how violence and its effects will be represented offer a judgment about that violence. . . . It makes a difference whether the image is beautiful or ugly. Those choices are both aesthetic and political."[76] I have demonstrated in this chapter some of the larger ramifications the abused-Salome trope can have. These directors have the power to reinforce or challenge toxic cultural ideas about female victimization, victim-blaming, and rape culture, and so it is vital for us as audience members and critics to think through the implications of their choices.

At its best, the addition of sexual violence to Strauss's *Salome* turns it into a story of righteous, incandescent female rage. At its worst, it makes this a maudlin tale of yet another woman victimized and broken by a cruel man gluttonous for power over her. There is no set of directorial choices that will necessarily distinguish the former from the latter when producing a *Salome* in this fashion. I have modeled a way of thinking through the effect that this production concept for *Salome* has on the story and its characters, and the work it does in the world of contemporary academic and popular feminist ideas. The most successful productions according to my framework are those that find ways to grant new agency to Salome's character in light of the agency she loses when her violence toward Jochanaan is pathologized.

The way acts of sexual violence are staged, if they are staged at all, in these productions is somewhat more complicated. An aestheticized depiction can have the benefit of focusing audience attention on Salome's suffering by removing potentially gratuitous nudity. And yet in our current cultural moment, in which we are struggling to see sexual violence understood as the egregious crime that it is, there is a benefit to depicting these acts in a way that gestures toward their harsh reality. But audiences are multifaceted, and there is also the risk that the same shockingly realistic representation of sexual violence that may help some audience members to appreciate that rape is a crime of domination rather than of lust, may serve to retraumatize others. There is not a single right way to ethically represent sexual violence. The stakes are too high for too many people for a single formula to be sufficient. I can only urge opera creators to think hard about what they want to achieve by putting sexual violence onstage and how to meet those goals as precisely as possible with their dramaturgical choices.

I advocate for a mode of criticism for opera production whose scope stretches beyond judgments about perceived authenticity and allegiance to the score to ask instead what kinds of stories we want to tell with the canon now. I do not believe that a production in which Salome is raped by Herodes, past or present, is an accurate interpretation of what Wilde and Strauss have written, but that is not the only valuable question to ask of this interpretation. I have asked instead how this reading works in practice: How does it affect the story and its characters? How does it influence our understanding of the work? Despite my disbelief that Strauss or Wilde intended a backstory about Salome being raped, Egoyan told me a coherent story in his production in partnership with Wilde's text and Strauss's music. I left the theater that night in 2013 troubled by the rape scene and its implications on the story in large part because Egoyan had made it work. But the power that a directorial concept can have to help us see new truths in the works we love is threatened if that concept itself becomes canon. I would be greatly saddened to see the rape-victim reading of *Salome* become the principal way that directors and audiences interact with the story, because more often than not the introduction of the rape storyline operates at the expense of what I have found to be the most compelling, revolutionary aspects of Salome's character—her unapologetically non-normative sexual desire and her absolute objectification of Jochanaan, which is still today a powerfully subversive position for a woman to take.[77]

Three

Die Entführung aus dem Serail and the Limits of Critique

Mozart's 1782 Singspiel, *Die Entführung aus dem Serail*, presents an abundance of problems to modern interpreters. The libretto by Friedrich Bretzner, adapted by Gottlieb Stephanie, tells the story of the nobleman Belmonte's heroic rescue of his lover, Konstanze, her maid, Blonde, and his servant, Pedrillo, from the Turkish seraglio of Bassa Selim and his henchman, Osmin. The constant threat of violence pervades all aspects of the story. Selim warns Konstanze that if she does not consent to love him, he will use force to compel her. Osmin, the Turkish *buffo*, describes in horrible detail all the ways he would like to torture and kill the men who plot to take the women away. Mozart's *alla turca* style in the overture and chorus numbers reinforces the Orientalism of the story, which is in itself problematic for some audiences today. But beyond the general tensions in presenting musical exoticism in the present day, *Entführung*'s characterization of the bumbling and murderous Osmin paints an appalling picture of the exotic Turkish man. The story ends with Selim setting the lovers free, and this act of mercy is construed as a victory of Enlightened thought—that magnanimous gift of the West—over Eastern obscurantism.

Originally intended to be premiered for the Russian Grand Duke Paul, *Entführung* is one of a number of Turkish novelties intended to celebrate the Russian defeat of the Ottomans in the previous decade and commemorate the Ottoman defeat at the siege of Vienna in 1683. Now that they were no longer considered a threat, representations of the Ottomans in Vienna in the 1780s were often farcical.[1] For *Entführung*'s earliest audiences, it is possible that the women were never perceived to be in any real danger at all, despite the constant threats of violence articulated by their captors. The

Turkish characters and the seraglio in *Entführung* have new meanings when performed in the West today. While in reality, Turkey's foreign policy in the twentieth century has made it a close ally of Western Europe and America, the Orientalist Turkish fantasy of *Entführung* is more likely to evoke Western anxieties about the Middle East, especially in North America post 9/11.

Despite its stereotypes and mockery of the East, *Entführung* is still performed regularly (in 2019, it saw thirty-three productions worldwide) and, more often than not, uncritically. The unblinking portrayal of palace guards in turbans and harem pants in many contemporary productions, including The Metropolitan Opera's most recent staging from 2016, is startlingly oblivious to contemporary concerns about cultural appropriation and ethical representation. This chapter considers two recent productions of *Entführung* that make an effort to address some of the representational problems in this opera: Calixto Bieito's 2004 production for the Komische Oper Berlin and Wajdi Mouawad's 2016 production co-commissioned by Opéra Lyon and the Canadian Opera Company. Both of these productions radically reinvent the story and, in particular, the representation of sexual violence.

Bieito's and Mouawad's productions take opposite approaches to interpreting and representing the violence in *Entführung*, and they illuminate how significantly a director's approach to staging sexual and gendered violence impacts an opera's meanings. Bieito's *Entführung*, set in a modern-day European brothel, takes seriously and amplifies the threats of violence and torture that litter the libretto, resulting in a production that stages multiple rapes and murders of sex workers. Mouawad attempts to neutralize the sexual violence of the story almost entirely by means of an ambitious reconceptualization of the narrative. He reimagines the original action of the Singspiel as a flashback narrated by Konstanze, Blonde, Belmonte, and Pedrillo in a series of newly written spoken scenes interspersed through the show. Konstanze and Blonde try to explain that their captors are misunderstood and actually treated them quite well. Mouawad's direction nullifies the violent language in the libretto by reimagining it as either affectionate joking or excusable outbursts that do not reflect the true feelings of the speakers.

The majority of this chapter focuses on Bieito's production by virtue of its multiple staged acts of sexual violence. I analyze the ways these acts are represented onstage, considering their resonance with rape myths and the context of performance. Many audience members and critics have objected to Bieito's staging of such graphic acts of violence, but using Mouawad's *Entführung* as a foil highlights some of the benefits to Bieito's controversial approach. While my analysis focuses on sexual violence, the dual representations of

Turkey are vital to the representation of women in these productions. Where Bieito sidesteps some of the potential for Orientalist caricature by setting his production in a brothel with all white singers, Mouawad invests in a reparative representation of Turkishness and of Islam. Both of these approaches face the Orientalism of this opera and attempt to address it in a twenty-first century context, but given the limitations of the source material, both approaches ultimately fall short. While Bieito removes the visual markers of racial or ethnic otherness, the references to Turkey remain and (perhaps inadvertently) invoke modern-day tensions about Germany's large marginalized Turkish population and the largely Eastern European makeup of Germany's sex trade. Ultimately, I consider the successes and the failures of these productions to produce critical commentary on Mozart and Stephanie's *Entführung*. This constitutes a fourth axis of analysis for this book: the risks and limitations of critiquing politically troublesome operas through staging.

Calixto Bieito's *Die Entführung aus dem Serail*

Since its premiere at the Komische Oper Berlin in 2004, Calixto Bieito's *Entführung* has generated ongoing controversy over its displays of nudity and explicit depictions of sex and violence onstage. The opening night crowd was divided between boos and fervent reassuring applause. Many audience members walked out opening night, and a representative from DaimlerChrysler was so outraged that he threatened to pull his company's sponsorship. Despite or because of the scandal, the production's renown brought it back to the Komische Oper stage several times before its final run in 2018.

Bieito's concept pulls *Entführung* from its Orientalist context and reimagines the seraglio as a modern-day European brothel. The stage is a gaudy pink, lit with colored lights, and plastered with images advertising women in lingerie. The most striking element of Bieito's mise-en-scène is a collection of glass-walled boxes onstage in which sex workers dance, strip, and perform sexual acts for clients in the background of much of the main action. Selim is a gangster who runs the brothel, and Osmin is his gold-chain-clad right-hand man. Blonde works at the brothel while Selim keeps Konstanze leashed in a small cage. When Belmonte infiltrates the brothel, he goes undercover not as an architect, as in the libretto, but in drag, presumably passing himself off as a sex worker. To make his concept work, Bieito adds to and alters the spoken dialogue, but manages to maintain a surprising amount of the original text. Toward the end of the opera, though, Bieito's concept departs from the original story, and the dialogue scenes are largely rewritten. After Belmonte

Fig. 7. Osmin (Andreas Hörl) and some of the sex workers beat Pedrillo (Thomas Ebenstein). *Die Entführung aus dem Serail*, directed by Calixto Bieito. (Photograph © Monika Rittershaus, reprinted by permission.)

and Pedrillo are reunited with their lovers, they arm themselves and shoot up the brothel, massacring all the clients, bodyguards, and sex workers onstage. They are still subsequently captured and forgiven by Selim, but the Pasha's forgiveness is no longer motivated by a desire to show mercy for mercy's sake. Now it seems to come from a genuine love for Konstanze. He unties Konstanze, gives her his gun, tells her he loves her, and then she shoots him. Blonde shoots Osmin shortly thereafter. The final celebratory chorus number exalting the Pasha's mercy is now twisted into a celebration of Belmonte, who dons a white suit and a pair of sunglasses and takes over Selims's role as head of the brothel. Konstanze, sitting at the front of the stage, sees what Belmonte has become, and after the final notes of music she shoots herself.

While Bieito's production offers a critical reading of a problematic opera, his approach is not itself immune to criticism. The strength of this production lies for me in the unblinking portrayal of sexualized violence, which makes it impossible for audiences to miss the themes of violence and consent already present in *Entführung*. Bieito also takes a clear stand on the brutality of the sex trade at a pivotal moment in German sex work legislation. In 2002,

Germany adopted the controversial Prostitution Act (ProstG) in an attempt to improve working conditions for sex workers.[2] This kind of contemporary resonance and political messaging is one of the most exciting things about *Regietheater*. Yet despite a compelling critical concept, the production's critique of misogyny sometimes gets lost in its graphic depictions of sexualized violence and its objectification of women's bodies. My analysis is based on a video recording of the premiere of the Komische Oper's production on June 20, 2004.

Violence and Desensitization

Sexual violence is pervasive throughout Bieito's production of *Entführung*. Selim, Osmin, Pedrillo, and Belmonte all commit acts of violence against women onstage including nonconsensual sex acts, sexual humiliation, and abuse of sex workers by pimps. Among the representations of these acts are several realistic simulations of extremely graphic violence against women. The depictions of acts of sexual violence in this production are the most graphic discussed in this book so far. I recognize the difficulty of viewing and even reading about these representations of violence, yet discussion of the details of these scenes is too important to my project to be omitted. Before moving into describing these depictions, I want to be upfront about the potential harms of engaging with graphic simulations of violence as well as the harms of ignoring them.

It is not controversial to suggest that over time exposure to violent imagery can lead to desensitization. The more we watch, the more we are comfortable watching. There is a culture of one-upmanship in *Regietheater* productions that attempts to overcome desensitization. Shocking audiences to jolt them out of their comfortable opera-watching reveries is a common goal in this art form, so for audiences who see a lot of *Regietheater* the shock value of the productions must logically continue to increase or at least modulate. There seems to be a certain kind of desensitization to the violence of *Regie* at work in reviewers of Bieito's *Entführung* who casually brush off the graphic violence of this production to the tune of "there goes Calixto, up to his tricks again."[3] Indeed, many commentators who have reviewed Bieito's *Entführung* group the representations of sexual violence in this production together with, for instance, nudity and representations of drug use into a single category of typical *Regietheater* scandal-mongering. In his 2013 history of opera production and staging, Evan Baker voices his distress about directors who "have inserted graphic sexual situations or seemingly pointless nudity into the dramaturgy of an opera, in some cases to excess, causing much revulsion" and uses this *Entführung* production as a case in point.[4] A reviewer for the Metropolitan Opera Guild expresses concern about the brutalization of sex workers in this production, but he connects it with his concerns about Belmonte's cross-dressing and a scene of homoerotic contact between women—as if rape might be effectively understood as an expression of queer sexuality.[5] A review for the *Irish Times* includes a quote from a spectator at the theater who said, "I don't know what all the fuss is about, if they knew anything about Mozart, they'd know that there's loads of this sort of thing in his letters."[6] I assume this audience member was referring to Mozart's well-documented appreciation for scatological humor. This too denies any real difference in kind between representing rape and torture and representing nudity and urination. It implies that any objection to this staging must be based merely in prudishness.

Although I approached this production as a researcher and informed about its contents, I could not share in the cynical immovability of many of the critics cited above. The most infamous scene of violence in this production is Konstanze's aria, "Martern aller Arten." My first experience watching this scene was through grainy archival footage on my laptop screen on a sunny afternoon—surely not Bieito's intended circumstances—and even then, I was so troubled by the staging that I needed to walk away from this research for several days. There is something striking about seeing this kind of violence in the context of live performance. Even a video of a live performance that took place fifteen years prior held for me a different kind of power than a similar depiction of violence represented in film—an aura of liveness. There is no camera work when you are looking at a stage; no one can frame the image or cut away at key moments to guide an audience member's eye. I was not asked to imagine anything but only to watch. I could not help but stare, horrified, at every moment.

Desensitization is not the only risk to viewing graphic depictions of fictional violence, though. Despite regular exposure to violent imagery in the media, I found this production difficult to bear at first watching and I still do, now. Watching the dehumanizing treatment of the women in this production stirred up the anxiety I carry as a woman navigating a patriarchal society; these representations of violence did not just make me feel uncomfortable, they made me feel afraid. As I discussed in the introduction to this book, in relation to Catharine Woodward's objection to Damiano Michieletto's *Guillaume Tell*, these kinds of representations have the potential to retraumatize survivors in their audiences, and given the prevalence of sexual violence in our society, this is not a risk we should take lightly.

My forthcoming descriptions of the acts of sexual violence in Bieito's production are not exempt from these risks. Yet not including the details of these representations would not be a suitable solution. Reviews of this production often invoke innuendo to discuss the sexual violence, and I worry that doing so makes it easier for them and their readers to include rape on these lists of non-violent depictions deemed to be in bad taste. My analysis of this production treats the representations of sexual violence as fundamentally different from the nudity, cross-dressing, and simulations of urination and drug use onstage. Based on the reviews cited above and others like them, sexual violence is grouped together with these other "scandalous" elements of Bieito's *Entführung* insofar as it is seen to threaten both the perceived seriousness of opera and the hegemony of the composer's wishes. These are not my concerns. My focus is on protecting not the legacy of the opera but the people who stand to be negatively impacted by its continued performance. Among this group I count not only audience members, but also members of identity groups that are stereotyped in the written text of *Entführung* and in the productions discussed here, namely women, Muslims, and sex workers.

In this chapter, I present a framework through which the choice to represent sexual violence in an opera like *Entführung* may be seen to be, perhaps paradoxically, the more ethical decision from a feminist point of view. However, beyond recognizing the choice to represent sexual violence at all as ethically defensible, I need to ask whether these representations in particular support or undermine that choice. To do so requires consideration of the details of these representations: What *exactly* is shown? And are the specific elements of those representations necessary and sufficient to the drama of the scene and the functioning of the director's critique? To this end, I describe the depictions of sexual violence in detail, prioritizing precise and unambiguous language. These descriptions occur in the section entitled "Performing Rape."

Sexual Violence and Agency in Captivity

Die Entführung aus dem Serail is a rescue opera, and as such, its female characters lack agency in the primary propulsion of the plot. The opera renders Konstanze and Blonde objects and Belmonte and Pedrillo subjects (the latter to a lesser extent due to his low class). The men rescue; the women are rescued. Mozart offers some critique of this formulation by giving Konstanze some of the most beautiful music in the opera. Her arias are show-stoppers and the power of her voice and rhetoric is undeniable, even as she finds herself helpless within the contraptions of the plot. Gretchen Wheelock reads

"Martern aller Arten" as "a powerful statement of resistance" proportional to the Pasha's power over her.[7] Bretzner also rewrites rescue convention to an extent; Belmonte is ultimately unsuccessful in his rescue attempt, and it is only because the Pasha chooses to be merciful that the central conflict of the story is resolved. Building off of *Entführung*'s eighteenth-century authors, Bieito also offers a critique of rescue convention, though it is in some tension with the work of his predecessors. Bieito's Pasha is so immediately frightening that his mercy at the end is hard to understand in terms of Enlightenment as Bretzner intended. His pity for Konstanze emerges from a violent, vengeful mania, and while it is presented as genuine, it does not feel earned by the story. Bieito's critique of the rescue formula comes instead from the revelation of Belmonte's priorities in the final scene. Belmonte's heroism erodes over the course of the third act. He relishes slaughtering the brothel's clientele and sex workers and emerges as the new Pasha, taking charge of what infrastructure remains. The hero becomes the villain, and the only escape left to a decidedly un-rescued Konstanze is suicide.

The finale of this perverted rescue-drama places Konstanze center-stage as she stares heartbroken into the audience. Bieito's production, like Mozart's music, centers on Konstanze's plight. Her suffering is of a different nature in this production, however. Whereas Bretzner's Konstanze seems to be truly torn between her affection for her captor and her allegiance to her betrothed, Bieito's Konstanze is terrified of Selim and lies about her affection to pacify him and protect herself. In the libretto, Konstanze's refusals of Selim's advances are successful; she resists him even in his position of absolute power. He tells her that he does not want to force her to love him—he wants her to choose to. Bretzner's Selim desires not just her body, but ideally her consent. Bieito's Selim is not concerned with consent. He speaks the same words, but as we watch him cage and abuse Konstanze, we know that they do not delimit his actions. Unlike Mozart and Bretzner's heroine, Bieito's Konstanze is not in charge of her fate at Selim's hands.

Selim's methods of exerting power over Konstanze operate in more insidious ways in Bieito's production as well. Toward the end of her aria, "Welcher Wechsel herrscht in meiner Seele," a weeping Selim attempts to strangle himself with the leash Konstanze has been wearing. She stops him and they kiss passionately. This scene evokes a darkly familiar tactic of sexual coercion in abusive relationships. Unwilling to be responsible for Selim's suicide, Konstanze's capitulation here is the result of his continued manipulation. In the dialogue that follows, Konstanze begins to assert herself against Selim for the first time in the opera. Selim tells her that by the next day she must love him, and she refuses. During their exchange, she unfastens her collar and hurls it to the ground. He whips her with his jacket and she retaliates, beating him with a leather whip. She kicks him in the chest, and he collapses to great cheers of support by the audience. For a moment, she has taken real action and has physically overpowered her captor. In retaliation, Selim forces Konstanze to watch Osmin torture and murder an unnamed sex worker onstage. After this scene, Konstanze is virtually catatonic for the rest of the opera. Even when she ultimately shoots Selim, this action lacks any sense of triumph—the same audience that cheered when she kicked Selim in the chest remains silent. Selim himself gives Konstanze the gun. By guiding her hand even in this final moment, Selim ensures his death reads less as murder and more as suicide.

Bieito presents Blonde in a very different light. From her first introduction, Blonde appears to be working at the brothel with Osmin as her pimp. In her first scene with Osmin, we watch their interaction devolve from coy play-fighting to brutal violence and humiliation. Blonde is written as a typical Mozartean maid, feisty and cunning, a forebear of *Le nozze di Figaro*'s Susanna, *Così fan tutte*'s Despina, and *Don Giovanni*'s Zerlina. In this production, Blonde treats Osmin with a sexualized version of her typical Mozartean sass, but it fails to keep Osmin in line. Blonde is one of the strong women of Mozart's oeuvre, but she does not stand a chance against Osmin as a twenty-first century mobster. In Mozart's *Entführung*, we are given every reason to assume that Blonde has resisted her captor due to sheer force of will and good humor, but Bieito dismantles her optimistic resistance before our eyes. Though in her first appearance she defies Osmin, it quickly becomes impossible to further believe Blonde's Mozartean bravado. After Osmin beats and humiliates her, she spends the remainder of the production self-medicating with pills and alcohol and staggering from one scene to the next in a haze. In the final scene, Blonde is morbidly fascinated by the dead bodies of her fellow sex workers. Unlike the Mozartean archetype, Bieito's Blonde loses her autonomy in this story almost immediately after her introduction. She still speaks some lines from the original libretto, saying that she will never be Osmin's slave, but as we watch Osmin overpower her and seize her earnings, it is clear that these words do not reflect reality in Bieito's seraglio.

Although Konstanze and Blonde are the only named women in the opera, Bieito populates his stage with a number of sex workers engaged at the brothel. These sex workers serve as elements of the mise-en-scène and props for the main characters. Throughout the opera, the sex workers have no agency and are consistently dehumanized. They are tools for Osmin to use against his enemies and to satisfy his own desires; they are effigies on whom Selim can inflict damage in order to hurt Konstanze; they are collateral damage, serving in their deaths to expose Belmonte and Pedrillo's true colors; and throughout all of this, they are scene dressing. After they are murdered, the bodies of these women remain onstage as props for Osmin to interact with through the opera's conclusion. Their deaths constitute a progression between two states of objectification—from sex toys to corpses. Bieito only shows us these sex workers in a large undifferentiated group. The production denies them their individuality and reduces them to their work and to their relationship with Osmin and the brothel. Even Blonde is at risk of deindividuation in this production as a sex worker herself. One early reviewer of this production actually failed to differentiate Blonde from the supernumerary sex workers, identifying her at one point not by name but as "a peroxide-blonde prostitute."[8]

Konstanze, then, is the only female character onstage who is able to even attempt to act as an agent in the story, and she is either undermined or punished at every opportunity. We watch her constant abuse, and after witnessing another woman be tortured and murdered just to teach Konstanze a lesson it is hard not to wonder if her resistance is really worth it. If she would have just slept with Selim, maybe that sex worker would still be alive. Furthermore, the time Konstanze does not spend in a cage or on a leash she spends in Selim's or Belmonte's arms. Despite her incredible strength of will in denying Selim's requests of her, she is trapped under the unending control and surveillance of one of these two men. In the end, Konstanze believes the only way she can bring her situation to an end is suicide. And based on everything we have seen in Bieito's production, this is not an illogical conclusion.

In the libretto, Konstanze and Blonde essentially function as objects for exchange in the conflict between Belmonte and Bassa Selim as representatives of the Enlightened West and the obscurantist East. Yet within that framework, Mozart's women exert power through their music: Konstanze through her vocal extravagances and Blonde through comic irreverence in the face of Osmin's threats. Bieito largely nullifies even this micro-agency in his representations of Konstanze and Blonde. In doing so, he makes a powerful statement about the ways in which women's agency can be compromised by men in the sex trade. This production points out that the agency we read onto Konstanze and Blonde through their music is a fantasy. By transplanting the story from an Orientalist daydream to contemporary reality, Bieito suggests that *Entführung* has been a story about sex slavery all along—as distasteful as this might be to some opera fans. But simply presenting this stark vision of women stripped of their agency does not in itself operate as critique. In the following sections, I examine the specific ways the creative team of this production render the acts of sexual violence onstage, and then consider the work these representations do in crafting Bieito's critique.

Performing Rape

The first scene of sexual violence occurs early in Act I during Osmin's aria, "Solche hergelauf'ne Laffen." After dismissing Belmonte, who is seeking entry into the palace, Osmin rages at Pedrillo, accusing him of lecherousness and laziness. The aria concludes with a laundry list of the startlingly violent ways in which Osmin wishes to see Pedrillo killed. In Bieito's staging of this scene, Osmin addresses Pedrillo, but he interacts primarily with an obsequious group of sex workers who surround him and laugh as he insults his rival. One sex worker in lingerie gives Osmin an erotic massage, and he pulls her down onto the ground where they caress each other sensually. Osmin simulates performing oral sex on her, and after responding positively at first, the woman suddenly screams—presumably he has bitten her—and tries to move away from him. Osmin grabs her by her ankles, drags her back toward himself, and pins her to the stage in the fetal position. He eventually lets her get up and directs his anger at Pedrillo for the remainder of the aria. This act of violence is the first time in the opera that we see Osmin exert his power over the women in the brothel. We learn that he can hurt them casually as it suits him.

Osmin inflicts a similar mix of sexual play and violence on Blonde in their Act II duet, "Ich gehe doch rate ich dir." In the written text, Blonde sings an aria in which she rebukes Osmin's attempts to be intimate with her, and then in this duet, she declares that she will never be his slave and threatens to scratch out his eyes, ultimately chasing him from the room. Bieito's staging of this scene begins with Blonde alternating between stomping around arms akimbo and coyly dancing for Osmin. In the duet, they argue and push each other around in a way initially played for comedy. At several points, Osmin removes articles of Blonde's clothing and attempts to initiate sex with her, and her refusals are characterized by an eye-rolling exasperation more than a real fear. Midway through the duet, however, Osmin adjusts his tactics and the stakes change. He drags Blonde to her feet by her hair and pours vodka all over her body before threatening her with a lighter. She bites his wrist, which causes him to drop the lighter and starts a vicious fight between them. The much larger Osmin pins Blonde to the ground and punches her hard in the stomach. She begins to cry, and Osmin urinates into a glass tumbler which he places next to her. The set rotates them out of view before Blonde can drink. Like in "Solche hergelauf'ne Laffen," Osmin's sexual playfulness transforms into brutality. He puts Blonde in her place with a combination of physical abuse and humiliation that reduces her to a shadow of herself for the remainder of the opera.

Selim's approach to sexual violence differs from Osmin's. Whereas Osmin's acts of violence are clumsy and spontaneous, Selim's are calculated and precise. The only explicit act of sexual violence he commits is a digital rape of Konstanze during her first-act aria, "Ach, ich liebte." In this aria, Konstanze sings about the pain of being separated from her betrothed, Belmonte. In Bieito's version, Konstanze is held in a small cage (perhaps a dog kennel). Over the course of the aria, Selim opens the cage and leads Konstanze out on a leash. While she sings, he escalates from kissing her ankles to penetrating her with his fingers. Osmin's abuses are shocking for their proximity to and growth out of comic amorous gestures; Selim's, by contrast, shock by their sheer depravity. Osmin's musical numbers above are comic, but "Ach, ich liebte" is in the high dramatic mode of an opera seria heroine. Bieito transforms Konstanze's soliloquy about her emotional suffering into a brutal, physical ordeal at the hands of her captor. This staging presents a disturbing parallel between the "Liebe Schmerz" Konstanze names in her aria as she mourns Belmonte and the twisted "Liebe Schmerz" of Selim's punishment for not loving him back.

Finally, there is the scene that seems largely responsible for the infamy of this production, "Martern aller Arten." In Konstanze's second aria, she is punished for the retaliatory violence she inflicts on Selim by being forced to watch Osmin violate and murder a sex worker. In the aria's written text, Konstanze defiantly tells Selim that she will willingly face any torment before she betrays her love, but ultimately, she requests Selim's mercy. As Konstanze sings, Osmin emerges with a sex worker in tow, and the two engage in apparently consensual sexual activity. After some kissing and foreplay, Osmin throws the woman onto her back on the ground at Konstanze's feet, and the woman laughs and beckons him to come closer. Osmin straddles the woman on his knees, and she performs fellatio on him. Selim holds Konstanze by her hair, making her watch. Osmin pulls a knife, which he shows to Konstanze. He pushes the woman's shoulders down onto the stage and stuffs a cloth into her mouth. When she sees the knife, the woman panics and struggles to get away, but Osmin's weight holds her in place. He systematically makes long cuts on her face, both her forearms, her back, her chest, and finally across her

Fig. 8. Selim (Guntbert Warns) leads Konstanze (Brigitte Geller) out of her cage on a leash. *Die Entführung aus dem Serail*, directed by Calixto Bieito. (Photograph © Monika Rittershaus, reprinted by permission.)

throat. After she has ceased moving, Osmin cuts off her nipple and presents it to Konstanze as she sings the climactic ending of her aria. This is the first death of a sex worker in this production, and it is excruciating to watch. Osmin's relaxed approach to the deed highlights the arbitrariness of this murder—the sex worker he chooses here is a stand-in for Konstanze to show her what will follow if she continues to resist Selim. The power of Konstanze's resistance, which Wheelock recognizes in this aria, is obliterated.[9] Konstanze's words invite Selim's torture and anticipate the freedom that will come from death, but there is no salvation in the death she is made to witness, and we will sense no salvation in her eventual suicide.

As with some of the productions of *Salome* in chapter 2, the context of performance within the fictional world of the opera and the thematization of spectacle and the gaze informs our spectatorship. The most infamous act of violence in Bieito's production situates sexual violence in this context. Selim forces Konstanze to watch as Osmin violates, tortures, and murders a supernumerary sex worker. The acts of violence serve primarily to teach Konstanze a lesson; they are, above all else, done to be seen. Osmin's abuse of the sex worker in "Solche Hergelauf'ne Laffen" may similarly be seen as, in part, a performance for the other sex workers and for Pedrillo to demonstrate Osmin's power over all of them. And although the other sexual assaults take place in private in the context of the story, our spectatorship of them from the audience is informed by the way women's bodies are represented as objects for display in this production's mise-en-scène. With *Salome*, the self-consciously spectacular elements of the Dance of the Seven Veils often had troubling implications when the Dance was replaced with a rape. In the case of Bieito's *Entführung*, though, I get the sense that the dissonance between watching the supernumerary sex workers perform in the background and watching the rape and murder of other sex workers in the foreground is the point. This production problematizes the tendency of its audience to gaze at the bodies of the supernumerary performers by pulling the curtain back on the dangerous and violent underworld they represent. Bieito's use of nudity and dramatic realism is a part of what makes his representation of violence so shocking, and it also raises questions about objectification and perspective with regards to our spectatorship of sexualized and suffering women's bodies.

Nudity has become one of the hallmarks of *Regietheater*, especially according to its critics. As I pointed out above, some reviews of this production do not differentiate between the graphic acts of sexualized violence and the appearance of nude bodies. I have no ethical quarrel with onstage nudity in itself. However, Bieito's particular uses of nudity in *Entführung* are wrapped up in his representations of sexual violence, its perpetrators, and its victims. There is a great deal of nudity in this production, though among the main characters of the opera, we see only Osmin fully nude. In the background, supernumerary sex workers and their clients appear nude, both to engage in simulated sex and, in the case of the women, to pose in glass boxes advertising their services. Bieito's use of nudity in this production is not uniform. Sometimes it highlights the comedy of the score, as when Osmin bounces on a bed with his genitals exposed. Other times it constructs the realism of the brothel, as in the case of the supernumeraries engaging in sex around the set. The two women whose nude bodies appear in the foreground of Bieito's staging are the two sex workers that are victims of Osmin's violence. The woman Osmin kills in "Martern aller Arten" has her body increasingly exposed while he tortures her. He pulls her dress and brassiere down so he can cut her back and chest, and as she writhes around on the ground, her skirt rides up, exposing her buttocks to the audience while she struggles to escape.

One of the dangers of putting sexual violence onstage is the potential eroticization of the violated female body. Theater scholar Charlotte Canning links staged sexual violence with pornography and outlines a number of alternative feminist modes of representation that focus on a stylization of the *idea* of rape rather than the physical act in an effort to eschew the pornographic potential of exposed women's bodies.[10] Canning's citation of pornography is interesting. In 1983, anti-pornography lobbyists Andrea Dworkin and Catharine MacKinnon drafted a set of ordinances that proposed treating pornography as a violation of women's civil rights in the United States. The ordinances were ultimately deemed unconstitutional on the grounds of freedom of speech protections, but the definitions of pornography in the proposed ordinances have been influential on continuing anti-porn campaigns in the US and Canada. Dworkin and MacKinnon proposed a list of conditions that when combined with "the graphic sexually explicit subordination of women through pictures and/or words" constitute pornography. The conditions relevant here are:

> a. Women are presented as dehumanized sexual objects, things or commodities; or . . . d. women are presented as sexual objects tied up or cut or mutilated or bruised or physically hurt; or e. women are presented in postures of sexual submission, servility, or display; or . . . h. women are presented in scenarios of degradation, injury, abasement, torture, shown as filthy or inferior, bleeding, bruised, or hurt in a context that makes these conditions sexual.[11]

Regardless of the potential political value of these ordinances, it is worth noting on how many counts Bieito's depictions of sex and sexual violence constitute the kind of pornography Dworkin and MacKinnon opposed. I will talk more about Bieito's representation of sex work later in this chapter, but it is certainly true that the nudity and sexual gestures of the supernumerary sex workers serve to commodify the women in the brothel. Their servility to Osmin's sexual whims is similarly clear. Conditions A and H apply to the sex worker Osmin kills as well as to Konstanze, whom Selim strips down to her undergarments while she is leashed and bound. The sexualization of the violence done to the women in this opera is especially clear in the last scene. When Belmonte and Pedrillo massacre all the available inhabitants of the brothel, many of the sex workers are killed while in the act of having sex with clients. This proximity of death and sex leads to a troubling sexualization of their naked and near-naked bodies, which lie strewn across the stage for twenty-two minutes until the end of the opera.

The erotic treatment and reception of the female body in scenes depicting rape and victims of rape onstage is an old problem in the theater. Elizabeth

Howe argues that the introduction of actresses to the English Restoration stage caused a spike in the portrayal of rape in English theaters. Rape was both "a way of giving the purest, most virginal heroine a sexual quality," and an excuse to expose naked female flesh.[12] Bieito's introduction of sexual violence to *Entführung* accomplishes both of these tasks. Konstanze is beyond reproach as a heroine in Bretzner's story—chaste and faithful even in the face of certain death. But in Bieito's torture chamber she is made to be Selim's sexual plaything. The problem with exposing women's bodies onstage, especially in proximity to representations of sexual violence, is essentially a problem of perspective. Bieito is a male director telling a story in which the sexual violation of women serves to inspire a male protagonist to action. In this context, it is also easy to recognize the way Bieito uses the exposed bodies of the women who represent the sex workers in this production to express his concept and his critique. Both within the story of the opera and outside of it, these women's naked bodies are wielded as tools by men.

When it comes to these scenes of violence, Bieito's production subscribes to an excruciating realism.[13] As a musical as well as a dramatic form, opera cannot be "realist" in the same way that theater or film can be. But given the genre's necessary suspensions of disbelief when it comes to music and singing, Bieito's *Entführung* is remarkably realistic. The violence onstage, like the sex, happens in full view of the audience without any veils of stylized movement or dance. The fight choreography is highly realistic and accentuated by convincing use of fake blood. This version is also cut down significantly from the original so that the action is always moving forward.[14] Bieito's newly written dialogue scenes are remarkably naturalistic. They employ different German dialects for different characters and discard the poetic scansion of the original. Even in the arias and other numbers, Bieito's singers are unusually active; almost every moment of music is filled with involved stage business. This level of naturalism is unusual in opera, and certainly contributes to the shock value of this production because the action in this realist mode is so horrifying.

Realism is not a value-neutral mode of representation, and within feminist theater criticism there are disagreements about its potential benefits. Elin Diamond summarizes the feminist attack on theatrical realism thusly: "Setting out to offer truthful versions of experience, realism universalizes but one point of view. . . . In the process of exploring social (especially gender) relations, realism ends by confirming their inevitability."[15] Elaine Aston attributes the allegedly objective perspective of realism to a male subject and a male gaze.[16] The point of view of *Entführung*'s narrative is certainly masculine; rescue operas typically tell tales of heroics in which women are objects of exchange between men, and *Entführung* is no exception.[17] Diamond and Aston might argue that by telling this story through a lens of theatrical realism, Bieito does nothing to challenge the masculine point of view of the story. A naturalistic aesthetic takes as a given that the world presented on Bieito's stage is the real world. And on this stage, where women are beaten, raped, and murdered without consequence, naturalism's attestation to reality can be seen as an acquiescence to the inevitability of violence against women.

Other feminist scholars of theater and literature have defended realism as an aesthetic not necessarily opposed to a feminist project. Patricia Schroeder and Kim Solga have both made cases for the feminist and even radical potential of theatrical realism.[18] These arguments hang on the enduring popularity of realist depictions among spectators and the intense identification with fictional characters and situations that realist depictions make possible. Throughout Bieito's production, Konstanze and Blonde have brutally realistic responses to the violence done to them. Their trauma plays out in different but recognizable ways: Blonde abuses pills and alcohol, and Konstanze becomes totally dependent on Belmonte after witnessing the sex worker's murder and eventually dies by suicide. In a sense, these characters can be more easily identified with because they behave more like real people than do their Mozartean archetypes—the feisty maid and the sentimental heroine. But despite Bieito's more realistic characterization, the caricatures persist and this dichotomy is jarring. Konstanze and Blonde, while their reactions to trauma are informed by a more realistic approach to the opera's plot, are still a far stretch from complex, responsible depictions of sexual assault survivors. Bieito's new dialogue is tilted toward the men in the opera. Most of the little that the women have to say and sing in this production was written for them by Stephanie and not Bieito, so it enforces their archetypal roles and does not respond to the violence done to them in between their words. Yet while Bieito does not give the women much to say, his use of the opera's music, especially in his staging of Konstanze's arias, goes some distance to generating empathy and encouraging audience identification with her experience.

The interaction of Bieito's stage business and setting with Mozart's music has fueled a good deal of the controversy in the popular press. Reviewers report cries of "poor Mozart" from the house at the public dress rehearsal and on opening night. Though this tendency to frame criticism of *Regie* productions of canonic operas as a defense of the composer's presumed intentions or wishes is common, it is rarely a very interesting way to evaluate a production in my view. In Bieito's *Entführung*, the argument that "that's not what Mozart wrote" is especially shallow because Bieito's staging is actually highly sensitive to details in Mozart's score. Despite the vast difference in tone between this and a more conservative production of *Entführung*, Bieito's dramaturgical style throughout is surprisingly well integrated with Mozart's music. Bieito recontextualizes the music in a variety of ways throughout his drama and harnesses it for his own dramatic project. Clemens Risi uses this production as one of his prime examples to demonstrate a technique in opera production in which a director "uses musical structures to legitimate his scenic choices."[19]

There is a kind of violence in the noisy, motoric drive of Mozart's Turkish marches in this opera. In her review of the production, musicologist Micaela Baranello comments on Mozart's *alla turca* style in *Entführung*, noting that "Bieito makes a lot of its gaudiness and maniacal repetitive energy."[20] This fusion of the comical and the violent does not feel entirely out of place, accompanying, for instance, Osmin jumping up and down naked on the bed in his first number. The brashness of the *alla turca* at the production's conclusion is somewhat more subversive. After the murders of Selim and Osmin, the chorus runs on, presumably representing the employees and patrons of the brothel who survived Belmonte and Pedrillo's earlier massacre. The final chorus is thick with percussion and bells, and the whole company accents practically every attack. In the instance of this final chorus and much of the *alla turca* throughout this production, I think that Bieito is capitalizing on the dissonance between the music and the experience of our main characters, pointing out that the jaunty Turkish music in this opera about captivity in a harem was problematic to begin with. The disjunction between the cheerful, comic *alla turca* music and the darkness that Bieito exploits in the opera's story characterizes this production as a whole. But within this frame, Bieito also plays off of Mozart's music in more specific ways in the scenes of sexual violence.

Osmin's abuses of the sex worker in "Solche hergelauf'ne Laffen" and of Blonde in "Ich gehe doch rate ich dir" also feature a disjunction between the comic character of the music and the seriousness of Osmin's violence, but in these cases it is a disjunction inherent in Osmin's character. Mozart plays Osmin's rage and threats of violence as comedy. Bieito's Osmin maintains the character's playfulness even while he commits acts of extreme violence onstage. In "Solche hergelauf'ne Laffen," Bieito aligns Osmin's movements with the music, implying that what we hear in Mozart's score is indicative of Osmin's point of view. Jens Larsen, as Osmin, runs his hands over the woman's body rhythmically with motions that largely correspond to the musical shapes he is singing. At one point, a sharply accented beat at the resolution of a cadence accompanies a sharp squeeze of the woman's buttock. These moments of correspondence between comic musical figures and Osmin's playful sexual gestures are fun to watch, and Larsen's execution of the staging is excellent. When Osmin bites the woman, her scream punctuates the musical fabric. It is a clear sonic marker that pulls us out of our alignment with Osmin's character. The comic gestures of Osmin's music now accompany the image of him pinning this woman to the stage while she cowers and cries. The music is still Osmin's, but now we are hearing it from the outside, and the same basic musical features feel sinister. The comic character of the music works in two ways in this scene: it gives us some insight into Osmin's twisted mind, which makes little distinction between sexual play and sexual violence, and it startles us with the dark reality of the story Bieito intends to tell us through this previously comic opera.

Osmin and Blonde's duet, "Ich gehe doch rate ich dir," works differently in its musical and scenic correlation. Over the course of the number, the balance of musical power shifts from Osmin to Blonde by way of changing who introduces new musical material and influences the register of the other character's music.[21] Blonde ends the duet in the more powerful position due to her musico-rhetorical prowess. In Bieito's conception of this story, though, Blonde cannot be allowed to win. In the final bars of the duet, Bieito has Osmin overpower Blonde and throw her to the ground. The orchestra finishes playing, and Osmin continues to beat Blonde in silence. There is a sense that the music of the duet was a delusion: both Blonde's delusion and ours. The comic music allowed us to exist for a moment in a different *Entführung* in which Blonde can control Osmin, but when the music fades we are left with only the sounds of Osmin's fists landing and Blonde's laughter turning to cries of pain. These sounds from the actors onstage, the beating and the crying, contribute to the sonic profile of Bieito's production. Like the sex worker's scream that marks the first act of violence Osmin commits, Blonde's sobs and the sounds of Osmin's fists characterize the seriousness of Bieito's concept amid and around the sounds of Mozart's music. The last sound we hear in Bieito's production is the gunshot that signifies Konstanze's suicide, which happens just after the final notes of the score have been played. These sounds decenter Mozart's music as the only sonic signifier during the musical numbers of the opera. Bieito's vision encroaches on what most opera-goers hold most dear in their favorite works—the sound of the music—and in so doing does not allow his listeners to simply close their eyes to block out the production (a popular tactic of the *Regie*-hating opera-goer).

Bieito stages Konstanze's two arias, "Ach, ich liebte" and "Martern aller

Arten," in a way that aligns spectators with Konstanze's experience of the events taking place onstage. These are both highly emotional and introspective tours de force for Konstanze, but in Bieito's production both are staged in ways that strip her of agency in the plot even as she seems to have so much in the music. In "Ach, ich liebte," Konstanze is violated by Selim and in "Martern aller Arten" she is forced to watch a murder. In both, Bieito harnesses the extravagance of her singing voice to express the powerful emotions of the character. Konstanze's high-flying coloratura passages in "Ach, ich liebte" become vocalized responses to the increasingly horrible things Selim does to her, culminating in the digital rape.[22] Similarly, in "Martern aller Arten," Konstanze's coloratura is associated with her responses to the action. These passages become shrieks that Konstanze releases when Osmin cuts the sex worker somewhere new or when the bleeding woman grasps at Konstanze's legs. Osmin slits the sex worker's throat on Konstanze's sustained high C. At the aria's conclusion, a long vocal trill scores the tremor of the sex worker's legs before she falls limp on the downbeat of Konstanze's cadence. The final coloratura passages, which are the most elaborate in the aria, are sung here in response to Osmin holding out the bloody nipple. Bieito's technique of aligning physical and musical gestures in his staging ensures that these scenes of violence do not feel entirely disconnected from Mozart's music. In addition to legitimizing the staging for the spectator, as Risi argues, the use of this technique in these two arias draws us closer to Konstanze's point of view.[23] She screams on our behalf as we join her in witnessing these acts of shocking brutality.

Production as Criticism

Bieito is using Mozart and Stephanie's written text to do something that it was not intended for. Rather than a comic work of entertainment, Bieito's *Entführung* is a dark, gritty examination of the sex trade. This production can also be understood as a cogent criticism of the opera's written text and its performance tradition. While the thesis that comes through most clearly in this production is that the sex trade is deeply exploitative and dangerous, ultimately, I find the secondary critical theme to be the most interesting element of this production.

Bieito's focus on the twentieth-century European sex trade allows him to transplant *Entführung* and bypass some of the problems of this opera's representations of Islam. However, whitewashing the characters and setting does not erase the troubling racial implications of setting an opera that stereotypes and villainizes Turkish people in a contemporary German brothel. Turkish immigrants make up the largest ethnic minority group in Germany, and the presence of this large primarily Muslim Turkish diaspora has been perceived by some as a threat to German social and political order.[24] A German audience might reasonably presume that the unnamed sex workers are Turkish or Eastern European, given the makeup of the sex trade in Germany and Western Europe more broadly.[25] The representations of the sex workers in Bieito's brothel as props and victims for powerful men is particularly troubling through this frame. That said, Bieito's decision to set *Entführung* in a contemporary brothel is not without critical merit. It is meaningful that in Bieito's production, it is not only Osmin and Selim that mistreat women and profit from their suffering. When Belmonte takes on the role of Pasha at the end of the opera, Bieito seems to be arguing that the problems of the sex trade are not problems of individual bad men but are systemic.

Bieito's production is clearly critical of European brothels, but its representation of the seraglio as a brothel is confusing and inconsistent from the perspective of the German sex trade in the early 2000s. Within the walls of Bieito's brothel, everything about the action seems to refer to an illegal underground operation. Selim and Osmin are dressed as and behave like gangsters, and for the most part criminal gangs run the illegal tier of the sex trade in Germany. Belmonte and Pedrillo's massacre of the prostitutes, patrons, and pimps in Selim's brothel may be seen to evoke the violence that goes on between rival gangs in Germany's red-light districts. And yet other elements of this production suggest this is a legal brothel, including types of advertisement typical to German brothels at the time. Bieito's set contains scrolling signs listing services offered by the sex workers inside and the glass boxes evoke window prostitution, which occurs in several German red-light districts.[26] The supernumerary sex workers, when their employers are not subjecting them to violence, go about their work relatively cheerfully. Their stage business is characterized by sassiness and humor. In short, their behavior easily leads a spectator to believe they are working by choice. This stands in stark contrast to the behavior of Konstanze and Blonde, who we know have been kidnapped and are being held against their will. It is hard to reconcile all the disparate elements of Bieito's brothel. This is a brothel that advertises, and so is presumably a legal one, but it is also a brothel in which uncooperative trafficking victims are leashed and held in cages, and in which any woman might be spontaneously murdered as a show of power.[27]

I do not mean to suggest that legal brothels never feature violence or exploit women, but this kind of representational blurriness between sex work and sex trafficking risks conflating the two in a troubling way, especially with regard to the agency of the women in Bieito's production. Prohibitionist feminists argue that sex work is necessarily violent and reinforces a system of patriarchal dominance, and that consent in relation to sex work is impossible.[28] For prohibitionists, the distinction between sex work and sex trafficking is meaningless because they do not believe that it is possible for a woman to truly consent to sex work in any case. A common criticism of this position is that the prohibitionist insistence that sex work turns women into objects makes it impossible to understand sex workers as agents capable of self-determination.[29] The unnamed women in Bieito's *Entführung* are examples of this model in action. These are women who are completely without power, who are unable to give or withhold consent, and who are treated literally as objects that the men can use to experience pleasure, make money, and demonstrate their power to others. Maybe the unnamed sex workers in this production are trafficking victims, like Konstanze and Blonde seem to be, and they behave cheerfully around the boss as a means of self-preservation. Or maybe this is an illegal brothel featuring both trafficking victims being held against their will (Konstanze and Blonde) and migrant sex workers who are choosing to work but are not recognized by the legal system (the supernumerary sex workers). Maybe the trappings of advertisements around the set are simple tools to aid the audience in identifying the setting as a brothel and are not meant to signify legality at all. The point is, Bieito's representation of the sex trade in this production is confusing and at times self-contradictory. I fear the production plays into the cultural idea that sex workers are necessarily victims of coercion and abuse, and it may suggest that the very specific horrors we witness are indispensable to any system of sex work.

Though this production's criticism of the sex trade is vague, I find Bieito's criticism of *Die Entführung*'s written text and performance history coherent and compelling overall. When I first started hearing about this production, the reigning opinion and consensus of many critics was that the sex and violence were gratuitous and Bieito was blatantly capitalizing on nudity and gore to sell tickets. I do not disagree that the explicit sex and violence in this production may be partially attributed to that *Regie* motivation to shock audiences and stoke controversy, and the risks of this aesthetic should not be understated. Bieito's production incessantly eroticizes suffering women's bodies and treats them as stage decoration throughout. These women are silent, without agency, and present only as receptacles of sex and of violence. The tendency of some spectators to take pleasure in depictions of rape goes unchallenged and may actually be encouraged by this staging.

However, the more time I have spent with this production, the more I have come to appreciate it as a work of opera criticism. Bieito makes the dark realities of captivity, torture, rape, and murder upsettingly explicit, but none of these elements of the story were invented for this production. Bieito's production suggests that *Entführung*, when you really listen, is a bleak and cruel story of misogynistic violence. The recognition that in some ways this staging is very much the story that Mozart and Stephanie wrote is uncomfortable and, for those among us who have taught or sung this opera without awareness of these realities, even embarrassing.

My appreciation for Bieito's critique of *Entführung* has not displaced my discomfort, but it has complicated it. This is by no means a flawless approach to calling out the violence in the opera; Bieito's approach perpetuates the objectification of women's bodies even as he critiques it. I feel that the strengths of this production as a criticism of the normalization of rape in the opera canon is ultimately a net positive in terms of representations of sexual violence on the opera stage. Yet I understand that my research in this area has steeled my nerves, and I have a particular appetite for blunt remonstration of the politics of works like *Entführung*. For many other critics and fans, Bieito's *Entführung* is too gruesome and careless in its representations of women, sex, and violence to be taken seriously in the way I have taken it seriously in this chapter. This is not a tension I am interested in resolving—indeed I think it is inherent to conversations about ethical representations of terrible acts. It is on this note that I now turn to a very different *Entführung*, in which the violence implicit in the opera is not amplified, it is extinguished.

Wajdi Mouawad's *Die Entführung aus dem Serail*

Opéra Lyon and the Canadian Opera Company co-commissioned Lebanese-Canadian writer/director Wajdi Mouawad to create a new production of *Entführung* in 2016. Mouawad's interpretation takes aim at the unflattering, uninformed representation of Islam in the opera. He remarks in his program note for the Toronto performances, "If I have a unique perspective to bring to Mozart's *The Abduction from the Seraglio*, it is the fact that I have been shaped equally by Eastern and Western culture, and as a result, I'm incapable of condoning one at the expense of the other."[30] Mouawad adds a new narrative frame to the story, beginning his production at a party celebrating the return of the lovers to Europe after their rescue. The events of the libretto become memories that the lovers share with each other and comment on from the present. Like Bieito, Mouawad uses as much of the original dialogue as he can and adds to it. But Mouawad's interpretation is carried by new dialogue in a way that Bieito's is not, so Mouawad's dialogue scenes are much longer and occur more frequently than Bieito's.

The lovers communally tell the story of the events of the opera with an interest in sharing their different perspectives. Konstanze and Blonde want to show Belmonte and Pedrillo that their captors were not as bad as they have been made out to be, while Belmonte and Pedrillo vilify the Muslim characters and hold them up for scorn. Over the course of the opera, Mouawad reveals that although Konstanze remained chaste, she has fallen in love with the Pasha. Meanwhile, Blonde had been in a consensual sexual relationship with Osmin, resulting in a pregnancy. Mouawad specifies in the prologue to his production that the women had been in captivity for two years.[31] It gradually comes out that Pedrillo also has mixed feelings about his captivity. In one of the new dialogue scenes, he expresses to Blonde that "there [in Turkey], like here [in Europe], I was in a master's service, they call me servant there, like here" and recalls wondering, "what's there at home to return to in such a rush?"[32] These explicit equivalences pervade Mouawad's new dialogue. Blonde and Konstanze both remark on the similarity between being a slave in the seraglio in Turkey and being a woman in patriarchal eighteenth-century Europe. Blonde tells Pedrillo that he, her fiancé, is exactly the same as Osmin, her slave master: "Here or there, there or here, you or he, he or you, neither is better than the other."[33]

Even with all of the new dialogue, there are some fundamental tensions between the story Bretzner wrote and the one Mouawad wants to tell. One of the ways this concept works in spite of these tensions is by questioning whether the text preserved from the original libretto is always trustworthy. Because Mouawad brings an element of self-conscious storytelling to the opera's narrative, we cannot necessarily take all of the musical scenes at face value. The presence of four narrators, each informed by their own biases and emotions, has the potential to shape the stories they tell. Mouawad also sows seeds of doubt about Stephanie's libretto with lines like this one from Konstanze in an added dialogue scene in the present: "Despite the cruelty of [Selim's] words, I knew he was a good man."[34] The words do not matter, Mouawad tells us. The libretto is fallible and incomplete; what the characters say is not necessarily indicative of who they are. Mouawad seems to share this conviction with his heroine. He wrote a synopsis in the program specific to his production that takes on some of the work of explaining his version of events. In the second scene between Konstanze and Selim, Selim's previously benevolent demeanor cracks and he tells her, "You won't have that

Fig. 9. Konstanze (Jane Archibald) and Selim (Raphael Weinstock) share a romantic moment. *Die Entführung aus dem Serail*, directed by Wajdi Mouawad. (Photograph © Michael Cooper, reprinted by permission.)

satisfaction [of suicide]. Here the road to death is a long, slow torture."[35] This moment feels extremely out of character for Mouawad's version of the Pasha, but he needs to say something to justify Konstanze's aria, "Martern aller Arten," which follows. In the synopsis for the next scene, Mouawad writes, "Selim, horrified by the threats he has just uttered, is called away by muezzin. The hour of prayer will give him back some sanity." This element of

Mouawad's story exists only in the program, which is acting here as a necessary supplement to an otherwise confusing bit of stage action.

Mouawad's ambitious production aims to address the Orientalist depiction of Islam in this opera and to empower and envoice Blonde and Konstanze. But given the written text of *Entführung*, which Mouawad adds to but otherwise does not significantly alter, this reparative project is not always successful. The representations of Konstanze and Blonde are confused and troublesome in the midst of Mouawad's apologetics for Selim and Osmin. My analysis of this production is based on a live performance in Toronto on February 22, 2018 and archival footage of the dress rehearsal.

Agency and the Absence of Violence

Then COC Artistic Director Alexander Neef introduced Mouawad's staging in his own note in the program. But whereas Mouawad's note focuses on redeeming the portrayal of the East in the opera, Neef wants to promote this production based on its gender politics. He writes that Konstanze prefigures "a more hopeful voice, in so far as she gains what the contemporary writer Rebecca Solnit identifies in her book of essays, *Men Explain Things to Me*, as a small but essential victory in women's ongoing struggle for equality: 'The ability to tell your own story.'"[36] He goes on to applaud Mouawad's production for "granting the opera's female characters a new audibility and ownership in the narrative: complex, fully human voices to share their perspectives on what the ostensible culture clash of an East/West binary looks like from their lived experience of it."[37] I find it noteworthy that while Mouawad describes his concept as primarily concerned with responsible cultural representation, Neef hardly mentions this element of the production and opts instead to align it with contemporary feminism. Another indication of the COC's desire to promote this production as specifically a feminist one is the inclusion in the program of an interview with soprano Jane Archibald, who sings Konstanze, in which she is quoted as saying that Mouawad approached *Entführung* "very much through a feminist lens" and that he allowed for her character to be "an actual human being."[38]

Mouawad certainly amplifies Konstanze's and Blonde's narrative voices in his production; he writes a great deal of new dialogue for them and much of the action of the original opera is inflected as a story they are telling Belmonte and Pedrillo. Yet centering the women's voices does not necessarily empower them. As a general rule in this production, Mouawad eliminates or dials down the violence against Konstanze and Blonde in the service of redeeming their captors. But the way that he removes the violence, and what takes its place, is important.

Selim and Konstanze's first scene together, built around her aria "Ach, ich liebte," bears little resemblance to the same scene in Bieito's production. Mouawad's Selim is soft spoken and gentle. He pleads with Konstanze to share the source of her unhappiness with him and when she resists, he assures her that he loves her. Raphael Weinstock's performance encourages us to believe him. Konstanze sings about missing Belmonte, but her affections are obviously split; Selim rests his head in her lap, and she strokes his hair for a time before abruptly stopping herself and standing up. She tells him in the following dialogue, "I never dreamed my heart would be so torn. Your two faces meld into one another. You are powerful, brilliant, and generous as no other man. He exudes innocence and youth. You make me tremble, while he makes my heart beat faster."[39] Mouawad allows a glimmer of Selim's domineering side to come through in this scene, but it is tempered with an insistence that his behavior is not entirely unreasonable. He tells Konstanze, "I couldn't bear seeing you turn to another. Not that. What man wouldn't say that about the woman he loves madly?"[40] Even when Selim explicitly threatens her with forced marriage (and its implied consummation), the larger context of Mouawad's new dialogue seems to ask, what man wouldn't? At one point when Konstanze resists Selim's advances, he suddenly asks her, "Do you think your world is better than mine?"[41] Konstanze's struggle against his attempt at forced marriage and rape is thus reframed as a question of East versus West. Mouawad recasts Konstanze's interest in protecting her bodily autonomy from her captor as a colonialist disdain for Eastern cultures. Mouawad's goal is to humanize the Muslim men in this opera, but a side effect of that humanization is to quietly excuse the misogyny that fuels these men's speech. Again and again, the new dialogue encourages us to sympathize with Selim even as he threatens to torture and rape Konstanze.

In Blonde and Osmin's scenes together, we are encouraged not to take their words at face value in order to humanize and redeem Osmin. Mouawad's dialogue encourages us to see Blonde's relationship with her captor as parallel to her relationship with Pedrillo. Before her first aria, "Durch Zärtlichkeit und Schmeicheln," Blonde wonders, "Why do I always fall for infantile men who never stop complaining?"[42] In having Blonde refer to Osmin as just another man she has fallen for, Mouawad momentarily disguises the fact that Blonde was given as a slave to Osmin. And moments later, when Bretzner's slave-master language comes up, Mouawad has Blonde direct her admonishments to both Pedrillo in the present and Osmin in the past: "Why do I always attract the good-for-nothings? Get it into your head that I don't like this. I'm telling you Pedrillo, as I told Osmin. Do you think you're dealing with a slave who, trembling, obeys your every command? I'll never fulfill that fantasy of yours."[43] Blonde makes the literal slavery of the seraglio indistinguishable from the figurative slavery of being a woman in misogynistic eighteenth-century Europe. When she finishes her aria about how to properly treat a woman, Osmin scornfully speaks his words from the original libretto: "Tenderness and flattery? We're in Turkey! I'm the master, you're my slave. I command, you obey."[44] Mouawad adds an aside from Pedrillo, who is listening in from the present and laughing: "It's the same in Europe!"[45]

In service of this equation of Pedrillo's and Osmin's relationships to Blonde, Mouawad goes out of his way to make Osmin as endearing as possible and Pedrillo a violent boor. The duet between Osmin and Blonde, "Ich gehe, doch rate ich dir," becomes a playful quarrel between lovers that builds up to the reveal to the audience that Blonde is pregnant. At the point in the text where Blonde threatens to scratch Osmin's eyes out, the pair roll around the stage giggling and cuddling. The light, jolly, buffa music is not entirely out of place for this staging of the duet, but the words of the libretto become entirely meaningless—Blonde's resistance is nullified. Pedrillo and Blonde's interactions in contrast are steeped in threats and mockery even when none are present in the original libretto. At one point, Pedrillo warns Blonde, "Be quiet or I'll behave like a Turk!"[46] This line is an effective distillation of Mouawad's message: European Pedrillo already exhibits all the bad behavior toward women that *Entführung* typically locates in Osmin and "Turkishness."

The vast majority of the new dialogue written for Konstanze and Blonde in this production serves to defend the characters of the men who hold them captive. One exception to this is in a brief conversation between the two women after Konstanze's aria "Welcher Wechsel." They only exchange a few lines, but it is the only scene they have alone together. It is notable that while in the original libretto they daydream about Belmonte and rescue, here they do not talk about the men at all. Still, their relationship is challenging to read in the midst of the contemporary value system of Mouawad's production, because while the women may behave as friends, Blonde is Konstanze's servant. In "Durch Zärtlichkeit," we see Blonde thinking through the figurative slavery of being a woman—and specifically a lower-class woman—in Enlightened Europe by equating her relationships with Pedrillo and Osmin. But she does not direct any of this revolutionary attitude toward her mistress.

Instead, Blonde comforts Konstanze, who is having a harder time adjusting to life in the seraglio by telling her, "I've often experienced exile. Changing countries and languages becomes an advantage in the long run, an identity."[47] Konstanze expresses envy for Blonde's courage, and Blonde jokingly suggests that they should change places before telling Konstanze, "Who understands me better than you, and you, better than me? We were mistress and servant, now we're two women, side by side."[48] This female camaraderie initially has a sheen of empowerment, but it quickly corrupts under scrutiny. This new equality that Blonde feels is possible in the seraglio because the class distance between them has dissolved, but it has dissolved because now they are both slaves. Mouawad romanticizes their captivity, first by having Blonde express gratitude for the learning experience, then by casting it as the catalyst to bring these two women together in a way that would have been impossible while they still had their freedom.

Like Bieito's *Entführung*, Mouawad's also offers a critique of the rescue genre. Bieito accomplishes this goal by revealing the hero to be no different than the villain at the opera's conclusion when Belmonte takes ownership of the brothel and leaves Konstanze very much un-rescued. Mouawad's critique is more subtle and hinges on the idea that the women did not necessarily need rescuing in the first place. His representation of Belmonte indicates that the rescue storyline is more about the ego of the hero than the needs of the damsel. During his aria, "Wenn der Freude Thränen fliessen," Belmonte sings about the joy of being reunited with his lover, but he addresses the entire aria to the audience and fails to interact with or even make eye contact with Konstanze who is onstage with him. In contrast to Belmonte's self-serving heroism is the behavior of the Muslim men. Mouawad gives the final line of dialogue in the opera to Selim, who tells Osmin, "Love your Blonde more than anything else and let her go."[49] So, ultimately, it is the Turkish men who prove themselves actually capable of selfless action to benefit the women they love, in contrast to Belmonte and Pedrillo, whose clueless callousness in the prologue is the impetus for the entire action of the opera. Bieito's rescue critique generates sympathy for the women who have been failed by the false heroics of their lovers, whereas Mouawad's generates sympathy for the women's captors, whom he assures us are the real heroes of this story once we get past our Western bias.

The problem with Mouawad's approach is best encapsulated in one of his added dialogue scenes after the lovers' quartet, in which the men question the women about their faithfulness:

> BLONDE. You wanted to save us only on the condition that we had
> been faithful to you . . .
> KONSTANZE. What would have happened if we hadn't been? Would
> you have left? On your boat? We don't want any of those unfaithful
> girls, now do we?
> BLONDE. The most unbearable part was that we were forced to lie to
> you to save our own lives![50]

At first, this is a strong criticism of the written text; Konstanze and Blonde point out the false virtue of the men who only want to rescue them from slavery under certain conditions. But Blonde goes on to tell Pedrillo, "Two years sleeping in the same house with a man who did nothing but seduce me and win me over, offering me gift after gift, making me the queen over everything, over his life, what did you want me to do?"[51] She is arguing here that she had no choice but to give in to Osmin's seduction, but Mouawad combines coercion and imprisonment with Blonde's tender feelings for Osmin. She had sex with him both because she could not effectively resist him any longer as her captor and because he made her happy. I think Mouawad is wrong to try to have this both ways. As a slave, Blonde cannot consent to sex with her master.

This issue of sex and romance with one's captor constitutes the central problem with Mouawad's concept in this production. It is difficult to accept Konstanze and Blonde's respective tender feelings for Selim and Osmin as real love blossoming across cultural borders when it looks so much more like Stockholm syndrome. Stockholm syndrome refers to a condition in which captives develop an emotional bond with their captors. The name was coined by the media in coverage of a bank robbery in Stockholm in 1973, in which four hostages held by the robbers defended their captors and refused to testify against them in court after being liberated. While not a medically accepted psychological disorder, Stockholm syndrome is widely familiar to the public in part thanks to its frequent occurrence as a trope in television and film. I recognize this trope in Mouawad's *Entführung* in the way this production romanticizes the captivity of the women and works hard to stoke compassion for their captors. A part of this problem lies in Stephanie's libretto. When Selim first asks Konstanze to give herself to him, she replies, "most generous man! If only I could."[52] It is not impossible that she is lying to him, but Mouawad takes this kind of language from Konstanze as the truth of the matter. He further extends this logic to Blonde's feelings for her captor, although she gives no indication in the libretto that she feels anything other than contempt for Osmin. Bieito's production is worth consideration here as a counterpoint. His staging highlights the ways in which Selim manipulates Konstanze's emotions to keep her under his control. The scene in which Konstanze stops Selim from strangling himself lays bare the extent of Selim's emotional manipulation. This scene casts the rest of the tender things Konstanze says to Selim in a new light. Bieito's Selim is severely unbalanced, and Konstanze says what she needs to say to keep herself alive and her hands free of his blood. Mouawad has us take Konstanze at her word when she speaks Stephanie's tender words to Selim, but Bieito's production encourages us to read this element of Konstanze's speech as either manipulation by Selim or self-preservation—that is, in the context of abuse.

Mouawad's *Entführung* tries to be reparative in its representations both of the Middle East and of women, but the feminist themes are inconsistent and confusing. He may have set out to redeem the Turkish characters by envoicing the women with a more multicultural sensibility, but within an eighteenth-century frame and to a modern audience it doesn't quite work. While it is admirable to assert that misogyny is misogyny no matter where it happens and that "Enlightened" Europeans are not exempt, Mouawad's insistence on claiming a direct moral equivalence is troubling. This production treads dangerously close to being an apologia for sex slavery and rape. Mouawad has reimagined the scenario of the opera to exclude the elements of force and coercion in the women's captivity. But a story about women being held as slaves in an eighteenth-century seraglio is problematic as a starting point for a story about cultural acceptance. Mouawad's focus on redeeming the Muslim characters in this opera is understandable—and to some spectators perhaps even a net positive—but he sacrifices the opera's female characters to the cause. Mouawad argues again and again that the women's experience in the seraglio is not fundamentally different from their experience in the systemic misogyny of Western Europe. While the latter is certainly not a system exempt from criticism, it is misguided to argue that it is no different from the literal captivity and slavery of *Entführung*'s fantasy seraglio.

Orientalism and Reparation

The strength of Mouawad's production lies in its commitment to updating the opera's representation of Islam. The aforementioned prayer session that Selim retreats to takes place onstage directly following intermission. Before Mozart's music resumes, a cantor—in Toronto, Iraqi actor/musician Ahmed Moneka—leads a group of the inhabitants of the seraglio, including Blonde and Pedrillo, in prayer. Mouawad brings a greater sense of realism to *Ent-führung*'s representation of Islam by introducing elements of actual religious practice. But this more sensitive and informed depiction of religion can do little to address the problem of generalization in this depiction of the East. In *Entführung*, as in so many Orientalist representations, ethnicity, geography, and religion are conflated to create a generalized monolithic other in relation to the West.[53] Mouawad's intervention in this opera as a Lebanese-Canadian creator is a productive one, but the Orientalist and misogynist logics of this story persist even in this relatively radical reconceptualization. Mouawad infuses elements of realism into the opera's depiction of the Middle East, but changing the Orientalist fantasies into more realistic depictions of another culture creates inconsistencies because *Entführung* was never really about Turkey, its people, or its religions. You can't take the Orientalism out of *Entführung* because without Orientalism there is no story left. The central conflict between the Orientalist other and the West presents a significant obstacle to reparative representation.

The women in both Bieito's and Mouawad's productions are largely without agency in the story. This is the case with the written text of *Entführung*, for the most part, and both of these productions amplify it. Bieito does this intentionally—he represents the underground sex trade as a horrific place for women where they are stripped of dignity and choice. They are raped and mutilated, and the only choice Konstanze ever has the opportunity to make is to kill herself. Mouawad also represents the women of *Entführung* with little agency in their story, but this feels more like an unfortunate side effect of his larger representational project. Mouawad uses Konstanze's and Blonde's voices to make the Muslim characters—the women's captors—more sympathetic. But without changing any more of the opera's written text, this leads to the women defending behavior that is clearly wrong, and it is difficult to know what to make of their insistence that they were happy in their captivity. Because the only speaking Muslim characters in the opera are men, empowering them can result in further disempowering Konstanze and Blonde—the only women the audience has any connection to.

In *Entführung*'s written text, there are no women in the seraglio besides Konstanze and Blonde, but both Bieito and Mouawad populate their stages with supernumerary women. For Bieito, these women are sex workers or maybe other captives, and for Mouawad they are presumably Turkish women living in the seraglio. None of these women speak or have any meaningful impact on the action—except, for Bieito, when they are the victims of rape and murder—but they are there, visible in the background through much of the opera. Both of these groups of seraglio women move cheer-fully through their daily tasks of emotional labor for the men of the seraglio. The sex workers in Bieito's production pleasure their customers and stroke Osmin's ego (among other things). The women in Mouawad's production teach their children and comfort Konstanze when she is struggling with her relationship with Selim.[54] Despite extensive additions and alterations to the dialogue scenes in the written text, neither director gives these background women anything to say.[55] For Mouawad in particular, these women stand out to me as a potential antidote to the male-dominated politics of cultural representation in this production. Their intersectional identities could have had great power in a reparative retelling of this story. Instead, what we get are the silent figures of women who represent not only a missed opportunity but still another reminder of the ways gendered representation feels like an afterthought in this production.[56]

In the best cases, inventive reimagining of Orientalist works can illumi-nate not only the racism within these works but also racism in our contem-porary culture. Anne Bogart's Bessie Award-winning *South Pacific* in 1984 moves the action to a rehabilitation clinic for veterans with PTSD. Bogart's approach shares similarities with Mouawad's in *Entführung*; while Rodg-ers and Hammerstein's numbers appear in order and without alteration, the narrative that connects them casts these numbers in a very different light. More recently, in 2017, New York's Heartbeat Opera produced a revised and trimmed version of *Madama Butterfly* called *Butterfly*. Like Bogart, director Ethan Heard removes the opera from its romantic exotic locale, which allows him to tell the story of a modern Asian woman and to avoid what he calls the fetishistic desire of audiences to witness Butterfly's ritual suicide.[57] GenEn-Co's *The Mikado: Reclaimed*, produced in Austin in 2016 and directed by kt shorb, uses music from *The Mikado* to tell a story about Japanese internment. This sampling of productions share a willingness to alter the written text to support their critical projects. This type of work has been largely carried out in smaller opera and musical theater companies. I hope that future years will see an increased willingness of larger companies to entertain productions that make significant intervention at the level of the written text. In the absence of such intervention, I feel it is time for opera companies to take a step back from some of these works.[58]

• • •

Both Bieito and Mouawad make radical efforts to critique the content of *Die Entführung aus dem Serail* within the confines of not altering any of the music or sung text. Bieito sets out to highlight the horrors of contemporary sex trafficking while Mouawad confronts the opera's racist depiction of the Middle East. Bieito brings every hint of violence in the opera's written text to the surface of his staging with excruciating explicitness. Mouawad uses the voices of the female characters as a framing device to counteract and cancel out all of that implied violence in the service of telling a story about cultural difference and respect. Both productions include moments of compelling critique of *Entführung*'s written text, but both create other representational problems in the process. The tension between the source material and the directors' concepts persists, and both of these productions feature some deeply flawed representations of women and of Turkey and Turkishness despite their reparative and critical aims.

When it comes to sexual violence, Bieito's and Mouawad's opposite approaches to the violence in the written text of *Entführung* can teach us something about the value of recognizing sexual violence even (or especially) when it is uncomfortable to do so. In the introduction to their essay collection, *Rape and Representation*, Lynn Higgins and Brenda Silver point out the simultaneous pervasiveness and invisibility of rape as a theme in our cultural texts. They suggest that therefore, for feminist critics:

> The act of reading rape . . . requires restoring rape to the literal, to the body: restoring, that is, the violence—the physical, sexual violation. The insistence on taking rape literally often necessitates a conscious critical act of reading the violence and the sexuality back into texts where is has been deflected, either by the text itself or by the critics: where it has been turned into a metaphor or a symbol or represented rhetorically as titillation, persuasion, ravishment, seduction, or desire.[59]

In the written text of *Entführung*, the sexual violence implicit in the scenario is made invisible by Selim's gentle entreaties to Konstanze, Blonde's good humor, the cheerful musical character, and a performance history that rarely challenges the opera's status as a charming—if a touch outdated—romp.

Bieito excavates *Entführung*'s invisible violence and holds it up for scrutiny. But the good that his production does in making this sexual violence visible is tempered by the specific ways in which he stages that violence. He objectifies the bodies of supernumerary sex workers. While the silent and exposed bodies of these women function in part as a criticism of the sex trade, they are also props to dress Bieito's stage. By contrast, Mouawad's stage action and additions to the libretto further the project of burying and abstracting the sexual violence of this story. To use Higgins's and Silver's language above, Mouawad masks the sexual violence through rhetorics of persuasion and desire.

As challenging and as flawed as Bieito's production is, I find his approach to the sexual violence in this story more compelling and more useful than Mouawad's. These productions stand as a pair of exemplars that demonstrate, perhaps counterintuitively, that putting less violence against women on stage is not necessarily the more feminist choice in staging the opera canon. Despite the risks of Bieito's production in terms of the potential for objectifying women's bodies and reveling in explicit sexualized violence, it forces us to confront the problems that already exist in *Entführung* and in our contemporary culture. I don't think the erasure of sexual violence in productions of works from the past is always or necessarily a bad thing. My main criticism of Mouawad's production in this regard is that it doesn't actually erase the sexual violence. If Mouawad—or, more likely, his producing companies—had been willing to make alterations to the opera's written text and not just additions to it, I would have been much more open to this story about cultural negotiation and bias. If the goal of this production is to recast the European men's objections as ignorance and racism, then remove the other legitimate motivations for them to distrust the Turkish characters, namely their very real capture of and threats against Konstanze and Blonde.

These two productions outline an overarching tension observable in this book between a particular European *Regie* culture that trades in shock and outrage and an Anglo-American culture concerned with the politics of representation in art works.[60] If there is a conclusion to be drawn from the comparison in this case study, it might be that these two schools of opera direction could stand to learn from one another. Bieito's production is daring, and his willingness to be scandalous—even to be hated—allows for interesting and original artistic choices. But he is also a bull in a china shop of representational politics. While I find elements of his production truly brilliant, it is also messy and brutal, and it reinforces negative stereotypes about sex workers. Mouawad wants to craft an ethical representation that pushes back against stereotypes, but in *Entführung*, he has done so in a way that anesthetizes the drama of the story and reinforces some of the opera's most troubling content.

Entführung can be a difficult opera for modern audiences, and I think that it should be. In this story, the women are reduced to merely a "site of transaction" between men, per Teresa de Lauretis, and by extension a site of transaction between cultures.[61] It is a story that celebrates the colonial project in its depiction of Selim, who stands apart from his brutish counterpart Osmin because he has been civilized by Enlightenment ideals. And it is a story whose tension arises from the constant, implicit threat of rape. Bieito and Mouawad both attempt to critique elements of the written text of this opera, but ultimately neither critique is entirely coherent. *Entführung*'s problems of misogyny and Islamophobia look different in these two productions, but in neither have they been solved despite extensive rewrites. To approach staging *Entführung* from a place of critique is, I believe, the best option if this opera continues to be programmed. And both Bieito and Mouawad have made valuable contributions to the performance history of this work through their efforts. Yet ultimately, I am not convinced that the written text of this opera will allow for a coherent, ethically defensible stage interpretation without significant alterations to the musical numbers in addition to the spoken dialogue. I am a great proponent of critical staging as an approach to challenging repertoire, but *Entführung* in particular simply may not be salvageable. It is a residue of the eighteenth-century Turkish opera fad that has lingered for as long as it has despite changing cultural sensibilities due to the canonicity of its composer. But its outmoded representations of gender, of violence, and of Turkishness chafe more and more as concerns about ethical representation come increasingly to the forefront of criticism and reception. Perhaps it is time to let this one go.

Four

Rape in/as Warfare

The Perils of Allegory

Sexual violence and war are inextricable in recorded human history. Raping the women of the enemy has been a mainstay of combat since antiquity and it persists despite increased scrutiny and legislation. It is not surprising that these dual atrocities, linked as they are in reality, often occur together in fictional representations of conflict as well. The opera canon is filled with wartime stories, especially in works from the nineteenth century. Great battles from history and myth offer opportunities for epic tragedies and tales of valor and showcase the pomp and spectacle of grand opera in massive choruses of soldiers and elaborate stage effects. *Regietheater* also loves wartime settings, but these are frequently stark and dystopian modern-day wars or occupations. It is here that sexual violence often emerges as a stark reminder of the horrific realities of war that might otherwise be lost in grand operatic spectacle. Treating wartime opera stories seriously (in the opinion of many critics, too seriously) points out and problematizes opera's predominantly aesthetic preoccupation with stories of war and oppression.[1] Sexual violence is a popular way for directors to achieve this level of increased seriousness. In many cases, staging sexual violence makes the stakes of a war plot more relevant by placing the focus on the individual suffering of innocents. Amplifying and even inventing violence in productions of canonic operas, especially operas set in wartime, can also function as a criticism of opera's tendency to dramatize scenarios of human suffering for the sake of entertainment.

This chapter considers the relationship between war and sexual violence in four *Regietheater* productions of four canonic operas: Tobias Kratzer's 2019 production of Verdi's *La forza del destino* for Oper Frankfurt, in which the third act takes place during the Vietnam War; Damiano Michieletto's 2015 production of Rossini's *Guillaume Tell* for the Royal Opera House, with the Austrian occupation of Switzerland updated to the twentieth-century; Tilman Knabe's 2007 production of Puccini's *Turandot* for the Aalto Theater Essen, set in a non-specific contemporary authoritarian state; and Calixto Bieito's 2000 production of Verdi's *Un ballo in maschera* for the Gran Teatre del Liceu, set in a non-specific contemporary police state.[2] All four productions take place under military rule, either amid combat or occupation, and feature acts of sexual violence supported and condoned by military structures. Staging sexual violence in wartime operas, including operas given wartime settings in production, is not merely a result of *Regietheater*'s economy of shock and scandal; these stagings frequently enact cultural anxieties about war and occupation and about the opera canon itself. Representing rape onstage in wartime operas can function to challenge and critique the normalization and valorization of warfare on operatic stages.

Public perception of the prevalence of wartime sexual violence increased as legal definitions shifted through the late twentieth century. In 1977, an amendment to the Geneva Conventions explicitly outlawed the rape of victims of armed conflicts, but it was only in the 1990s, in response to a number of specific conflicts, that international governing bodies began to recognize the full scope of wartime sexual violence.[3] In 1993, instances of widespread gang rape and sexual slavery of Muslim women in Bosnia and Herzegovina were classified as crimes against humanity for the first time. Then in 1998, the United Nations ruled that rape could be an element of genocide, after witnessing how during the Rwandan Genocide Tutsi women were systematically raped in an attempt to destroy their ethnic group. Finally, in 2008, the United Nations adopted language that categorizes rape and sexual violence as war crimes. These landmark decisions have led to gradual acceptance of the idea that sexual violence is not a side-effect or coincidence of war, but a weapon of war employed systematically in military conflicts for purposes up to and including genocide.

The idea that sexual violence could be a weapon of war came to wide public attention during the Balkan Conflict, and these four wartime opera productions capitalize on the popular association between rape and war that followed. In her ground-breaking volume on the rape camps in Bosnia and Herzegovina, Alexandra Stiglmayer argues that although popular wisdom has typically excused wartime rape as a natural result of enforced chastity among young soldiers, we might better understand the motivations for these rapes in terms of existing structures of misogyny. She writes:

[The soldier] rapes because he wants to engage in violence. He rapes because he wants to demonstrate his power. He rapes because he is the victor. He rapes because the woman is the enemy's woman, and he wants to humiliate and annihilate the enemy. He rapes because the woman is herself the enemy whom he wishes to humiliate and annihilate. He rapes because he despises women. He rapes to prove his virility. He rapes because the acquisition of the female body means a piece of territory conquered. He rapes to take out on someone else the humiliation he has suffered in the war. He rapes to work off his fears. He rapes because it's really only some 'fun' with the guys. He rapes because war, a man's business, has awakened his aggressiveness, and he directs it at those who play a subordinate role in the world of war.[4]

Stiglmayer's justifications here touch on issues of objectification, dehumanization, and male dominance common to many feminist interpretations of wartime rape. The feminist scholars who populate this chapter have shaped popular understandings about the nature of rape and its interaction with military conflict, and their interpretations of wartime rape in terms of power, dominance, and misogyny are at work in the operatic representations of sexual violence by Michieletto, Bieito, Kratzer, and Knabe.

Sexual Violence and Agency in Armed Conflict

Sexual violence attacks and limits the bodily autonomy and the agency of its victims. Feminist philosopher Anne Cahill argues that the act of rape "constructs male sexuality in a particular way such that it constitutes a way of imposing harm, pain and powerlessness" and "constructs female sexuality in terms of passivity, victimhood, and lack of agency."[5] In the real world, women who experience sexual violence do not necessarily lose their agency. There are many ways in which women can resist the powerlessness that their attackers may try to impose. Representations of rape often focus on a powerless victim, though. In an effort to condemn sexual violence, representations of its objects tend to lean into their victimization to show how damaging rape is to the body and the mind. But this leaves us with countless depictions of women who are only noteworthy for their status as victims and who have no opportunity to express their agency.

Damiano Michieletto's *Guillaume Tell* fits into this representational framework with its depiction of an attempted gang rape of a Swiss woman. Michieletto updates Schiller's story of the fourteenth-century Austrian oppression of the Swiss people to a non-specific twentieth-century occupation by a brutal military force. In the second scene of the third act, the Austrian soldiers are celebrating the hundredth anniversary of their rule in Switzerland. In Michieletto's production, when the ballet movement begins, a few soldiers select a woman from the chorus of Swiss prisoners and drag her forward.[6] They offer her a glass of champagne, and when she refuses it and runs, about half a dozen soldiers surround her and force her to drink while they pour their own champagne over her head. She runs again, and this time is caught by a soldier sitting at a long communal table. He holds her in his lap while others grope her and try to reach up under her dress. Now when she breaks free, it is Rodolphe, the captain of the guard, who catches her and brings her to Governor Gessler. Gessler initially presents a veneer of kindness, touching her shoulder as if to comfort her and moving her wet hair out of her face. He draws his gun and taunts her with it playfully. In the presence of the gun, the terrified woman momentarily stops fighting. Gessler tries to kiss her mouth, and she pushes him. Furious, he gestures for his men to take her away. They force her onto the tabletop and strip her, obscuring her from the audience with their bodies. She stands up and wraps the tablecloth around herself, crying and shaking her head no. The men jump and dance around below her, beating their fists on the table in unison. They seize her, pull her to the ground, and pile on top of her, pulling the cloth away. Suddenly, Tell appears in the fray as if from nowhere and the woman escapes offstage.

This display of violence communicates to the audience the nature of the Austrian oppression of Switzerland and the role that sexual violence can play in systems of political control. Eileen Zurbriggen posits that war and rape are correlated because they are both supported and justified by what she calls the traditional or hegemonic model of masculinity. One of the dimensions of masculinity that she explores in relation to both war and rape is dominance/power/control.[7] Studies have consistently found that men with high levels of power motivation are more likely to display coercive sexual behaviors and are also more likely to enter a war and have success as soldiers.[8] Power motivation is a common and tangible element of the representations of rape in combat zones in this production. When the Austrian soldiers assault the Swiss woman, it is not only for their own pleasure; it is an implicit threat to the other Swiss people who are watching and a reminder of their powerlessness. While rape is a crime against an individual, the meaning of rape in war is not individualistic. The women who are raped in armed conflicts are representatives of their ethnic groups and stand-ins for their husbands, brothers, and fathers.[9] In this way, martial rape is an act of terrorism toward the enemy group at large, used to maintain and express control.[10]

Calixto Bieito's production of Verdi's *Un ballo in maschera* for the Gran Teatre del Liceu in 2000 features the rape of a young man by police in a military state. Though not strictly a war setting, this production is still closely related to the theme insofar as it shows state-sanctioned sexual violence as a tactic to punish civilian disobedience under a military government. We are first introduced to the young man in a large ensemble scene at the home of the witch and fortune teller, Madame Arvidson (Ulrica).[11] In this production, Bieito has set this scene in a brothel and made Madame Arvidson its proprietor. The young man appears to be a sex worker. He is costumed provocatively in leather pants and a shiny silver shirt unbuttoned and hanging off his shoulders. Throughout this scene, he is used quite literally as a set piece; various characters physically move him around the stage as they caress his body. At the end of this scene, he gets on his knees in front of King Gustavo (Ricardo) and steals his wallet under the pretense of offering to perform fellatio. During the long orchestral interlude that introduces the next act, the young man from the brothel runs onstage, pursued by four police officers. They catch him, beat him, and strip him naked. Three officers hold the young man down while the fourth lowers his pants and rapes him. Anckarström (Renato), who in this production is the King's military captain, enters and watches from upstage. After the rape, another of the officers fishes the man's belt from his clothes and strangles him with it. The officers retrieve the stolen wallet from the dead man's pants and deliver it to Anckarström as they leave the stage. The naked body is left in the field as a clear message about how little this man's life is worth to the establishment. The rape and murder may also communicate a direct threat to Madame Arvidson, the young man's employer, who was in some tension with Gustavo in the previous scene. It is relatively unusual to see a man depicted as the victim of rape on the opera stage, but this character's representation sexualizes and objectifies him in a way that closely aligns him with the women who are more typically the receptors of operatic sexual violence. Inger Skjelsbæk has argued that war rape must always be understood in terms of the masculinization of the perpetrator and the feminization of the victim. She writes, "the ways in which masculinization and feminization polarize other identities are intimately linked to the overall conflict structure, and it is this mechanism which can make rape a powerful weapon of war."[12]

This scene in Bieito's *Ballo* portrays rape as primarily a means of asserting dominance and power. Susan Brownmiller uses the prevalence of rape within men's prisons to support her argument that rape is not a crime of passion but of violence. Prison rape, she argues, is "an acting out of power roles within an all-male authoritarian environment in which the younger, weaker inmate . . . is forced to play the role that in the outside world is assigned to women."[13] Brownmiller's argument here appears overly reductive in light of contemporary conversations about the imprisonment of transgender women and non-binary people in men's prisons, who we now know suffer sexual violence at much higher rates than men. Yet Brownmiller's view of prison rape as primarily about violence and control rather than primarily about sex is at work in the portrayal of the rape of this sex worker in Bieito's *Ballo*.[14] In this production, rape is a tool used to maintain the power dynamic in this exclusively male political structure. Bieito suggests that sexual violence exists alongside and intermingled with political violence. The ease with which the soldiers transition from rape to murder and Anckarström's utter lack of surprise suggest that the military system of Gustavo's Sweden does not meaningfully distinguish sexual violence from other means of control and punishment.

In these scenes from *Tell* and *Ballo*, sexual violence is not only a method of control and terrorism but an act of dehumanization. Ann Cahill defines rape as "an act that destroys (if only temporarily) the intersubjective, embodied agency and therefore personhood of a woman."[15] The dehumanization and objectification inherent to sexual violence is reinforced in wartime settings as women are commonly perceived as representations of an enemy nation or race. Brownmiller describes the bodies of raped women during war as "ceremonial battlefields" on which conflicts between men are played out in miniature.[16] We have seen already that the victims of rape and attempted rape in *Tell* and *Ballo* are both unnamed and non-singing supernumeraries who are introduced to the story for the purpose of being raped as symbols of the ravages of war. In Tilman Knabe's 2007 *Turandot*, the victim—Turandot herself—exerts much more power in the story, yet the dehumanization inherent to rape persists.

Despite Turandot's relative power and agency in the opera, Calaf dehumanizes and ultimately rapes her in order to achieve his political goals. Knabe's *Turandot* is set in a totalitarian state whose aging dictator is near death. Calaf, exiled from a foreign kingdom, wins Turandot's hand and thereby a seat of political power. Knabe states clearly in the program that Calaf's desire for Turandot is about the power of her position; Calaf is not a "languishing lover" but "a clever, highly strategic politician."[17] In the final act, after Calaf has answered the riddles and Turandot has failed to guess

Fig. 10. Turandot (Iréne Theorin) in her wedding dress is surrounded by the apparitions of her previous suitors while Calaf (Dario Volonté) holds their baby. *Turandot*, directed by Tilman Knabe.
(Photograph © Joerg Landsberg, reprinted by permission.)

his name, Knabe sets the final scene in a small bedroom on an otherwise dark and empty stage. Everything until this point has taken place out in the open, under constant surveillance of guards and the populace. Now, Turandot and Calaf are alone. In the libretto, Calaf kisses Turandot despite her violent protestations. She pleads, "do not profane me," "no one will ever possess me," and "stranger, do not touch me."[18] In Knabe's staging, Calaf throws Turandot down on the bed, kneels between her legs, and rapes her. Whereas the stage directions in the libretto specify that Turandot is transfigured by the stolen kiss, Knabe's Turandot is broken and resigned through the opera's conclusion. This production cuts the portion of the ending when Turandot sings about her awakening to love, so she sings only a few short lines after the rape, including "I am ashamed."[19] As the chorus sings a climactic reprisal of the melody of Calaf's aria "Nessun dorma," Calaf walks away from Turandot carrying a baby doll smeared with what looks like blood and afterbirth. He holds the child up triumphantly over his head on one side of the stage as the climactic music swells.

Both Knabe and the musical director Stefan Soltesz refer to Turandot as a vehicle for power in Calaf's eyes.[20] After the kiss, or in this case rape, Turandot tells Calaf that he has won his victory and that now he can leave. She does not understand that the rape itself is not the prize, it is simply politically expedient. It binds Turandot to Calaf and assures he will reign as Emperor in her father's place, and the resultant child ensures the continuing power of his political dynasty. Calaf wants to conquer Turandot, and he does this not just by outsmarting her, but by impregnating her. During the war in the Balkans, the aggressors "used rape not only as a tool of war, but also to implement a policy of impregnation in order to further the destruction of one people and the proliferation of another—a policy of genocide by forced impregnation."[21] Turandot is a vehicle for power for Calaf, and she is also a vessel for his politically legitimate heirs. Calaf does not treat Turandot like a person with autonomy. To him, she is only her bloodline and her fertile body. Turandot's dehumanization is especially jarring because she is not only a named character, unlike the rape victims in the other productions, but the opera's eponymous character. Her immense power and agency from the opera's start is stripped away after Calaf answers her riddles. In the opera's final scene, after the rape, Calaf and Turandot pose in their wedding clothes as if for a portrait, before Calaf walks away with the baby to celebrate his victory. Turandot stands motionless in her white dress like a photograph of herself reduced to a single purpose—providing legitimacy to Calaf's reign.

Rape is an act of dehumanization because it strips its victims of their agency and bodily autonomy. In *Turandot*, Knabe illuminates this characteristic of rape by demonstrating how even a woman as powerful as Turandot can be reduced to just a body by a colonizing force. Her lack of agency in the final scene of this production is powerful because it is unexpected. In *Tell* and *Ballo*, the victims of sexual violence are also objectified and dehumanized by powerful men. But these unnamed characters are not just bodies to their attackers, they are also essentially just bodies to their directors. The bodies of the dancers who represent the victims serve the needs of the productions in that they allow Michieletto and Bieito to comment on the atrocities of military dominance. Critics sometimes resist feminist theories of rape because they fear these theories risk reducing women to victims and actually increasing their powerlessness.[22] I think theorizing, representing, and talking about rape is vital to the feminist project, but representations of rape like those in *Tell* and *Ballo* give me pause. These unnamed characters are only their victimhood. Rape is no less abhorrent a crime when we do not know anything about its victims, but opera is a storytelling medium. The story that these scenes tell is that military oppression is brutal and disregards the humanity of the oppressed, but the way that they tell this story is by creating characters who exist only to be assaulted.

Rape in/as Performance

The acts of sexual violence in these productions are all performed for these operas' audiences. But while the rapes in *Turandot* and *Ballo* happen in private, Michieletto's *Tell* and Kratzer's *Forza* use rape and the threat of rape as public spectacles to raise the morale of Austrian and American troops, respectively. These productions both present the basic assumption that sexual violence is an effective tool of peer bonding for soldiers. Susan Brownmiller suggests that gang rape may even have been one of the earliest forms of male bonding.[23] Though the scenes of sexual violence in *Tell* and *Forza* are drastically different in tone, both rely on our recognition that sexual violence, and gang rape in particular, can function to sow solidarity among its perpetrators.[24]

This third act of Verdi's *La forza del destino* is set during the eighteenth-century War of Austrian Succession. Tobias Kratzer's 2019 production for Oper Frankfurt transposes the action to the Vietnam War. Act 3 scene 3, in which the soldiers have a moment of rest and recreation, becomes for Kratzer a performance given for the troops by a trio of Playboy Bunnies who are airlifted in, in an allusion to the 1979 film *Apocalypse Now*.[25] One of the Bunnies is a singing role, Preziosilla, who appears twice in the opera to encourage the men to enlist and then enjoy military life. In a performance area amid the transfixed soldiers, the women don rubber masks and play out a short mime scene. Two dancers wearing JFK and Marilyn Monroe masks flirt over a birthday cake until they are interrupted by a dancer in a Nixon mask, who takes the cake from Marilyn and shoves it into JFK's face, who then collapses. The woman who had been wearing the JFK mask trades it in for an Asian conical hat and slinks around the stage menacingly as the soldiers boo. The dancer in the Marilyn mask takes it off, and hands an oversized strap-on dildo to Nixon. As the chorus bursts into a refrain of "long live the madness of war," Nixon grabs the dancer in the conical hat by the hips and simulates raping her while the third dancer stands behind Nixon with a hand on her shoulder, egging her on.[26] The soldiers dance and thrust along with the mock rape as they sing, and they burst into laughter and applause as the number concludes. While the rape fantasy represented here is an allegorical one, it is an unnamed, non-singing woman in a sexy costume who takes on the role of the Vietnamese enemy. Her already-objectified body,

Fig. 11. Preziosilla (Tanja Ariane Baumgartner) entertains the crowd of American soldiers in Vietnam. *La forza del destino*, directed by Tobias Kratzer. (Photograph © Monika Rittershaus, reprinted by permission.)

which had moments before been titillating the amassed soldiers, easily transitions from a sexual object meant to draw the men's lust to a despised object meant to draw their hatred. To heighten the gendered dynamics of *Forza*'s mock rape, the dancer in the Nixon mask wears a comically oversized phallus, and struts around the stage flexing her muscles. The skit leverages the idea of rape as a vehicle to express hatred of the Vietnamese other by mapping racialized identity onto femininity.

Where Kratzer's soldiers bond over a crass representation of rape, Michieletto's soldiers in *Guillaume Tell* bond over watching and participating in the real sexual assault of a young woman selected from among their Swiss captives. Catharine MacKinnon describes the sexual violence at the Serbian rape camps in Bosnia and Herzegovina as representing "live pornography"; in addition to filming the rapes, MacKinnon claims that the Serbian forces would invite their fellow officers to come and watch them. One soldier, she writes, compared this experience to going to a movie theater.[27] The rape scene in Michieletto's *Tell* clearly evokes these real-world stories about the utilization of rape as a spectacle for entertainment.[28]

Fig. 12. A Swiss woman (Jessica Chamberlain) is restrained and groped by a group of Austrian soldiers. *Guillaume Tell*, directed by Damiano Michieletto. (Photograph © Donald Cooper, reprinted by permission.)

The rape in *Guillaume Tell* takes place during a ballet movement, and like Salome's Dance of the Seven Veils in chapter 2, staging sexual violence to music intended for dance and spectacle can encourage an audience to take voyeuristic pleasure in the representation of sexual violence. But Michieletto's choreography in this scene provides a sophisticated reading of the opera's written text that makes it clear who this music is for and who is harmed by it. Michieletto does not add sexual violence to the ballet scene so much as he accentuates and makes explicit the sexual violence that is already there. In the written text of *Guillaume Tell*, the Austrian soldiers force the Swiss women among their prisoners to dance with them during this scene; this is an act of violence and coercion predicated on sex. In Michieletto's production, the undercurrents of sexual coercion are brought to the surface: in place of a dance, the ballet accompanies the sexual assault of one Swiss woman. Governor Gessler whispers something to the captain of the guard just before the soldiers pull the Swiss woman out of the crowd, so we can assume that Gessler orders this act of sexual violence. The assault serves both to entertain the other soldiers and to terrorize and threaten the Swiss chorus.

Although Michieletto dispenses with a traditional ballet for this scene, his choreography is consistent with the idea that this is functional music played and heard as part of the Austrian soldiers' celebration. In the written text of *Guillaume Tell*, this music is already dissonant with the experience of the Swiss people. Michieletto's performance text accentuates this feature of the written text in the way he choreographs the motions of the Austrian soldiers, whose experience of the scene aligns with the music, versus the Swiss woman, whose experience of the scene is dissonant with the music. When the Swiss woman first interacts with Governor Gessler, we see the way that Gessler's actions align with the music and the Swiss woman's do not. The orchestral texture thins, and a short unison scalar passage of descending sixteenth notes in the strings corresponds with Gessler running his fingers down the woman's arm twice (the first and third bars of Example 1). Michieletto is depending on that same *Regietheater* technique, discussed in chapter 3, in which staging choices are legitimated by their alignment with musical structures.[29] The concordance emphasizes that while this music has an estranging effect on the audience and the Swiss characters, it fluently scores the actions and motivations of the Austrian soldiers.

Music Example 1: Rossini, *Guillaume Tell*, Act 3, scene 2, no. 16, 16–21 bars after letter C.

Gessler continues to be attuned to the music of Rossini's ballet through the remainder of this scene. The following section, marked Allegro vivace, is a little waltz that begins with an eight-bar theme in the strings and woodwinds that hurtles up an arpeggio to a towering peak emphasized by a cymbal crash on the second beat of the bar before winding its way back down the scale to repeat (Example 2). The first time this musical figure appears, the crashing top note of the phrase corresponds with Gessler thrusting his gun suddenly in front of the woman's face. On the repeat of the theme, Gessler repeats this threat, surprising the woman again with the gun in her face on the emphasized beat. A little while later, this theme appears twice more (17 mm. before letter A in the Allegro Vivace). The first time, the emphasized beat at the top of the arpeggio coincides with Gessler suddenly grabbing the woman's face. He holds her tightly and slowly moves in to kiss her lips. The phrase repeats for a final statement, and this time the woman, in a desperate attempt to escape, pushes Gessler away just before the accented beat. It is possible that this was simply a small mistake in the execution of the complicated chore-ography of this scene, but I interpreted her timing as an interruption of his next intended move. It begins to feel as if in the world of the opera, Gessler is intentionally mapping his movements onto the dance music he hears for fun. He certainly conceives of his torture of this woman as a game; is it also a dance?

Music Example 2: Rossini, *Guillaume Tell*, Act 3, scene 2, no. 16, beginning of Allegro vivace.

The other Austrian soldiers seem to show similar awareness of the music in the next part of this scene. When the woman stands up on the table wrapped in the tablecloth, the waltz concludes and the next section begins, marked Presto in 2/4. This section repeats the pastoral music from the begin-ning of the *Pas de soldats* but faster. At the new tempo, this already rapid-fire melody feels increasingly frenetic. The soldiers pound the table rhythmically with the quarter notes, dancing to the music as they keep time with their fists. In this moment, it is especially clear that the characters can hear the music; they are able to accurately dance and play tabletop percussion on the beat. They perform for one another, contributing to the music played for their celebration while tormenting the Swiss woman.

The actions of the perpetrators of violence in this scene are dancelike in the way they are mapped onto musical features. But the Swiss woman who is the victim of this violence experiences the music of the scene and the context of performance differently. She does not move to the music, as the men do, but against it. While their fist-pounding accentuates the existing beat, her vocalizations interrupt the oblivious frivolity of the dance music as she grunts with exertion and screams. By adding something new to the soundscape, the woman's vocalizations decenter music as the only sonic source of meaning in this scene. The uncomfortable juxtaposition of the soldiers' celebration and the Swiss prisoners' terror is translated into sound as these vocalizations of pain and fear punctuate and disrupt the blithe veneer of the dance music. And because these vocalizations and her movements are so determinedly not dancelike, they allow the audience a way of engaging with the scene as something other than the merry spectacle the soldiers take part in. The ballet is an ironic backdrop for the horror of the scene rather than an invitation to witness the assault as a pleasurable spectacle. The Swiss woman's rhythmically irregular activity allows us to see her attempted rape not *as* a dance but *during* a dance.

Sexual Violence and Critical Staging

All four of these productions contain clear critiques of war and authoritarianism. I have found this to be the case in general for productions that add a wartime setting in production distinct from what is in the written text. There are a couple of directorial short-hands that tend to arise in the service of critiquing war in this context. One of them is the inclusion of scenes of sexual violence, which I will return to shortly. Another is fascist iconography. *Regietheater* frequently takes aim at jingoism, and in the German context of so much *Regietheater*, this is often accomplished with reference to Nazi symbols.[30] The intrusion of these powerful images from the real world can shock audience members out of their absorption in the fictional worlds of the operas and the enjoyment of the music. Joy Calico has theorized that *Regietheater* in general operates by creating in its spectators what Bertolt Brecht called the alienation or estrangement effect (*Verfremdungseffekt*).[31] Calico argues that in nonliteral stagings of canonic operas, the experience of estrangement comes from the disruption of expectation, and specifically the "rupture between what is seen and what is heard."[32] The goal of estrangement is not only the disorientation of thwarted expectations, but also the recognition that follows. *Regietheater*, like Brecht's epic theater, bestows agency on its spectators by asking them to rethink what they have previously taken for granted. This kind of spectating can be pleasurable, but it can also be used to forward a socio-political critique.[33]

Kratzer's *La forza del destino*, Michieletto's *Guillaume Tell*, Knabe's *Turandot*, and Bieito's *Un ballo in maschera* all contain clear critiques of fascism. Whereas in *Tell*, the fascist regime is the enemy Austrian force that subjugates the Swiss protagonists in the written text, *Forza*, *Turandot*, and *Ballo* tease fascist undertones out of the chorus scenes that in the operas' written texts generally serve as uncritical celebrations of the glory of war or the homeland. In Kratzer's *Forza*, the rollicking chorus number "Rataplan" accompanies a group of American soldiers amusing themselves by shooting a revolver loaded with a single bullet at a Vietnamese POW until eventually one of them kills him. The soldiers sing, "your glorious wounds will be rewarded by your triumph. . . . Victory shines brighter for the courageous soldier."[34] Kratzer undercuts the grandiosity of this sentiment by drawing attention to a different vision of war that focuses on the dehumanization of the enemy and the reckless sadism that soldiering can foster. *Ballo*'s "O figlio d'Inghilterra" and *Turandot*'s "Ai tuoi piedi ci prostriam" are stirring hymns sung by the people to their leader. Though the leaders in question are both the "good guys" in their respective operas, both of these productions have the chorus perform a Sieg Heil salute during these numbers.[35] These moments of relatively uncritical expressions of musical patriotism and love for one's leader become, in these stagings, fanatical fascist gestures.[36] All three of these chorus scenes, from *Forza*, *Ballo*, and *Turandot*, represent conventional operatic use of the chorus, but Kratzer, Bieito, and Knabe all use their staging to mine a darker message out of these scenes. These symbols alienate us from the beautiful and triumphant music of these choruses by connecting this music to the historical and contemporary reality of fascism.[37]

The fascist state depicted in Knabe's *Turandot* warrants a bit of additional attention for its interaction with the exoticism of the opera's written text. Knabe's setting for the opera is not clear; the house program says only that it is a totalitarian regime. Knabe has suggested that he thinks Puccini and his librettists were commenting on contemporary Italian fascism in the 1920s; however, politically, it was safer to move the setting away from Italy, "so it retains something that is timeless and universal."[38] Knabe retains this timelessness and universality in *Turandot*'s representation of fascism; the program notes make reference to a series of different fascist regimes including North Korea and the Third Reich. On stage, however, there are visible markers of ethnicity that are not entirely coherent. Like many opera casts, this one is predominantly (though not exclusively) composed of white singers, so the indication of ethnicity comes primarily from costuming. Turandot is blonde and wears costume pieces including dress pants, a cardigan, a trench coat, and a white wedding dress and veil. Her father, the aging emperor, has white wispy hair. On the other hand, Ping, Pang, Pong, the emperor's soldiers, and all of the civilians have black hair, and many are wearing wigs to achieve this. In my interpretation, this creates an apparent racial distinction between the ruling class and the public in this system. Calaf's position in this structure is unclear; he wears military fatigues until he dons his wedding tuxedo, and the performers wear their natural hair.[39]

The visual distinction between Turandot and her father and the people they rule heightens the perception that this is a populace controlled by people who do not represent them. However, Turandot's whiteness in this production gives me pause. Like Salome, this is another operatic anti-heroine being made white at the same time that she is made a victim of sexual violence. This is a striking coincidence. Cultural discourse around sexual violence frequently focuses on white women to the exclusion of marginalized groups who experience endemic sexual violence—at present, notably, trans women of color and Indigenous women and girls. And the victimhood of white women has a long history of use as a tool of white supremacist oppression.[40] I am not suggesting this is why Turandot is white in this production, but this context is present and legible nonetheless. I don't think the solution is for us to depict more rapes of women of color in opera. However, the overwhelming whiteness of operatic casts and creators in Europe and North America can lead to a myopic white frame in a lot of this work that I hope we can move past by diversifying the voices telling operatic stories.

The shared critical vocabulary between the four wartime productions in this chapter extends to their inclusion of sexual violence as a feature of these fascist and proto-fascist regimes. Kasper Holten defended the inclusion of rape in Michieletto's *Guillaume Tell* staging by implying that the existence of rape in real-world warfare is justification enough to include it in operatic representations of war. Holten refutes Catharine Woodward's accusation that the rape was gratuitous by framing gratuitousness as a question of realism—it cannot be gratuitous if it reflects reality. The distinction between useful and gratuitous representations of sexual violence will not be consistent between different critics and spectators, but the fact of the existence of sexual violence in wartime does not itself settle the matter. There are situations in which the inclusion of sexual violence not explicitly called for in an opera's score can be ethically productive by prompting critical analysis and advancing pertinent cultural conversations. But even from a position of accepting that adding violence to a work can be done ethically, the often sensationalized violence of the *Regietheater* aesthetic can feel like a bridge too far. There is undeniably a character of one-upmanship regarding the shock value of some of these productions; there are directors and producers that thrive on the controversy generated by outrageously lurid renditions of beloved operas.

I find *Regietheater* stagings of operas the richest and most compelling when they critique the operas they adapt. That sexual violence in conflict zones is a bad thing is not a particularly interesting take. But Michieletto's *Guillaume Tell* and Knabe's *Turandot* both level powerful critiques against not just sexual violence but the ways sexual violence is either glossed over or glorified in the written texts of *Tell* and *Turandot*—and, indeed, in many operas of the performance canon. Critics of *Regietheater* are quick to dismiss productions that interpolate acts of violence or sexual content into familiar works with claims about the authorial intent of the composer (and, less often, the librettist). Reviews of Michieletto's *Tell*, for instance, frequently characterize the assault scene as "unprompted either by music or libretto,"[41] and argue that it was in "blatant contradiction to the spirit of the music,"[42] or similarly, that Michieletto is determined to "privilege concept over music."[43] In general, I do not find arguments about authorial intent particularly useful for judging the efficacy or quality of *Regietheater* concepts, but in this case these criticisms are particularly inappropriate because the written text of *Guillaume Tell* thematizes sexual violence already. Michieletto does not so much invent a rape story as he calls attention to a rape story that was already there.

In the third-act ballet in *Guillaume Tell*, the Austrian soldiers force the Swiss women to dance for them. But even outside of this scene, *Tell's* libretto alludes to other acts of sexual violence. Early in the opera's first act, the shepherd Leuthold explains that he killed one of the Austrian soldiers because that soldier had attempted to abduct his daughter. Given the context of a military occupation, this alone may be readily interpreted as intent to rape, but there is even more clarity in the libretto's source material. In Schiller's play it is not Leuthold but Baumgarten who kills an Austrian soldier, and it is in defense of his wife, not his daughter. Baumgarten explains that he did what any man would do: "I exercised my rights upon a man who would befoul my honor and my wife's."[44] In the credits for a commercial DVD of Michieletto's ROH *Tell*, the woman that is raped in the ballet scene is called "Leuthold's daughter," so the inclusion of the rape scene is linked directly to the existing allusion to sexual violence in the first act of the opera. Michieletto capitalizes on this undercurrent of sexual violence in a number of ways throughout his production in addition to the attempted gang rape in the ballet. The opera's opening scene typically depicts the bucolic bliss of the Swiss people who are happy at work while a fisherman sings a love song. Michieletto's production opens grimly: the fisherman is intoxicated and staggers through the assembled company as he sings, stopping at one point to roughly grope the breasts of a woman in the chorus. She resists and he leaves her alone, but there is little response from anyone else onstage. From the opera's first scene, we see that sexualized violence is not unusual here, and that the Swiss women do not occupy a social position of much respect, even in their own community. Later, Mathilde, an Austrian woman in a relationship with one of the Swiss men, is threatened and harassed by both her lover and Governor Gessler. Michieletto avoids making sexual and gendered violence exclusively the problem of the enemy Austrians and shows that it is also pervasive within the ranks of the Swiss themselves. This is an interesting perspective for a wartime story. Michieletto's production offers some resistance to *Tell*'s romantic narrative of the heroic Swiss people overcoming their oppression.[45] The heroes are not themselves immune from oppressive behavior along gendered lines.

The inclusion of representations of sexual violence serves the story Michieletto is telling about the harsh realities of war. He engages with the idea of sexual violence in a relatively sophisticated way by depicting smaller pervasive forms of gendered violence in addition to the shocking rape scene in the third act. But although I think the presence of the gang rape in the ballet may be justified by both the plot of the opera and the rest of the production, the specific representation of rape performed in the dress rehearsal may have contained gratuitous elements. In the first version of the scene, the Swiss woman's naked body was exposed in full to the audience and the stage action included some more graphic allusions to rape. I was unable to access any footage of this performance, but Catharine Woodward mentions a moment in which Gessler shoves his gun between the Swiss woman's legs, which was not included in the later version. Holten reported that the changes to the scene made between the dress rehearsal and opening night were spurred by the comments made by Woodward and others. He characterizes the changes as "tweaks" and insists that the scene "has not changed in its essence. It is the same duration and makes the same point that we find valid for the theatrical context."[46] If we take Holten at his word, then Michieletto deemed the full nudity of the dancer and some of the more explicit gestures—such as Gessler simulating rape with his gun—to be nonessential to the drama. The choice to do without these elements is not only more sensitive to the risks of representing sexual violence on stage, but it also streamlines the staging of the ballet so that every action is necessary and in service of Michieletto's vision. With so little visible nudity and no simulation of sexual penetration onstage, this scene captures the fear and the humiliation that the soldiers achieve through this sexual violence while side-stepping at least some of the pornographic potential of putting rape onstage.

So the sexual assault serves the sense of realism in Michieletto's approach to the setting and functions in the plot to illustrate how bad the Austrian occupation is. But there is another layer of criticism at work here, too. The ballet scene can also be read as a critique of *Guillaume Tell* the opera and other war operas in general, which all too often glorify and romanticize war and the military. Typical stagings of the *Tell* ballet feature a corps of dancers who perform a charming folk-inspired dance number, extraneous to the plot, in which the men happen to wear military costumes and the women, peasant attire. By highlighting the darkness that is already in this story about resistance under a brutal oppressor, Michieletto challenges our tendency to see this opera as something primarily optimistic. His staging of the ballet holds an unflattering mirror up to the audience. He seems to ask, why are you so shocked to see a prisoner of war being abused when you came to an opera about a violent and unjust military occupation? We so often attend the opera to evaluate the voices and the orchestra and to revel in the lush, expensive design, even while we watch depictions of women suffering and dying onstage. Michieletto's ballet foregrounds the spectacle of suffering and makes it impossible to ignore.

Like *Guillaume Tell*, the written text of *Turandot* features both allusions to sexual violence and acts that can be interpreted as sexually violent. Turandot's resistance to being married stems directly from fear of ending up like her ancestor, Princess Lo-u-Ling, who was "dragged by a man like you, stranger, into the dreadful night where her sweet voice was silenced."[47] This line is commonly understood as an indication that Lo-u-Ling was raped as well as murdered by the usurper.[48] Later, when Calaf wants to kiss Turandot, she resists, saying, "the agony of my ancestor will not be repeated."[49] The language of Turandot's protestations makes it clear that she perceives any kind of intimate contact with Calaf to be a dire threat to her safety, in light of what happened to Lo-u-Ling. Calaf talks about his desire for Turandot almost exclusively in terms of winning or conquering her. "Nessun dorma" famously ends with his threefold repetition of "vincerò!" Turandot's reaction to Calaf successfully answering her riddles indicates that she had been confident the riddles were unanswerable—her way of ensuring she would not be forced into an unwanted marriage without having to explicitly refuse. Calaf and Turandot's kiss in the third act of the opera is already an act of sexual violence. It is an intimate, romantic act that Turandot actively resists, and it is clear from the text that Turandot understands this act as being commensurate with Lo-u-Ling's rape and murder. A production that treats this scene and the rest of the dénouement like a romance in which Turandot is radically transformed by Calaf's affections normalizes the idea that women sometimes need to be forced into intimacy, that it is ultimately for their own good, and that they will be grateful in the end.

The brutal rape in Knabe's *Turandot* is supported by more than the character of the libretto. Whereas Michieletto's *Tell* plays off the cheery dance music of the ballet to contrast the brutal stage action, Knabe's rape scene in *Turandot* is actually well supported by Alfano's music.[50] Roger Parker describes the musical realization of this scene as "brief and violent to the point of brutality. . . . *Tristan*-like dissonance piles on dissonance and then releases onto a sequence of rhythmically irregular, triple forte bangs on the drum, bassoons, and trombones. If this is a representation of sex, then the act is a barbaric, messy business, overwhelmingly concerned with power."[51] Knabe seems to hear this sequence of rhythmically irregular strikes at the moment of the kiss in essentially the same way that Parker does: in his production, these percussive strikes align with the sharp thrusts of Calaf's hips (Example 3). There is a long pause notated in the score at this moment during which Knabe's Calaf stands, refastens his pants, and leaves Turandot lying motionless on the bed. Parker's reading of the music of this scene, from its violence to its equation of sex and power, comes to life on Knabe's stage.

Knabe and Michieletto take the same kind of approach to their representations of rape and attempted rape in their productions that Bieito did for his *Entführung* in chapter 3. All three of these productions recognize the sexual violence that is often obscured in production and reception of the operas they adapt, and all three move that violence into the spotlight. Axel Englund calls this strategy a "hyperbolic gambit": recognizing that male violence is the norm in opera, a hyperbolic onstage representation of that violence resists the norm by making it impossible to ignore.[52] Englund argues that "this mode of critique is a risk activity with high stakes: it may be potentially productive, but it is also liable to misfire in various ways."[53] One of these risks is that no degree of onstage violence is so repulsive that it will necessarily preclude secret titillation for some audience members. I think this is particularly likely in Bieito's *Entführung*, given that the women who carry out pornographic scenes in the background of the main action are the same women who go on to be tortured, raped, and killed. The other risk is that "the affective impact becomes too strong to be justifiable."[54] This is clearly on display in Catharine

Music Example 3: Puccini/Alfano, *Turandot*, Act 3, scene 1, 10–11 bars after number 38.

Woodward's criticism of Michieletto's *Tell*, which she feels goes too far and poses too great a risk to sexual assault survivors. In Englund's discussion of the hyperbolic gambit, he identifies Bieito's *Entführung* and Michieletto's *Tell* as two of the most notorious productions in this mode. Micaela Baranello similarly connects these two productions while considering the blurry line that exists "between exploitation and productive meaning."[55] I think it is actually Knabe who makes the most effective use of this directorial gambit. The act is brutal enough that its inclusion in this opera is shocking and extremely disquieting. However, it happens quickly and unceremoniously. This serves the story Knabe is telling—the rape is simply a means to an end for Calaf—and it also forestalls the potential erotic enjoyment of the spectacle. There is no visible nudity and the rape is not drawn out; it is over almost immediately.

One principal difference between the scenes of sexual violence in Michieletto's *Tell* and Knabe's *Turandot* is that although sexual violence is present in the written texts of both operas, it is characterized in opposite ways. In the written text *Guillaume Tell*, the sexually violent acts are portrayed as bad things that the oppressors do; Michieletto needs only make these acts more visible to an audience that may prefer not to think about them. In *Turandot*, Knabe has more work to do because the written text of the opera does not portray Calaf forcing himself on Turandot as a bad thing but as the transformative moment that makes her fall in love with him. By turning the stolen kiss into a rape, Knabe is not only criticizing the reception and performance history of *Turandot* but also the written text in a deep and damning way. Supporting this critique is the omission of the seventy bars of music of Turandot's transfiguration.[56] With this passage gone, there is nothing left to soften the sense of her defeat. Her final proclamation, "his name is Love!'" rings hollow as she stands alone in the bedroom where we just saw her raped.[57] The fact that the music of this production supports the critical dramatic project is no doubt one of the strengths of Knabe's and Soltesz's *Turandot*. While the alienation effect discussed above is a central aesthetic of *Regietheater*, some cooperation between music and drama can go a long way to making a conceptual production coherent. Optimistically, I hope we might see more of this kind of collaboration between stage director and music director in service of interpretive projects in *Regietheater* productions in the future.

Rape as a Metaphor

I have argued that the unnamed, unsinging characters in Bieito's *Un ballo in maschera* and Michieletto's *Guillaume Tell* are not so much characters with agency as they are symbols of the ravages of war. To borrow Brownmiller's parlance, they are "ceremonial battlefields"—sites of conflict between warring men. In this formulation, sexual violence is a metaphor for other types of violence and domination. Rape represents war. A metaphorical understanding of rape is discernible even in the ways wartime rape is legislated. In 2005, Amnesty International's fact sheet about violence against women in armed conflict read that women "experience armed conflicts as sexual objects, as presumed emblems of national and ethnic identity, and as female members of ethnic, racial, religious, or national groups."[58] Indeed, war rape is seen as a tool of genocide when it is carried out "with intent to destroy, in whole or in part, a national, ethnical, racial or religious group, as such."[59] When soldiers rape women in the context of war, the intent is already in a sense metaphorical—the humiliation and abuse of women symbolizes the domination of a land and people. Rhonda Copelon writes that the fact "that the rape of women is also designed to humiliate the men or destroy 'the enemy' itself reflects the fundamental objectification of women. Women are the target of abuse at the same time as their subjectivity is completely denied."[60] Their individual domination is a metaphor for the large-scale domination of their homes and people.[61]

The metaphorical weight of wartime rape has long been a useful tool in the theater. It is not often feasible to show the larger-scale tactics of warfare on the stage; huge bloody battles typically resist live representation. Wartime rape, though, is interpersonal in its scope while still representing the conflict at large. Theater historian Jennifer Airey writes of the political resonance of rape narratives on England's Restoration stage: "Acts of rape in political tracts and stage plays . . . transform the female body into a symbol of the suffering nation, a physical representation of the horrific consequences of Catholic, Cavalier, Whig, Tory, Dutch, or Stuart rule."[62] In these productions of *Ballo* and *Tell*, we see little to no military combat on stage. Instead, we see acts of sexual violence that illustrate the power and dominance of a military force over a vulnerable enemy. In Knabe's *Turandot*, Calaf's victory is primarily a political one, and he demonstrates his dominance over Turandot's kingdom and people by raping her. The rape skit in Kratzer's *La forza del destino* is transparently symbolic: the woman who is raped represents the whole nation of Vietnam, or maybe the Vietnam War; the rapist is Nixon, America's final Vietnam president; and Nixon is being supported by Preziosilla dressed in the American flag. The idea of rape is leveraged as an appropriate vehicle to express a hatred of the Vietnamese other.

But while rape can certainly be an effective metaphor for war, the widespread use of rape as a way of representing other horrors is troubling. Airey goes on to warn about the potential dangers of transforming rape into "an artistic and allegorical symbol," noting that these representations "transform that very real pain into social and political metaphors."[63] Similarly, Lisa Fitzpatrick notices that contemporary theater often stages rape in wartime as "a metaphor or as an allegory for forms of oppression other than gendered oppression."[64] These theatrical uses of rape imagery, like the operatic uses throughout this chapter, depend on rape's status as a master trope for the violation of women by the patriarchy, but also of oppressed groups more generally. Literary theorist Sabine Sielke argues that such broad deployment of rape as a trope works to "diffuse the meaning of rape."[65] Using rape to stand in for other harms assumes an audience for whom rape itself is not an active, even ever-present, threat. The allegorical rapes in these productions demonstrate the baseness of the soldiers and lay plain the horrors of military occupation. But for some in the audience, especially those who have been or fear they may be sexually assaulted, this rape is not shocking as a symbol of another terrible thing, but as a terrible thing in and of itself. It is hard to see rape as standing for something else when the specter of rape is dominant in one's life. Catharine Woodward is getting at this problem when she writes that as a woman, she feels she is having the horrors of rape highlighted *at* her all the time. In these productions, it feels like rape is being used as a metaphor by men for men to say, "look how bad it is there, women are raped with no regard." But many women may not recognize such a distance—we are raped here, too.

Employing wartime rape as a metaphor also deindividuates its victims and perpetrators. Focusing only on the harm rape does to the social body or to a particular class of people disguises both the specific injury done to the individual victim and the agency of the perpetrator. Literary scholar Régine Michelle Jean-Charles writes of political rape that "violence, while inexorably political, is not always a consequence of (state) politics" and considers "what happens when, rather than focusing on the context of conflict, we focus on the material, psychological and bodily significance of sexual violence for the individual subject."[66] Audience members are not given the opportunity to focus on the individual significance of the acts of sexual violence in *Ballo* or in *Tell* as the victims vanish from the story as soon as they have served their dramatic purpose—to be assaulted. Both these victims are unnamed characters not present in the operas' written texts. Though the young man in *Ballo* gets some stage time before he is raped and murdered, the young woman in *Tell* is not necessarily familiar to the audience at all when the soldiers begin to torment her. While there is a way that these productions criticize the way that wartime rape itself deindividuates victims by reducing them to their ethnic group or class, Bieito and Michieletto enact the very thing they critique by using the bodies of these two supernumerary dancers as solely the receptors of simulated violence.

• • •

Sexual violence is a short-hand that *Regietheater* directors often use to concisely communicate the horrors of warfare and authoritarianism. Staging scenes of sexual violence sets the stakes of the conflict and personalizes the threat that the enemy poses. It is an effective metaphor for the ravages of war and it can serve as a stinging critique of the normalization of rape at wartime and the romanticization of war in opera. Still, it does so at high risk. These representations often depend on representations of rape victims as objects, stripped of their agency (*Forza*), and they may reinforce toxic rape myths about who deserves to be raped (*Ballo*). There is also the risk of retraumatizing survivors of sexual assault, as Catharine Woodward pointed out in her exchange with Kasper Holten about Michieletto's *Tell*.

The potential harm caused by exposure to depictions of sexual violence does not end with trauma survivors. In Woodward's response to Holten's point that it is important to highlight violence against women in war zones, she explains, "it feels like I am having it highlighted *at* me all the time, often in a way that serves just to make me feel more vulnerable."[67] There are familiar fears that exposure to violent imagery desensitizes spectators to real-world violence, but what Woodward is getting at here is something more like hyper-sensitization. New understandings about what constitutes rape have made the prevalence of sexual violence in our culture increasingly visible in recent years. That visibility is positive insofar as it encourages changes in the ways we think about and legislate sexual violence, which has long been normalized or ignored in our culture. But for women who are socialized under the threat of sexual violence, this visibility may not always feel so progressive. Cahill argues that "the threat of rape is a formative moment in the construction of the distinctly feminine body, such that even bodies of women who have not been raped are likely to carry themselves in such a way as to express the truths and values of a rape culture."[68] While the inclusion of rape in these opera productions critiques nationalist and misogynistic oppression, it does so by reinforcing gender roles ascribed by rape culture: men—soldiers, conquerors, police—have all the power, and there is nothing their victims can do to stop them. Woodward's description of having rape highlighted *at* her all the time resonates with my own experiences of deep unease when surprised by an act of sexual violence represented onstage. My fear of sexual violence is never far away, and these reminders do not so much serve to teach me about the horrors of rape as they do reinforce those fears that I already carry.

I agree with Woodward that content warnings are valuable in protecting vulnerable audience members from unexpected representations of triggering imagery. But beyond content warnings, in this book I have advocated a way of thinking about representations of sexual violence in opera in a way that is guided by an ethical interest in its victims and their portrayal onstage. A content warning is not a free pass to stage rape carelessly. The conclusion to Woodward's story about *Tell* is a happy one for me not because Holten added a content warning to the website but because Michieletto returned to the rehearsal room to find a way to maintain his vision for the scene while eliminating the excess. If a director can represent rape less explicitly or if they can reduce the amount of nudity of rape victims without fundamentally changing the effect of the scene, it is responsible to do so. This is not to say that there is no place on the contemporary opera stage for explicit representations of rape and violence against women. Calaf's rape of Turandot in Knabe's production, perhaps ironically, felt like a purging of misogyny from the story achieved by making that misogyny plain.

Balancing the risks and benefits of staging sexual violence is a delicate activity, and not one where I believe there are correct or incorrect solutions. For me, that balance depends on showing only as much as is needed to accomplish the critical goals and no more. It also depends on the written text of the opera—does the sexual violence come from within or from without, and what critical work does it do? Of the four productions that feature sexual violence as an element of their representations of unjust power and domination in this chapter, I am only convinced that the inclusion of sexual violence is justified in two of them. The rapes in Bieito's *Un ballo in maschera* and Kratzer's *La forza del destino* both serve to criticize elements of modern warfare and soldiering, but I suspect that these directors could have accomplished their goals without recourse to such brutally explicit (*Ballo*) and perversely comic (*Forza*) scenes of sexual violence. Michieletto's *Guillaume Tell* and Knabe's *Turandot* are different cases, in large part because both *Tell* and *Turandot* contain underlying themes of sexual violence already. These operas support the directorial addition of the rape scenes, and the productions by Michieletto and Knabe offer compelling examinations of the written texts of the operas and the non-critical way in which directors and audiences often interact with them.

Directors and producers must balance the risks of harm from depicting rape onstage with the potential benefits of dramatizing social commentary. But in operas like *Guillaume Tell* and especially *Turandot*, which contain sexual violence just below the surface, there are potential harms in ignoring the tacit allusions to rape as well. There is a risk that a sexual violence survivor may experience retraumatization from witnessing Turandot's rape in Knabe's production, but even in the absence of an explicit rape, the written text of this scene thematizes sexual violence and reinforces harmful cultural ideas about consent. The rape in Knabe's *Turandot* is shocking, but the rape does more than just shock. By incorporating an explicit rape, Knabe calls attention to and criticizes the virulent misogyny that is already foundational in this opera's written text.

While I ultimately feel that by my own framework the scenes of sexual violence in both *Tell* and *Turandot* are justified, my experiences as a spectator of these two productions differ significantly. Michieletto's ballet scene, even in its revised version, made me feel tense and unsettled. Watching it multiple times in a row to take notes and study the interaction with the music was a trying experience. It is only in retrospect that I appreciate the way this scene refuses to gloss over the violation of the Austrian soldiers forcing the Swiss women to dance with them. Viewing Knabe's *Turandot*, however, was a cathartic experience from the start. The rape scene is vicious and sickening, and I had a powerful emotional response; but in all, I have never enjoyed *Turandot* more. I appreciate this production more than any other production in this book, which I attribute to a number of things. First, the written text of *Turandot* has always bothered me more than any other opera I have discussed here, not because it is the most misogynistic—that would be a difficult distinction to grant—but because its misogyny may be the most neglected. I have only rarely seen the forced kiss and Turandot's transfiguration in the last act held up for scrutiny. When I have seen other productions of *Turandot*, the happy ending feels not only hollow but offensive; the triumphant reprise of "Nessun dorma" by the chorus makes me deeply uncomfortable when presented uncritically.

To continue to perform an opera like *Turandot* in an ethical way demands that we engage with the dark and messy realities of the story it tells. In the house program for *Turandot*, Knabe describes the opera as a male fantasy in which three men (Puccini and librettists Adami and Simoni) "brutally destroy the only women in the opera: one [Liù] kills herself and the other [Turandot] is abused. To put it cynically: Long live the patriarchy."[69] There is a rebellious character to this kind of *Regietheater* that I find vital and exciting in the opera world. By staging a rape and cutting Turandot's transfiguration, Knabe refuses to tell the story of *Turandot* as written. His production rejects the norm of male violence by pushing the forced intimacy in the third act into the spotlight and making it impossible to ignore. This choice casts the rest of the opera's conclusion in a very different light. It is still uncomfortable listening to "Nessun dorma" and the rest of the celebratory music at the opera's close in Knabe's production. But it is a different kind of discomfort—it is one I feel I get to share with other audience members and with the creative team. It is a discomfort that invites us to think deeply about this opera and our relationship to it.

Conclusion

The opera canon can sometimes feel like a collection of problems. It is a parade of misogyny, racism, and assorted other forms of bigotry that remind us of some of the worst things the forbearers of Western art music believed about the world. And also, I love it. This book was generated by the tension between the deep discomfort I feel watching casual or gratuitous representations of sexual assault and the pleasure I nonetheless experience when I attend my favorite operas. This pleasure makes me unwilling to simply stop watching and listening to *Don Giovanni*, *Turandot*, and other operas where I know in advance I am likely to be deeply troubled by the depiction of sexual violence. And this pleasure is part of what motivates me to want to see the way we talk about and produce these operas get better.

Production is the best tool we have to explore and evolve our relationship to the canon. Through production, directors, producers, technicians, and performers co-create performances that are informed by, but not limited to, the written texts of our canonic inheritance. This work keeps old artworks alive and relevant, and it also gives modern-day creators the opportunity to intervene in the more troubling elements of these stories. *Regietheater*'s detractors often frame these interventions as attacks on the operas and their composers, but they sell the operas short when they try to shield them from criticism. We do a disservice to opera when we decline to engage deeply with what the canon means to us today and how its works are different in our context. Refusing to engage with contemporary ideas in the way we produce and talk about opera makes these works old and irrelevant by deciding a priori that they have nothing new to say to us.

While *Regietheater* has enormous potential to do positive, reparational work within the opera canon, there are obvious and urgent flaws with the current state of affairs. Some tropes of *Regie* productions, especially in Germany, have become so familiar to audiences and critics that they lose a lot of their impact. And efforts to shock audiences into paying attention and thinking critically can be carried out in incredibly risky ways, as demonstrated in particular in Bieito's *Entführung*. *Regietheater* in current practice is also marked by whiteness. The case studies in this book are glaringly white, even when the operas being produced feature exotic locales and racialized characters. Bieito's *Entführung*, Knabe's *Turandot*, and the majority of the productions of *Salome* in chapter 2 move stories about a racialized other into a white, Western context. Casting white singers to play racialized characters is an issue that has been increasingly scrutinized in recent years as debates about the use of blackface and other skin-darkening makeup in opera have been more mainstream.[1] But the whitewashing happening in the productions in this book is not only a matter of casting but of costume and setting as well. White men are overrepresented among the directors in this book and also among opera directors in general. I think the whiteness of many of these productions is a default state: in order to place the emphasis of the production on sexual violence, race and ethnicity are overlooked or downplayed. In North American and European cultures, whiteness is frequently perceived as neutral—a lack of race—and so making these characters white can be seen as an attempt to decline to engage with race. I am also sensitive to the focus in these productions on the victimhood of white women, which is a mainstay of white supremacy.

When staging operas that feature Orientalism in their written texts, whitewashing the stories in production can be understood as a tactic to sidestep the racism. This might be a particularly appealing option in operas where the exotic music has lost some of its specific signifying power to time; for example, while the Chinese music in *Turandot* still sounds Chinese to modern audiences, the Turkish music in *Entführung* does not sound Turkish outside of its association with a specific eighteenth-century European musical trope. Yet I worry that eliminating race from these operas just replaces one white racial frame with another one: instead of whiteness standing in contrast to a racialized other, whiteness is invisible as the default state of humans. I am not suggesting that these are choices being made intentionally by these opera creators. Rather, I think the whiteness of the opera industry and of directors specifically in North America and Europe limits the perspectives and the stories that audiences have access to. Mouawad's *Entführung* for Lyon and Toronto is a great step toward bringing new perspectives into opera through production. Though I have my misgivings about elements of the approach to gender and violence in this production, I am glad it exists and I hope to see more work in this vein.

Regietheater and opera production in general would be served by a greater diversity of creators. I want more voices bringing more perspectives to these works to move beyond *Regie*'s tired tropes of mobsters and Nazis toward a future where opera production is a creative enterprise more often than it is not. Dylan Robinson has suggested the radical potential of *Regietheater* as a practice of positionality that acknowledges and foregrounds the relationship between author, performer, and listeners.[2] He cites Spivak on deconstruction as critical intimacy to argue that this work can be motivated by a love of the text and the art form.[3] I am excited to see the stories that my contemporaries want to tell about and through the works of the canon. The discomfort I have felt as an audience member at the opera that inspired this book is a result of my unwillingness to just leave. I want new ways to engage with these texts that I love but that also trouble me.[4] And I want to see the ways that others who feel like I do have dealt with the curious combination of their own discomfort and pleasure.

I think that bringing more voices and more perspectives into opera will improve the art form and support its longevity; but ultimately, I don't think this is the best motivation for this work. Although I love opera and want to see it survive, the urgency of making operatic representations and practices more ethical comes from the risk to the people who participate in and spectate opera more than from the risk to the genre. Musicologists sometimes espouse a belief in having an ethical responsibility to operatic works themselves.[5] I fear that this focus on protecting the legacy of canonic artworks and their long-dead creators can shift our attention away from the responsibility we owe to the living people who interact with these artworks today, especially when those people belong to equity-seeking groups that are not typically represented fairly or at all in the written texts of these operas.

When I have criticized directors and producers in this book, it has generally been for failing to take responsibility for the work their productions do and especially the harm they might cause others. Staging canonic operas that contain distressing and potentially harmful content without comment or intervention is not ethically neutral; it upholds and perpetuates the outdated and often deeply misogynistic and racist politics of these works in the present day. I want artists to consider the role their work might play in creating a better world. This impulse is visible in many of the productions I have discussed in the preceding chapters; using operas of the canon to criticize violence, racism, and misogyny is a valuable ethical project. These interventions are the most effective and the most radical when they balance care for others with that critical agenda. With representations of sexual violence in particular, the needs of women, especially survivors of sexual assault, may be anticipated and tended to as a central priority and practice.

While the focus of this book has been the representational issues of putting sexual violence onstage, the presence of sexual violence can be felt at every level of contemporary operatic discourse and practice. The opera industry itself is a minefield of harassment and abuse, and the ethical stakes of staging sexual violence do not end with the consequences for audiences watching these productions. Directors work through the bodies of singer-actors to craft these representations, and there are risks associated with onstage simulations of intimacy and violence. I have spent enough time around opera singers to know that being a woman in this industry almost necessarily means having had bad experiences with reckless approaches to staging intimacy without sufficient training or support. Singers are frequently asked to improvise scenes of intimacy in rehearsal with few if any guidelines given to ensure that all parties are comfortable and safe. This carelessness of approach and lack of oversight is not always harmful, but it can be a perfect storm for harassment and hostile work environments. It is not an exaggeration to say that every woman in the industry I have asked has a story about a time they felt uncomfortable or unsafe in a rehearsal room due to a director's approach to representing intimacy.

Practices of intimacy direction are one concrete way that opera creators can center care for performers as well as for audience members. Intimacy directors, also called intimacy choreographers or coordinators, advocate treating onstage intimacy with the same kind of care and control necessary for onstage violence.[6] Intimacy directors choreograph scenes of intimacy or sexual violence precisely, so that the representation communicates what it needs to, and the performers involved know exactly what to expect. They also take responsibility for the performers' emotional safety, serving as advocates for them when required. There are a number of practical obstacles to the large-scale implementation of the principles of intimacy choreography and the hiring of more intimacy directors, including budgetary concerns and the typically very short rehearsal periods for opera compared with straight theater. But still, some opera companies are beginning to bring in intimacy directors to work on productions featuring scenes of intimate contact felt to be especially risky or delicate.

Intimacy direction asks some of the same questions of directors and performers that I have asked in this book. For instance, the first of five pillars of safe intimacy in rehearsal and performance, assembled by Intimacy Directors International, is "context": "All parties must be aware of how the scene of intimacy meets the needs of the story and must also understand the story within the intimacy itself. This not only creates a sense of safety, but also eliminates the unexpected and ensures that the intimacy is always in service of the story."[7] Ideally, adherence to this directive would ensure that conversations like the ones that led to the toning down of the rape scenes in Egoyan's *Salome* and Michieletto's *Tell* happen in the rehearsal room before a new production becomes public. Moving forward, I hope to see more work done on the connection between ethical onstage representations of sexual violence in opera and approaches to the practice of staging that prioritize safety and consent for the singers and promote critical thinking about the role and intention of representations of intimacy and of violence in operatic storytelling.

My dual goals of improving the relevance and longevity of opera and of caring for opera's creators and audiences are frequently aligned, as they are in practices of intimacy direction that improve a story's cogency and coherence while also protecting the physical and emotional safety of performers. Still, anticipating that these goals of making better operatic art and caring for people may in some cases be set in opposition, I turn to William Cheng's advice from the introduction to his book *Loving Music Till It Hurts*. He urges us to "love music, and love people. If ever in doubt—or if forced to choose—choose people."[8] In negotiations with the opera canon in production, I believe choosing people means remembering that the responsibility opera creators owe to living people should outweigh any perceived responsibility to the operas themselves. This often looks like loosening the grip of the composer's imagined intentions in favor of a contemporary critical awareness of the works of the canon and their impact in the world today.

I am excited about the evolution of opera through new works that engage with social issues in contemporary, ethically informed ways. There are contemporary opera composers working through many of the same issues I have raised in this book by crafting representations of sexual violence that focus on the experiences of survivors. Laura Bowler and Laura Lomas's 2022 *Blue Woman* at the Royal Opera House is one excellent example. Yet even as the number of new operas that deal sensitively with issues of gender, race, and violence increases, performances of the canon continue to make up the majority of work done at almost all major opera houses. I am therefore unwilling to either ignore or give up on the canon in my desire to see operatic practices and representations improve.

The misogynistic representation of sexual violence is one problem in the opera canon, which is also marked by racism, antisemitism, ableism, homophobia, and a host of other bigotries. Sexual violence has been my entry point for making arguments and recommendations that apply to the opera industry at large as we continue to negotiate with the canon as scholars, creators, producers, critics, and lovers of opera. I hope that this book might inspire and support studies of some of these other representational issues of the canon not just on the page but also on the stage. Opera lovers are quick to attest to the power this art form has to speak to its audiences through music in a way that can feel more direct and intimate than straight theater. If opera indeed has this special rhetorical power, surely it makes understanding, critiquing, and shaping the messages that it conveys particularly important. Investing in rethinking and remaking the canon in a way that supports contemporary values and priorities is not easy, but I believe it is the way that we keep opera alive and ensure that its stories support a future we want.

Appendix

Don Giovanni Productions

Director	Setting	Approach to Written Text
Calixto Bieito	Barcelona ca. 2000	Rampant and explicit sexual violence, no humor
Jonathan Kent	Twentieth-century Europe	Conservative and conventional representation of the women
Rufus Norris	Twentieth-century Europe	Explicit sexual violence, nuanced representation of the women
Marshall Pynkoski	Seventeenth-century Seville	Comic presentation, heroic representation of Don Giovanni
Jean-François Sivadier	*ambiguous*	Realistic approach to the women's emotions and trauma
Francesca Zambello	Seventeenth-century Seville	Subtle changes to give the women more agency

Notes

Introduction

1. "Sia questa mia risposta al tuo giurar."

2. Ellie Hisama, "John Zorn and the Postmodern Condition," in *Locating East Asia in Western Art Music*, ed. Yayoi Uno Everett and Frederick Lau (Middletown, CT: Wesleyan University Press, 2004), 72–84.

3. See, for instance, the 2018 *Washington Post* exposé on sexual harassment in classical music. Anne Midgette and Peggy McGlone, "Assaults in dressing rooms. Groping during lessons. Classical musicians reveal a profession rife with harassment," *Washington Post*, July 26, 2018, https://www.washingtonpost.com/entertainment/music/assaults-in-dressing-rooms-groping-during-lessons-classical-musicians-reveal-a-profession-rife-with-harassment/2018/07/25/f47617d0-36c8-11e8-acd5-35eac230e514_story.html

4. Data from operabase.com. 2018–2019 is the most recent season not affected by disruptions due to COVID-19.

5. See Elizabeth Hudson, "Gilda Seduced: A Tale Untold," *Cambridge Opera Journal* 4, no. 3 (1992): 229–51, http://www.jstor.org/stable/823693

6. Axel Englund, *Deviant Opera: Sex, Power, and Perversion on Stage* (Berkeley: University of California Press, 2020), 6.

7. Another common *Regietheater* trope is the critique of fascism and particularly Nazism, as we will see in chapter 4.

8. Englund, *Deviant Opera*, 6.

9. See, for instance: Catherine Clément, *Opera, or the Undoing of Women*, trans. Betsy Wing (Minneapolis: University of Minnesota Press, 1988); Susan McClary, *Feminine Endings: Music, Gender, and Sexuality* (Minneapolis: University of Minnesota Press, 1991); Carolyn Abbate, "Opera; or, the Envoicing of Women," in *Musicology and Difference: Gender and Sexuality in Music Scholarship*, ed. Ruth A. Solie (Berkeley: University of California Press, 1993), 225–58; Ralph Locke, "What Are These Women Doing in Opera?" in *En travesti: Women, Gender Subversion, Opera*, ed. Corinne E. Blackmer and Patricia Juliana Smith (New York:

Columbia University Press, 1995), 59–98; Abbate, *Unsung Voices: Opera and Musical Narrative in the Nineteenth Century* (Princeton: Princeton University Press, 1996); Mary Ann Smart, ed., *Siren Songs* (Princeton: Princeton University Press, 2000); Melanie Unseld, *"Man töte dieses Weib!": Weiblichkeit und Tod in der Musik der Jahrhundertwende* (Stuttgart: Metzler, 2001); Joseph Kerman, "Verdi and the Undoing of Women," *Cambridge Opera Journal* 18, no. 1 (2006): 21–31, https://doi.org/10.10 17/S0954586706002072

10. A panel discussion at the 2016 annual meeting of the American Musicological Society called "Sexual Violence on Stage" resulted in the 2018 colloquy on sexual violence in opera published in the *Journal of the American Musicological Society*. The six essays of the *JAMS* colloquy "build on earlier scholarship to suggest ways in which scholars and opera professionals can begin to resist the tradition of rape culture embedded in Western opera by making ever more deliberate choices about our own performative acts of interpretation—be it as producers, stage directors, performers, composers, or scholar-teachers." Three essays in the *JAMS* colloquy, by Micaela Baranello, Ellie Hisama, and Richard Will, discuss production and performance issues. Suzanne G. Cusick and Monica Hershberger, "Introduction," in "Colloquy: Sexual Violence in Opera: Scholarship, Pedagogy, and Production as Resistance," *Journal of the American Musicological Society* 71, no. 1 (2018): 217–18, https://doi.org/10.1525/jams.2018.71.1.213

11. Naomi André, *Black Opera: History, Power, Engagement* (Urbana: University of Illinois Press, 2018), 26.

12. Roger Parker, "Reading the *livrets*, or the Chimera of 'Authentic' Staging," in *Leonora's Last Act: Essays in Verdian Discourse* (Princeton: Princeton University Press, 2014), 128.

13. I am indebted to Linda Hutcheon and Michael Hutcheon, who have broken ground on the topic of opera in production with so much of their work, and to David Levin, Clemens Risi, and Axel Englund for their monographs analyzing opera productions and the ways that the meaning of operas shift in performance. Linda Hutcheon and Michael Hutcheon, "Adaptation and Opera," in *The Oxford Handbook of Adaptation Studies*, ed. Thomas Leitch (Oxford: Oxford University Press, 2017), 305–23; Linda Hutcheon and Michael Hutcheon, "Opera: Forever and Always Multimodal," in *New Perspectives on Narrative and Multimodality*, ed. Ruth Page (London: Routledge, 2009), 65–77; David Levin, *Unsettling Opera: Staging Mozart, Verdi, Wagner, and Zemlinsky* (Chicago: University of Chicago Press, 2007); Clemens Risi, *Oper in Performance: Analysen zur Aufführungsdimension von Operninszenierungen* (Berlin: Theater der Zeit, 2017); Englund, *Deviant Opera*.

14. Levin, *Unsettling Opera*, 3. See also Nina Penner, *Storytelling in Opera and Musical Theater* (Bloomington: Indiana University Press, 2020), 4–5.

15. Roland Barthes, "From Work to Text," in *Image, Music, Text*, trans. Stephen Heath (New York: Fontana Press, 1977), 157.

16. Barthes, "From Work to Text," 159–60.

17. Levin, *Unsettling Opera*, 11.

18. Dylan Robinson suggests the value of fostering an awareness of the "primary audience" imagined by arts organizations and recognizing the relationship between this imagined audience and an individual audience member who may identify with the values of the primary audience or may feel alienated from it. Similarly, in her theorization of the oppositional gaze, bell hooks argues that Black female spectators actively refuse to identify with a film's imagined spectator. Dylan Robinson, *Hungry Listening: Resonant Theory for Indigenous Sound Studies* (Minneapolis: University of Minnesota Press, 2020), 125; bell hooks, "The Oppositional Gaze: Black Female Spectators," in *Black Looks: Race and Representation* (1992; repr., New York: Routledge, 2015), 115–32.

19. Considering alternate or peripheral perspectives as sources of knowledge is a feature of the feminist epistemology of standpoint theory, originally formulated by Marxist feminists Sandra Harding and Nancy Hartsock and expanded by Black feminists including Patricia Hill Collins. Nancy Hartsock, "The Feminist Standpoint: Developing the Ground for a Specifically Feminist Historical Materialism," in *The Feminist Standpoint Theory Reader: Intellectual and Political Controversies*, ed. Sandra Harding (New York: Routledge, 2004), 35–54; Patricia Hill Collins, "The Social Construction of Black Feminist Thought," *SIGNS: A Journal of Women in History and Culture* 14, no. 4, Common Grounds and Crossroads: Race, Ethnicity, and Class in Women's Lives (Summer 1989): 745–73, https://www.jstor.org/stable /3174683

20. Clément, *Opera, or the Undoing of Women*.

21. For a few high-profile examples, see: Eleni Hagen, "Don Giovanni," "Resources for Educators," Kennedy Center website (Washington, 2019), https:// www.kennedy-center.org/education/resources-for-educators/classroom-resourc es/media-and-interactives/media/opera/don-giovanni/; Heidi Waleson, "Ladies' Man," *Wall Street Journal*, Oct. 20, 2011, https://www.wsj.com/articles/SB1000142 4052970204346104576636932497242112; "Mozart's 'Don Giovanni' from Houston Grand Opera," *NPR Music*, Nov. 2, 2007, https://www.npr.org/templates/story /story.php?storyId=15828636

22. Catharine Woodward, "Shock Factor," blog post on *Opera Div*, June 30, 2015, https://operacat.tumblr.com/post/122857938113/shock-factor

23. Kasper Holten, "Exclusive: An Open Letter from Kasper Holten on William Tell," *Slipped Disc*, July 1, 2015, https://slippedisc.com/2015/07/exclusive-an -open-letter-from-kasper-holten-on-william-tell

24. Jonathan Owen, "The Violence Epidemic: Half of Women in Britain Admit They Have Been Physically or Sexually Assaulted According to Shocking New Figures," *Independent*, March 5, 2014, https://www.independent.co.uk/news /uk/home-news/the-violence-epidemic-half-of-women-in-britain-admit-they-ha ve-been-physically-or-sexually-assaulted-according-to-shocking-new-figures-916 9143.html. The statistics in the article come from the Violence Against Women report by the European Union Agency for Fundamental Rights.

25. Kasper Holten, letter quoted in Woodward, "Shock Factor." It is significant that staging sexual violence is so popular as a strategy to make audiences uncom-

fortable in *Regietheater* productions. In chapter 4, I consider rape's status as a metaphor for representing other forms of violence.

26. Holten, "Exclusive: An Open Letter."

27. Bessel A. van der Kolk and Jose Saporta, "The Biological Response to Psychic Trauma: Mechanisms and Treatment of Intrusion and Numbing," *Anxiety Research* 4 (1991): 199, https://doi.org/10.1080/08917779108248774

28. While Gilligan's book is commonly cited as the progenitor of care ethics, Patricia Hill Collins has argued that it might be better understood as an African American phenomenon. Patricia Hill Collins, *Black Feminist Thought: Knowledge, Consciousness, and the Politics of Empowerment* (Boston: Unwin Hyman, 1990). See also Katie G. Cannon, *Black Womanist Ethics* (Atlanta: Scholar's Press, 1988).

29. Carol Gilligan, *In a Different Voice: Psychological Theory and Women's Development* (Cambridge, MA: Harvard University Press, 2016).

30. Critics include: Lawrence Kohlberg, "The Current Formulation of the Theory," in *Essays on Moral Development* (San Francisco: Harper and Row, 1984), 2:229; Jürgen Habermas, *Moral Consciousness and Communicative Action* (Cambridge, MA: MIT Press, 1990), 179–81; Bill Puka, "The Liberation of Caring; A Different Voice for Gilligan's 'Different Voice,'" *Hypatia* 55, no. 1 (1990): 59, https://doi.org/10.1111/j.1527-2001.1990.tb00390.x

31. Joan Tronto, *Moral Boundaries: A Political Argument for an Ethic of Care* (New York: Routledge, 1993), 96.

32. Tronto, *Moral Boundaries*, 105.

33. James Thompson, "Towards an Aesthetics of Care," in *Performing Care: New Perspectives on Socially Engaged Performance*, ed. Amanda Stuart Fisher and James Thompson (Manchester: Manchester University Press, 2020), 430–41.

34. Thompson, "Towards an Aesthetics of Care," 439.

35. *The Rape of Lucretia* is a story from ancient Roman history of the rape and suicide of a noblewoman that precipitated a rebellion against the Roman Kingdom. It has been treated by artists throughout the Western tradition including Ovid and Shakespeare. *Susannah* is an adaptation of the Apocryphal story of Susannah and the Elders. In Floyd's opera, Susannah is raped by one of the priests who unjustly accused her of improper conduct.

Chapter 1

1. Feminist philosopher Kate Manne proposes shifting our conceptualization of misogyny from the point of view of the accused to the point of view of its targets. In the fictional realm of *Don Giovanni*, I propose a similar shift by focusing not on whether Giovanni truly hates women or loves women but on the impact his actions have on the women around him. Kate Manne, *Down Girl: The Logic of Misogyny* (New York: Oxford University Press, 2018), 59–61.

2. Zambello's production premiered at the Royal Opera House in 2002 and was remounted in 2003, 2007, and 2008. The analysis in this chapter is based on the DVD recording of the 2008 production with Simon Keenlyside in the title role.

3. Extensive studies have been done measuring rape myth acceptance in various groups beginning with Martha R. Burt, "Cultural Myths and Supports for Rape," *Journal of Personality and Social Psychology* 38, no. 2 (1980): 217–30, https://psycnet.apa.org/doi/10.1037/0022-3514.38.2.217. The results have generally suggested that rape myth acceptance significantly influences the perceptions of jurors in rape cases. Jennifer Temkin, "'And Always Keep A-Hold of Nurse, for Fear of Finding Something Worse': Challenging Rape Myths in the Courtroom," *New Criminal Law Review* 13, no. 4 (2010): 710–34, https://doi.org/10.1525/nclr.2010.13.4.710. Russell Norton and Tim Grant have suggested "rape stereotype" would be more accurate. Russell Norton and Tim Grant, "Rape Myth in True and False Rape Allegations," *Psychology, Crime & Law* 14, no. 4 (2008): 275–85, https://doi.org/10.1080/10683160701770286

4. Rosalind Gill, *Gender and the Media* (Cambridge: Polity Press, 2007), 140.

5. Ronald C. Kessler et al., "Trauma and PTSD in the WHO World Mental Health Surveys," *European Journal of Psychotraumatology* 8, no. 5 (2017), section 3.3, https://doi.org/10.1080/20008198.2017.1353383

6. Bieito's production is the only one of the six discussed here that does not stage a fight in this scene. His interpretation is discussed in detail below.

7. Temkin, "'And Always Keep A-Hold of Nurse,'" 715.

8. Staging sexual violence against anonymous women as a tactic to establish a gritty setting or inform audience opinion about the abuser is a trope that recurs throughout many productions in this book. The risks and drawbacks of victimizing unnamed, unsinging women characters to these ends will be discussed in chapter 3.

9. This production, like all productions at the English National Opera, is sung in English. The translation of *Don Giovanni* used in this production was written by Jeremy Sams.

10. The Giovannis in Kent's, Sivadier's, and Zambello's productions all wear half-masks over the top portions of their faces. Norris's Giovanni does not wear a mask, but it is dark and he changes clothes after the rape. Anna does not appear to recognize him when they next meet. Suspension of disbelief is already necessary to accommodate Anna's failure to recognize Giovanni in this scene.

11. Large-scale studies of European countries, Canada, and the United States have found that between half and 75% of rapes are committed by assailants the victim knows. On American college campuses, a study found this number may be as high as 84%. Of these, a significant percentage of assailants are current or former intimate partners. United States Department of Justice, Office of Justice Programs, Bureau of Justice Statistics, National Crime Victimization Survey, 2010–2016 (2017); Jan van Dijk, John van Kesteren, and Paul Smit, "Criminal Victimisation In International Perspective: Key Findings From the 2004–2005 ICVS and EU ICS," Netherlands Research and Documentation Centre in Cooperation with the United Nations Office on Drugs and Crime (UNODC) and the United Nations Interregional Crime and Justice Research Institute (2007); Jo Lovett and Liz Kelly, "Different Systems, Similar Outcomes Tracking Attrition in Reported Rape Cases Across Europe," Child and Woman Abuse Studies Unit, London Metropolitan University, funded by the European Commission (2009).

12. Gill, *Gender and the Media*, 145.

13. Ann Wolbert Burgess and Lynda Lytle Holmstrom, "Coping Behavior of the Rape Victim," *American Journal of Psychiatry* 133, no. 4 (1976): 413–18, https://doi.org/10.1176/ajp.133.4.413

14. Susan Brownmiller, *Against Our Will: Men, Women and Rape* (New York: Bantam, 1976), 346–47.

15. Richard Will, "*Don Giovanni* and the Resilience of Rape Culture," in Cusick et al., "Colloquy: Sexual Violence in Opera," 222.

16. "Tacito a me s'appressa, e mi vuole abbracciar: sciogliermi cerco, ei più mi stringe; grido: non viene alcun. Con una mano cerca d'impedire la voce, e coll'altra m'afferra stretta così, che già mi credo vinta."

17. For instance, while Allanbrook sees Donna Anna's heroic style as necessarily undercut dramatically by its buffa context, Hunter argues that in eighteenth-century opera buffa, the high style could be used seriously or as parody. Wye Jamison Allanbrook, *Rhythmic Gesture in Mozart: Le nozze di Figaro and Don Giovanni* (Chicago: University of Chicago Press, 1983), 228–29; Mary Hunter, "Some Representations of *Opera Seria* in *Opera Buffa*," *Cambridge Opera Journal* 3, no. 2 (1991): 107, https://doi.org/10.1017/S0954586700003426

18. Kristi Brown-Montesano, *Understanding the Women of Mozart's Operas* (Berkeley: University of California, 2007), 2. Brown-Montesano surveys leading interpretations of Donna Anna from early Don Juan stories to the present in her chapter "Feminine Vengeance I: The Assailed/Assailant."

19. E. T. A. Hoffmann's reading of the opera has been highly influential on this point. Hoffmann represents Anna and Giovanni as star-crossed lovers, whose paths tragically cross too late. E.T.A. Hoffmann, "Don Juan: A Fabulous Incident which Befell a Travelling Enthusiast," in *E. T. A. Hoffmann and Music*, ed. and trans. R. Murray Schafer (Toronto: University of Toronto Press, 1975), 63–73.

20. Candida L. Saunders, "The Truth, the Half-Truth, and Nothing Like the Truth: Reconceptualizing False Allegations of Rape," *British Journal of Criminology* 52, no. 6 (2012): 1152, https://doi.org/10.1093/bjc/azs036. The study Saunders cites was done with a police department in the UK, but similar disparities are widespread and well documented. A survey of other sources from the 1990s to 2010 can be found in Saunders's introduction.

21. Brent E. Turvey, *False Allegations: Investigative and Forensic Issues in Fraudulent Reports of Crime* (London: Academic Press, 2018), 192.

22. Gill, *Gender and the Media*, 142.

23. Saunders differentiates between "false complaints," in which rape allegations are completely fabricated, and "false accounts," in which an allegation of rape contains falsehoods. False complaints, like the one Anna makes here, are considered rare, even among police and prosecutors. Saunders, "The Truth, the Half-Truth, and Nothing Like the Truth," 1167.

24. Lori Haskell and Melanie Randall, "How Trauma Affects Memory and Recall," in *The Impact of Trauma on Adult Sexual Assault Victims*, submitted to Research and Statistics Division, Justice Canada (2019), https://www.justice.gc.ca

/eng/rp-pr/jr/trauma/p4.html. This research paper published on Justice Canada's website summarizes the findings of a great deal of recent research from neuroscientists, psychiatrists, psychologists, and legal scholars.

25. Haskell and Randall, "How Trauma Affects Memory and Recall."

26. Cathy Caruth, ed., *Trauma: Explorations in Memory* (Baltimore: Johns Hopkins University Press, 1995), 153.

27. Erin O'Callaghan, Veronica Shepp, Sarah E. Ullman, and Anne Kirkner, "Navigating Sex and Sexuality after Sexual Assault: A Qualitative Study of Survivors and Informal Support Providers," *Journal of Sex Research* 56, no. 8 (2019): 1045–57, https://doi.org/10.1080/00224499.2018.1506731; Willy van Berlo and Bernardine Ensink, "Problems with Sexuality after Sexual Assault," *Annual Review of Sex Research* 11, no. 1 (2000): 235–57. http://dx.doi.org/10.1080/10532528.2000.10559789

28. See Brown-Montesano, *Understanding the Women of Mozart's Operas*, chapter 1.

29. Kristen N. Jozkowski et al., "Gender Difference in Heterosexual College Students' Conceptualizations and Indicators of Sexual Consent: Implications for Contemporary Sexual Assault Prevention Education," *Journal of Sex Research* 51, no. 8 (2014): 909–10, 913, https://doi.org/10.1080/00224499.2013.792326. See also Terry Humphreys, "Perceptions of Sexual Consent: The Impact of Relationship History and Gender," *Journal of Sex Research* 44, no. 4 (2007): 313–14, https://doi.org/10.1080/00224490701586706

30. "Io so, che rado colle donne voi altri cavalieri siete onesti e sinceri."

31. Catharine A. MacKinnon, "Rape: On Coercion and Consent," in *Applications of Feminist Legal Theory*, ed. D. Kelly Weisberg (Philadelphia: Temple University Press, 1996), 474.

32. Scott A. Anderson, "Conceptualizing Rape as Coerced Sex," *Ethics: An International Journal of Social, Political, and Legal Philosophy* 127, no. 1 (2016): 50–87, https://doi.org/10.1086/687332

33. Anderson, "Conceptualizing Rape as Coerced Sex," 75.

34. Anderson, "Conceptualizing Rape as Coerced Sex," 79.

35. A helpful survey of many of such studies can be found in Claire R. Gravelin, Monica Biernat, and Caroline E. Bucher, "Blaming the Victim of Acquaintance Rape: Individual, Situational, and Sociocultural Factors," *Frontiers in Psychology* 9 (2019): 2422–50, http://doi.org/10.3389/fpsyg.2018.02422

36. Giovanni says he cannot bear to see Zerlina's beauty "mistreated" by Masetto. The Italian verb, "strapazzare," is translated in the subtitles of Bieito's production as "abused."

37. Judith Herman. *Trauma and Recovery: The Aftermath of Violence—From Domestic Abuse to Political Terror* (New York: Basic Books, 1997), 1.

38. "La burla mi dà gusto."

39. Sex by deception is not strictly defined as rape under the law in Canada or the United States, though common law practices tend to criminalize deceptive sexual relations. Amit Pundik, "Coercion and Deception in Sexual Relations,"

Canadian Journal of Law and Jurisprudence 28, no. 1 (2015): 97–127, https://doi.org/10.1017/cjlj.2015.19; Jed Rubenfeld, "The Riddle of Rape-by-Deception and the Myth of Sexual Autonomy," *Yale Law Journal* 122, no. 6 (2012–2013): 1372–669, http://hdl.handle.net/20.500.13051/4879

40. For the impact this rape myth has on legal blame attribution, see Emily Finch and Vanessa E. Munro, "Juror Stereotypes and Blame Attribution in Rape Cases Involving Intoxicants: *The Findings of a Pilot Study*," *British Journal of Criminology* 45, no. 1 (2005): 25–38, https://doi.org/10.1093/bjc/azh055

41. Marc LeBeau and Ashraf Mozayani, *Drug-Facilitated Sexual Assault: A Forensic Handbook* (London: Academic Press, 2001).

42. An influential 2001 study found that approximately half of all sexual assault cases in America involve alcohol consumption by the perpetrator, victim, or both. Antonia Abbey et al., "Alcohol and Sexual Assault," *Alcohol Research & Health* 25, no. 1 (2001): 43–51.

43. Allanbrook argues that in Elvira's introduction in the opera, Mozart's music undercuts and mocks her character, making her impossible to take seriously. Allanbrook, *Rhythmic Gesture in Mozart*, 238–40.

44. Though it does not appear in any of the productions in this chapter, one trope I have noticed in some modern productions of *Don Giovanni* is making Elvira pregnant. Even if it is never addressed in the opera's text, a visibly pregnant Elvira can be much more sympathetic to an audience as she continues to pursue Don Giovanni in spite of continued mistreatment.

45. The productions by Bieito and Pynkoski do not include "Mi tradì," which Mozart added to *Don Giovanni* for its 1788 Vienna premiere.

46. Wye Allanbrook, Mary Hunter, and Gretchen Wheelock, "Staging Mozart's Women," in *Siren Songs*, ed. Mary Ann Smart (Princeton: Princeton University Press, 2014), 58.

47. Allanbrook, Hunter, and Wheelock, "Staging Mozart's Women," 58.

48. This production swaps "Mi tradì" with Donna Anna's aria "Non mi dir" so that the former occurs in between the graveyard scene and the dinner scene. I discuss the dramatic significance of this change later.

49. Herman, *Trauma and Recovery*, 34.

50. Laura S. Brown, "Not Outside the Range: One Feminist Perspective on Psychic Trauma," in Caruth, *Trauma: Explorations in Memory*, 102.

51. Allanbrook notes that the character archetypes in *Giovanni* are particularly rigid. She writes that in the world of *Don Giovanni*, the "human inhabitants are necessarily diminished in complexity by the overshadowing presence of the superhuman and daemonic." Allanbrook, *Rhythmic Gesture in Mozart*, 199.

52. "Introducing . . . Don Giovanni!" *Glyndebourne.com*, https://www.glyndebourne.com/festival/introducing-don-giovanni

53. Pynkoski presents this choice as one of accuracy and not of preference. The cover of the program booklet features an enlarged photograph of Mozart's catalogue of works with the words "opera Buffa in 2 Atti" circled in red.

54. Marshall Pynkoski, "Director's Notes," program for *Don Giovanni* (Toronto: Opera Atelier, 2019), 22.

55. In his notes on the production, Sivadier explains that we know from the first bars of the overture that Don Giovanni is going to die. Given his inevitable and endless death, "Don Giovanni has nothing else to do but theater" ("Don Giovanni n'a rien d'autre à faire que du théâtre"). Jean-François Sivadier, "Le rire et l'effroi: Entretien aven Jean-François Sivadier, metteur en scène," program for *Don Giovanni* (Festival d'Aix-en-Provence, 2017), 19.

56. ". . . un espace exposé, une arène, un ring, une piste de cirque, la scène d'un théâtre . . ." Sivadier, "Le rire et l'effroi," 20.

57. Sivadier argues that the confluence of different genres and different archetypes results in the characters becoming "not images but human beings: attractive, foolish, abject, fallible, capable of reasonable or irrational acts" ("Ce ne sont pas des images mais des êtres humains, séduisants, fous, abjects, faillibles, capables d'actes raisonnables ou irrationnels)." Sivadier, "Le rire et l'effroi," 21.

58. Richard Will argues that in the 2000s and 2010s, "graphic and gritty have become the new normal for Mozart." Will, "*Don Giovanni* and the Resilience of Rape Culture," in Cusick et al, "Colloquy: Sexual Violence in Opera," 220.

59. John Terauds, "Is Don Giovanni a #MeToo Monster or an Honest Seducer? Opera Atelier Weighs In," interview with Marshall Pynkoski, *Toronto Star*, October 28, 2019.

60. Pynkoski, "Is Don Giovanni a #MeToo Monster or an Honest Seducer?"

61. Laura Attridge, interview with the author, 18 September 2019.

62. Statistics from Operabase.com

Chapter 2

1. Oscar Wilde, *Salomé*, in *The Plays of Oscar Wilde* (New York: Vintage Books, 1988), 118.

2. Wilde, *Salomé*, 117.

3. Mary Simonson, "Choreographing Salome: Re-creating the Female Body," in *Body Knowledge: Performance, Intermediality, and American Entertainment at the Turn of the Twentieth Century* (New York: Oxford University Press, 2013); Davinia Caddy, "Variations on the Dance of the Seven Veils," *Cambridge Opera Journal* 17, no. 1 (2005): 37–58, https://doi.org/10.1017/S095458670500193X. The phenomenon was known as "Salomania."

4. Susan Anita Glenn, *Female Spectacle: The Theatrical Roots of Modern Feminism* (Cambridge, MA: Harvard University Press, 2000).

5. Arnold Schoenberg, for instance, referred to the power Expressionism has to represent the artist's inner processes. Jelena Hahl-Koch, ed., *Arnold Schoenberg/Wassily Kandinsky: Letters, Pictures and Documents* (New York: Faber, 1984), 98.

6. Gary Schmidgall, "Richard Strauss: Salome," in *Literature as Opera* (New York: Oxford University Press, 1977), 251.

7. Lawrence Kramer, "One Coughs, the Other Dances: Freud, Strauss, and the Perversity of Modern Life," *Muzikološki Zbornik* 45, no. 2 (2009): 33–44, https://doi.org/10.4312/mz.45.2.33-44

8. Sander L. Gilman, *Disease and Representation: Images of Illness from Madness to AIDS* (Ithaca: Cornell University Press, 1988), 168.

9. In a 1999 interview, Egoyan attributes his artistic fixation on father-daughter incest to a young woman he loved in his youth who was abused by her father. Brian D. Johnson, "Atom's Journey: Canada's Celebrated Director Reveals the Rite of Passage behind His Cinematic Obsessions," *Maclean's*, September 13, 1999.

10. The reason for this asymmetry, they argue, is that in mother-son incest, the son is challenging the father's ownership of his wife, whereas in father-daughter incest, there is no challenge of ownership. Judith Herman and Lisa Hirschman, "Father-Daughter Incest," *Signs* 2, no. 4 (Summer 1977): 735–56.

11. For a more thorough discussion of 1980s and 1990s feminist incest narratives and *The Sweet Hereafter*, see Melanie Boyd, "To Blame Her Sadness: Representing Incest in Atom Egoyan's *The Sweet Hereafter*," in *Image and Territory: Essays on Atom Egoyan*, ed. Monique Tschofen and Jennifer Burwell (Waterloo, ON: Wilfrid Laurier University Press, 2007), 275–93.

12. Atom Egoyan, "Staying Open," interview by Cindy Fuchs, *Philadelphia City Paper*, December 25, 1997–January 1, 1998.

13. Atom Egoyan, interview with the author, 6 March 2019. In Wilde's play, the page of Herodias is male, and in love with Narraboth (the young Syrian). In Strauss's setting, the role of the page is written for contralto, and is most often sung by a woman. Some productions of the opera, including Egoyan's, make the character of the page female instead of treating it as a pants role.

14. David Levin, "Operatic School for Scandal," in *Operatic Migrations: Transforming Works and Crossing Boundaries*, ed. Roberta Montemorra Marvin and Downing A. Thomas (Burlington: Ashgate, 2006), 243.

15. Atom Egoyan, interview with Stephen Weir, "Atom Egoyan on Canadian Opera Company Toronto Salome," YouTube video, 4:55, posted by "Canada Art Channel," April 20, 2013, https://www.youtube.com/watch?v=96WsfJ8FziY. Video archived at: https://archive.org/details/egoyan-coc-interview

16. Atom Egoyan, "Director's Notes," program for *Salome* (Toronto: Canadian Opera Company, 2013), 2.

17. Kay Armatage notes the power and penetration suggested by Herodes's flashlight at this moment in the Dance sequence. She writes, "if he doesn't look directly upon Salome's body, Herodes at least demonstrates that he has the luminous weapon that would allow him to do so." Kay Armatage and Caryl Clark, "Seeing and Hearing Atom Egoyan's *Salome*," in *Image and Territory: Essays on Atom Egoyan*, ed. Monique Tschofen and Jennifer Burwell (Waterloo: Wilfred Laurier University Press, 2007), 322.

18. Caruth, *Trauma: Explorations in Memory*, 4. Emphasis in original.

19. Egoyan, interview with the author.

20. "Ich habe deinen Mund geküsst, Jochanaan." For quotations from the libretto, I will use Wilde's English in text.

21. While Herodes literally weaponizes the blindfold, Egoyan weaponizes the very idea of invisibility—the capacity of an individual to control access to what

is and is not seen. Egoyan wields a kind of blindfold against his audience in the Dance of the Seven Veils: he covers the proscenium with a cloth to block the stimulating visual spectacle we expect and makes us watch a brutal and unexpected rape instead.

22. The earlier version of Egoyan's production did not make as much of the blindfold prop. In 2002, Herodes strangled Salome with his bare hands, the blindfold not having figured into the final scene as much.

23. Melanie Boyd faces a similar conundrum in her analysis of the incest storyline in *The Sweet Hereafter*. On Egoyan's choice to depict the relationship between Nicole and her father as quasi-consensual, Boyd asks, "How should politically concerned viewers judge the revision? Do we condemn its failure to represent an innocent victim, or celebrate its ability to represent an empowered one?" Boyd, "To Blame Her Sadness," 277.

24. Linda Hutcheon and Michael Hutcheon, "'Here's Lookin' at You, Kid:' The Empowering Gaze in 'Salome,'" *Profession* (1998): 11–22, https://www.jstor.org/stable/25595633; Lawrence Kramer, *Opera and Modern Culture: Wagner and Strauss* (Berkeley: University of California Press, 2004). Kramer argues that Salome ultimately loses the power she seizes in the Dance, while Hutcheon and Hutcheon believe that Salome is empowered by being gazed at throughout the opera.

25. Simonson, "Choreographing Salome," 47.

26. Salome is one of those opera heroines, like Juliette and Cio-Cio San, who is a young teenager in the story but tends to be perceived as older by virtue of being portrayed by adult women and sung with immense vocal authority.

27. Salome's infantile regression prompted one reviewer to note that when Salome turns into her own baby doll, "she says 'I want the head of Jochanaan' with the sound of 'Titti wants an ice cream.'" Markus Schwering, "Oper Bonn: Matrosenmädel im Kaffeehaus," *Kölner Stadt-Anzeiger*, Feb. 2, 2015.

28. Sunnegårdh sang Salome in 2013. The role was performed by Ljuba Kazarnovskaya in 1996, and by Helen Field in 2002.

29. McVicar's production was remounted in 2012 and 2018.

30. Michael sang Salome in the 2008 production. Several other sopranos have also taken the role in McVicar's production over the course of its life at the ROH.

31. Mary Ann Doane, *Femmes Fatales: Feminism, Film Theory, Psychoanalysis* (New York: Routledge, 1991), 2. Emphasis in original.

32. The fun of diagnosing one Straussian heroine with recourse to another is not lost on me.

33. Negrin's production was remounted in 2018 at the Asociación Bilbaína de Amigos de la Ópera in Bilbao, Spain, and had been scheduled for a 2020 revival at the Houston Grand Opera before cancelation due to COVID-19.

34. Francisco Negrin quoted in Federico Simón, "Mujeres trágicas tras el telón," *Ediciones El País*, June 2, 2010.

35. She asks for the head eight times before Herodes agrees and goes through the gamut of German verbs to request: "ich möchte . . . will ich . . . ich verlange von dir . . . ich fordre . . . gib mir . . . *den Kopf des Jochanaan.*"

36. Castellucci's *Salome* is not necessarily a victim of sexual assault, but this is

one interpretation of the staging. She is costumed in a white dress with a large red spot on the back at the height of her buttocks. The spot appears to be blood, but this could be a sign of menstruation, speaking to Salome's womanhood and fertility— this connects with the significance of the full moon in the libretto—or the blood could indicate violent sexual penetration, likely from an abuse. There is no violence in the Dance of the Seven Veils, but Salome lies motionless on a stone, evoking images of the ritual sacrifice of young women.

37. Castellucci's Salome is also not killed at the opera's conclusion, but she is not given a revenge arc like the Salomes in this section are.

38. Levin, "Operatic School for Scandal," 248. Levin also writes that he finds Strauss's opera deeply problematic and appreciates that Egoyan's production begins to suggest how and why.

39. Caryl Clark, "The Dirt on Salome," in *Performing Salome, Revealing Stories*, ed. Clair Rowden (Farnham, UK: Ashgate), 170.

40. The historical Salome and Herod Antipas were actually related by blood, but that element of their family history is not included in the text of Wilde's *Salomé*. The Herodian Dynasty was quite incestuous: Herod Antipas was the half-brother of Salome's father, the half-uncle of her mother, and the first cousin of her grandmother.

41. Lena Dominelli, "Betrayal of Trust: A Feminist Analysis of Power Relationships in Incest Abuse and its Relevance for Social Work Practice," *British Journal of Social Work* 19, no. 4 (1989): 297, https://doi.org/10.1093/oxfordjournals.bjsw.a055541

42. For more on the connections of typical "masculine" sexuality with violence and "feminine" sexuality with pain, see Irina Anderson and Kathy Doherty, *Accounting for Rape: Psychology, Feminism and Discourse Analysis in the Study of Sexual Violence* (London: Routledge, 2008), 6.

43. Female painters are relatively well represented among these depictions. See Artemisia Gentileschi, *Judith Slaying Holofernes* (1610) and Elisabetta Sirani, *Judith and Holofernes* (mid-seventeenth century).

44. I direct interested parties to Alexander Serov's 1863 opera *Judith*.

45. Ellie Hisama, "A Feminist Staging of Britten's *The Rape of Lucretia*," in Cusick et al., "Colloquy: Sexual Violence in Opera," 240.

46. Levin, "Operatic School for Scandal," 246–47.

47. Lucy Nevitt, *Theatre & Violence* (New York: Palgrave Macmillan, 2013), 33.

48. Egoyan, interview with the author.

49. Egoyan, interview with the author.

50. Kramer, "One Coughs, the Other Dances," 41.

51. Robin Holloway, "'Salome': Art or Kitsch?" in *Richard Strauss: Salome*, ed. Derrick Puffett (Cambridge: Cambridge University Press, 1989), 149.

52. Derrick Puffett, "Postlude: Images of Salome," in Puffett, *Richard Strauss: Salome*, 164.

53. Kramer, "One Coughs, the Other Dances," 40.

54. Caddy, "Variations on the Dance of the Seven Veils," 56. Ultimately, though,

Caddy argues that the music in the Dance of the Seven Veils is elastic, and its role in the drama shifts according to the dancer and the historical and narrative context.

55. Holloway, "'Salome': Art or Kitsch?," in Puffett, *Richard Strauss, Salome*, 149.

56. Egoyan, interview with the author.

57. Egoyan, interview with the author.

58. Kramer, "One Coughs, the Other Dances," 41.

59. Egoyan, interview with the author.

60. Nevitt, *Theatre & Violence*, 21–22. Emphasis in original.

61. Nevitt, *Theatre & Violence*, 22.

62. Levin, "Operatic School for Scandal," 246.

63. Paul Robinson, "It's Not Over Until the Soprano Dies," *New York Times Book Review*, January 1, 1989, https://www.nytimes.com/1989/01/01/books/it-s-not-over-until-the-soprano-dies.html; Abbate, "Opera; or, the Envoicing of Women." Both articles are responses to Clément, *Opera, or the Undoing of Women*.

64. Griselda Pollock, *Vision and Difference: Femininity, Feminism, and the Histories of Art* (New York: Routledge, 1988), 218.

65. Caruth, introduction to "Recapturing the Past," in *Trauma: Explorations in Memory*. Emphasis in original.

66. Gill, *Gender and the Media*, 139.

67. Gill, *Gender and the Media*, 141.

68. Lisa Fitzpatrick has commented on the prevalence of these two contrary approaches to staging rape in spoken theater: methods focused on the harsh reality of sexual violence and methods that seek to present affective and subjective experiences of rape. Lisa Fitzpatrick, *Rape on the Contemporary Stage* (London: Palgrave Macmillan, 2018), 215.

69. I find Salome's violent tendencies particularly cathartic because this subversion of gendered expectations and values takes place in the context of a story drawn from one of the most foundational texts in Western culture (the Bible) told through one of its most elevated art forms (opera).

70. Petra Dierkes-Thrun has observed two large trends in contemporary interpretations of Wilde's *Salomé*: "One is to enlist Wilde in contemporary antihomophobic projects via a sentimentalization and allegorization of his personal struggles; the other is to present Salomé as a feminist icon by focusing on the liberating force of her excessive sexuality." Dierkes-Thrun, *Salome's Modernity: Oscar Wilde and the Aesthetics of Transgression* (Ann Arbor: University of Michigan Press, 2011), 161.

71. In 1977, Lindsay Kemp led an all-male production of Wilde's play in which he played the title character. During the Dance of the Seven Veils, Kemp stripped away his drag to reveal his own body. More recently, the Lazarus Theatre Company's decision to cast a male actor as Salomé in their 2019 production at the Greenwich Theatre in London indicates the continuing presence of a queer interpretation of this character. See also: Elaine Showalter, "The Veiled Woman," in *Sexual Anarchy: Gender and Culture at the Fin de Siècle* (New York: Viking, 1990), 167–68.

72. Reading Salome as a stand-in for Wilde also guided Kate Millett's 1970

characterization of *Salomé* as "a drama of homosexual guilt and rejection," and Patrick Conrad's 1978 film *Mascara* which, as Carolyn Abbate writes, "asks us to consider whether Salome is revealed (as the final veil falls) as a man—not literally a biological man, but bearing nonetheless some frightening sign of maleness, symbolizing visually her usurpation of powers conventionally assigned to men." Kate Millett, *Sexual Politics* (Garden City, NY: Doubleday, 1970), 153; Abbate, "Opera; or, the Envoicing of Women," 225.

73. Review quoted in James H. Johnson, "Antisemitism and Music in Nineteenth-Century France," *Musica Judaica* 5, no. 1 (1982–83): 85, https://www.jstor.org/stable/23687595. Ralph Locke includes Salome in his discussion of the trope of the Orientalist woman as desirable and also dangerous. Ralph P. Locke, "Constructing the Oriental 'Other': Saint-Saëns's 'Samson et Dalila,'" *Cambridge Opera Journal* 3, no. 3 (1991): 269, http://www.jstor.org/stable/823619

74. Tamara Bernstein, a music critic for *The National Post*, accused Egoyan of pumping up the antisemitism in *Salome* in his production. Besides Bernstein's review, the reception of the productions in this chapter almost never feature any commentary on the representation of Jewishness in the opera, even though it is a significant concern in the scholarly discourse around *Salome*. Bernstein, "A Night of Violation, Both Musically and Personally," *National Post*, January 23, 2002.

75. Egoyan, interview with the author.

76. Nevitt, *Theatre & Violence*, 23.

77. **Postscript:** In February of 2023, after I completed this manuscript, Egoyan's *Salome* returned to the Canadian Opera Company. I attended on opening night and was excited to see another change to the Dance of the Seven Veils, continuing the process of abstraction of the representation of Salome's assault. Notably, Salome danced for much longer, and when the men eventually appeared, the struggle was represented without the physical contact and choreographed fighting of 2013; the focal point of the shadow ballet was Salome alone in the center, struggling, writhing, and clutching at herself amid the looming figures of the men. Clea Minaker worked with revival choreographer Julia Aplin to represent the rape in a way that is emotionally vivid while avoiding the explicit simulation of violence. I find this most recent iteration of the Dance in Egoyan's production to be the most effective yet at communicating the impact of sexual violence on its subject without the potentially gratuitous distraction of the details of the act itself.

Chapter 3

1. Larry Wolff, *The Singing Turk: Ottoman Power and Operatic Emotions on the European Stage from the Siege of Vienna to the Age of Napoleon* (Stanford: Stanford University Press, 2016), chapter 5.

2. Prior to ProstG, German courts repeatedly ruled that prostitution was immoral and so contracts regarding sex work were null and void. ProstG removed most of the morality language from the relevant laws in order to legalize promotion of prostitution (pimping), to recognize contracts between sex workers and their

clients as well as sex workers and their employers, and to grant sex workers access to employment benefits including healthcare and social security.

3. This kind of sentiment is expressed in: Derek Scally, "Sex, Drugs and . . . Opera," *Irish Times*, July 3, 2004, https://www.irishtimes.com/news/sex-drugs -and-opera-1.1147637; Jochen Breiholz, "Die Entführung aus dem Serail," *Opera News*, June 29, 2004, Metropolitan Opera Guild, https://www.operanews.com/op eranews/review/review.aspx?id=359&issueID=15; Jane Paulick, "A Violent, Drug-Addled, Hooker-Filled Opera Angers Sponsors," *Deutsche Welle*, June 24, 2004, https://www.dw.com/en/a-violent-drug-addled-hooker-filled-opera-angers-spons ors/a-1245750

4. Evan Baker, *From the Score to the Stage: An Illustrated History of Continental Opera Production and Staging* (Chicago: University of Chicago Press, 2013), 378–79. See also Scally, "Sex, Drugs and . . . Opera."

5. Breiholz, "Die Entführung aus dem Serail." Similarly, a critic for the *Telegraph* troublingly described a scene of dismemberment of a dead sex worker as "S&M." Michael White, "Hell Is Not under the Stage," *Telegraph*, September 21, 2004, https://www.telegraph.co.uk/culture/theatre/drama/3624283/Hell-is-not -under-the-stage.html

6. Scally, "Sex, Drugs and . . . Opera."

7. Allanbrook, Hunter, and Wheelock, "Staging Mozart's Women," in Smart, *Siren Songs*, 47–48.

8. Paulick, "A Violent, Drug-Addled, Hooker-Filled Opera."

9. Allanbrook, Hunter, and Wheelock, "Staging Mozart's Women," in Smart, *Siren Songs*, 50–57.

10. Charlotte Canning, *Feminist Theaters in the U.S.A.: Staging Women's Experience* (London: Routledge, 1996), 169–71.

11. Andrea Dworkin and Catharine MacKinnon, "Model Antipornography Civil-Rights Ordinance," *Pornography and Civil Rights: A New Day for Women's Equality*, Appendix D, http://www.nostatusquo.com/ACLU/dworkin/other/ordin ance/newday/AppD.htm

12. Elizabeth Howe, *The First English Actresses: Women and Drama 1660–1700* (Cambridge: Cambridge University Press, 1992), 43–44. Similarly, Jennifer Airey writes: "some plays foreground the physicality of the act of rape in the eroticized spectacle of the actress's violated form—the titillating promise of sexual situations and naked female flesh could certainly help attract an audience." Airey, *The Politics of Rape: Sexual Atrocity, Propaganda Wars, and the Restoration Stage* (Newark: University of Delaware, 2012), 26.

13. I am using "realism" interchangeably with "naturalism" to refer to a general aesthetic of mimetic representation. In theater studies, these terms have at times distinct and nuanced meanings, which I do not wish to evoke here.

14. Bieito's version of *Entführung* is just under two and a half hours and was performed with no intermission.

15. Elin Diamond, *Unmaking Mimesis* (London: Routledge, 1997), xiii.

16. Elaine Aston, "Feminist Theories of Representation: The Case against

Realism," in *An Introduction to Feminism and Theatre* (London: Routledge, 1994), 35.

17. Beethoven's *Fidelio* is a notable exception as a rescue opera where the soprano rescues her husband.

18. Patricia R. Schroeder, *The Feminist Possibilities of Dramatic Realism* (Madison, NJ: Fairleigh Dickinson University Press, 1996); Kim Solga, *Violence Against Women in Early Modern Performance: Invisible Acts* (Basingstoke: Palgrave Macmillan, 2009).

19. Risi, *Oper in Performance*, 34. My translation.

20. Micaela Baranello, "Die Entführung aus dem Serail, or, Men Who Hate Women," *Likely Impossibilities*, June 2, 2013, http://likelyimpossibilities.com/2013/06/die-entfuhrung-aus-dem-serail-or-men.html

21. Berta Joncus, "'Ich bin eine Engländerin, zur Freyheit geboren': Blonde and the Enlightened Female in Mozart's *Die Entführung aus dem Serail*," *Opera Quarterly* 26, no. 4 (2010): 574, https://doi.org/10.1093/oq/kbq050. See also Matthew Head, *Orientalism, Masquerade and Mozart's Turkish Music* (London: Royal Musical Association, 2000).

22. This aria is one of Risi's examples as well. Risi, *Oper in Performance*, 34–35.

23. In her review, Baranello notes that most of the reviews she has read of this production are written by men and tend to focus on the male gaze in their analysis of "Martern aller Arten." By contrast, she says that she found herself identifying powerfully with Konstanze in this scene and writes that "the production's equal (if not greater) weight on the women's perspectives is one of its most remarkable aspects." Baranello, "Men Who Hate Women."

24. Katherine Pratt Ewing, "Living Islam in the Diaspora: Between Turkey and Germany," *South Atlantic Quarterly* 102, no. 2–3 (2003): 405–31, https://doi.org/10.1215/00382876-102-2-3-405

25. For a discussion of the East/West European representational framework of sex trafficking rhetoric, see: Rutvica Andrijasevic, "The Figure of the Trafficked Victim: Gender, Rights and Representation," in *SAGE Handbook of Feminist Theory*, ed. Mary Evans et al. (London: SAGE Publications, 2014), 359–73.

26. Window prostitution involves sex workers dancing or otherwise advertising themselves in small cubicles visible from the street that open onto private rooms in which they work—for instance, in Amsterdam's red-light district.

27. The production team consulted with Hydra, a Berlin sex workers' advocacy group, about some of the representations in this production. Originally, bass Jens Larsen says he was going to cut off the sex worker's ear during "Martern aller Arten," but the women in Hydra said the nipple would be more realistic. While I applaud the team for consulting with these women, doing so is not an automatic guarantee that the representation will be legible or critically sound. Roger Boyes, "Opera So Lewd It Makes Berlin Blush," *Times*, June 26, 2004, https://www.the times.co.uk/article/opera-so-lewd-it-makes-berlin-blush-v9sdntsf9wn; Alan Riding, "Definitely Not Your Mother's Mozart Opera," *New York Times*, July 10, 2004, https://www.nytimes.com/2004/07/10/arts/definitely-not-your-mother-s-mozart -opera.html?smid=url-share

28. See Catharine MacKinnon, *Toward a Feminist Theory of the State* (Cambridge, MA: Harvard University Press, 1989); Andrea Dworkin, *Life and Death: Unapologetic Writings on the Continuing War Against Women* (New York: Free Press, 1997); Melissa Farley and Vanessa Kelly, "Prostitution: A Critical Review of the Medical and Social Sciences Literature," *Women and Criminal Justice* 11, no. 4 (2000): 29–64, https://doi.org/10.1300/J012v11n04_04; Janice G. Raymond, "Ten Reasons for *Not* Legalizing Prostitution and a Legal Response to the Demand for Prostitution," *Journal of Trauma Practice* 2, no. 3–4 (2004): 315–32, https://doi.org/10.1300/J189v02n03_17; Kathleen Barry, *The Prostitution of Sexuality* (New York: New York University Press, 1995); Sheila Jeffreys, *The Idea of Prostitution* (Melbourne: Spinifex, 1997); Donna M. Hughes, *The Demand for Victims of Sex Trafficking* (Kingston: University of Rhode Island, 2005).

29. Carol Wolkowitz, *Bodies at Work* (London: SAGE Publications, 2006).

30. Wajdi Mouawad, "Director's Notes," *Die Entführung aus dem Serail*, program for Winter 2018 (Toronto: Canadian Opera Company, 2018), 28.

31. Stephanie's libretto does not specify the length of captivity.

32. Wajdi Mouawad, *Die Entführung aus dem Serail*, 2016. "Was gab es bei mir Zuhaus so wichtiges, um so zu hetzen? Dort wie hier stand ich bei einem Herrn in Diensten, dort wie hier nannte man mich Diener, aber dort schien die Sonne, wenn es hier regnet." For dialogue quotations, I will use the English translation as projected in the surtitles at the COC in 2018.

33. "Ob hier oder dort, dort oder hier, ob du oder er, er oder du, der eine taugt nicht mehr als der andere!"

34. "Und trotz der Grausamkeit seiner Worte wusste ich, dass er gut war."

35. "Dieses Vergnügen wirst du nicht finden. Der Tod geht hierzulande, mit Martern aller Arten, langsame und schmerzhafte Wege."

36. Alexander Neef, "A Message from General Director Alexander Neef," program for Winter 2018 (Toronto: Canadian Opera Company, 2018), 5.

37. Neef, "A Message from General Director Alexander Neef," 5.

38. Jane Archibald quoted in Catherine Kustanczy, "'An Actual Human Being': Jane Archibald Talks about Konstanze and Working with Wajdi Mouawad," program for Winter 2018, 39.

39. "Nie hätte ich geahnt, dass mein Herz einmal so zerrissen wäre. Eure Gesichter fließen ineinander. Du bist mächtig, brillant, großzügig wie kein anderer Mann, während seines geprägt ist von Unschuld, von Jugend, und wenn du mich erzittern lässt, so lässt er mein Herz höher schlagen."

40. "Aber ich könnte es nicht ertragen mitanzusehen, wie du dich einem anderen zuwendest. Das nicht! Welcher Mann sagte das nicht über die Frau, nach der er verrückt ist?"

41. "Meinst du, deine Welt wäre besser als die meine?"

42. "Warum kriege ich immer die Kindsköpfe ab, die immer nur am Klagen sind!"

43. "Warum locke ich immer die größten Nichtnutze an! Mach dir ein für alle Mal klar, dass mir das hier nicht gefällt! Das sag ich dir, Pedrillo, Osmin hatte ich das auch so gesagt! Du bildest dir wohl ein, es mit einer Sklavin zu tun zu haben,

die zitternd deinen Befehlen gehorcht? Solchen Phantasien gibt man sich bei mir nicht hin, bei mir benimmt man sich anders."

44. "Zärtlichkeit und Schmeicheln! Wir sind in der Türkei! Ich bin dein Herr und du bist meine Sklavin: ich befehle, du gehorchst!"

45. "In Europa läuft das genauso!"

46. "Sei bloß still oder ich mache dir den Türken!"

47. "Ich habe mehrfach das Exil erlebt. Das Land zu wechseln und die Sprache, macht man sich mit der Zeit zu einem Gewinn, zu einer Identität."

48. "Wer könnte mich besser verstehen als du, und ich, als dich? Wir waren Herrin und Dienerin, jetzt sind wir zwei Frauen, Seite an Seite."

49. "Liebe deine Blonde über alles und lass sie gehen."

50. "BLONDE. Ihr wolltet uns gerne retten, unter der Bedingung, dass wir euch treu geblieben sind . . . KONSTANZE. Was wäre passiert, wenn wir es nicht gewesen wären? Wärt ihr wieder losgesegelt, auf eurem Schiff? Untreue Frauen wollen wir nicht? BLONDE. Am unerträglichsten war, dass ihr uns gezwungen habt, euch anzulügen, um unser Leben zu retten."

51. "Zwei Jahre lang im Hause eines Mannes zu schlafen, der mich unentwegt zu verführen versucht, mich zu erobern, der mir ein Geschenk nach dem andern macht, mich zu seiner Königin bestimmt, zur Königin seines Lebens, was soll ich denn machen?"

52. "Großmütiger Mann! O daß ich es könnte, daß ich's erwidern könnte."

53. Edward Said, *Covering Islam: How the Media and the Experts Determine How We See the Rest of the World* (1981; repr., New York: Vintage, 1997).

54. The supernumerary women in Mouawad's production were costumed in floor-length red dresses. In 2018 in Toronto, promotional posters for Hulu's adaptation of Margaret Atwood's *A Handmaid's Tale* adorned bus shelters right outside the theater. The accidental visual similarity did not help matters.

55. Consider Sara Ahmed's words: "Becoming a feminist was about becoming audible, feminism as screaming in order to be heard; screaming as making violence visible; feminism as acquiring a voice." Sarah Ahmed, *Living a Feminist Life* (Durham: Duke University Press, 2017), 73.

56. I am reminded of Gayatri Chakravorty Spivak's analysis of hegemonic Western feminism and the silence of its subaltern subjects. In the context of my production analysis, my subjects are not actual Eastern European or Arabic women but rather the representations of such women constructed by the production teams and especially the directors of these operas. Feminine agency looks different in different cultural contexts and the intersections of gender with race, ethnicity, nationality, and religion are rich and complex. But I find these complexities generally absent from the representations of "Turkish" women in these productions of *Entführung*. Gayatri Chakravorty Spivak, "Can the Subaltern Speak?" in *Marxism and the Interpretation of Culture*, ed. Cary Nelson and Lawrence Grossberg (Urbana: University of Illinois Press, 1988), 271–316; Gayatri Chakravorty Spivak, "The Rani of Sirmu," in *Europe and Its Others*, ed. Francis Barker (Colchester: University of Essex Press, 1985), 146–58.

57. Mary von Aue, "A Radical Redo for 'Madama Butterfly'—to Save It?" *New York Times*, May 19, 2017, https://www.nytimes.com/2017/05/19/arts/music/a-rad ical-redo-for-madama-butterfly-to-save-it.html

58. The Boston Lyric Opera canceled a planned production of *Madama Butterfly* in 2020 and instead began "The Butterfly Process," a series of conversations with artists and community members about the history and legacy of *Butterfly* in the context of a period of heightened racism against Asian American communities.

59. Lynn A. Higgins and Brenda R. Silver, "Introduction: Rereading Rape," in *Rape and Representation*, ed. Lynn A. Higgins and Brenda R. Silver (New York: Columbia University Press, 1991), 4.

60. Magnus Tessing Schneider identifies a similar "ethical turn" in American opera scholarship in the last quarter century. Magnus Tessing Schneider, *The Original Portrayal of Mozart's Don Giovanni* (London: Routledge, 2022), 213.

61. Teresa de Lauretis, *Alice Doesn't: Feminism, Semiotics, Cinema* (Bloomington: Indiana University Press, 1984), chapter 5.

Chapter 4

1. British music critic Hugo Shirley has similarly remarked that grand opera "tended to favour history and its battles for the scenic opportunities they afforded rather than for the lessons they taught." Hugo Shirley, "Mariinsky's *Les Troyens*—A Bad Night for Berlioz and Edinburgh," *Spectator*, September 6, 2014.

2. Knabe's *Turandot* was remounted in 2015 and 2018.

3. The Third Geneva Convention "relative to the Treatment of Prisoners of War," adopted in 1929, specifies that POWs are to be humanely treated and protected from violence, but acts of sexual violence are not specifically named.

4. Alexandra Stiglmayer, "The Rapes in Bosnia-Herzegovina," in *Mass Rape*, ed. Alexandra Stiglmayer (Lincoln: University of Nebraska Press, 1992), 84.

5. Ann J. Cahill, *Rethinking Rape* (Ithaca: Cornell University Press, 2001), 27.

6. The ballet movement has been subject to significant cuts in this ROH production, including cutting the choral numbers entirely. It is common practice to make cuts to the long dance movements of French grand opera in contemporary performance. Even with the cuts, this orchestral interlude is over five minutes long.

7. Eileen L. Zurbriggen, "Rape, War, and the Socialization of Masculinity: Why Our Refusal to Give Up Wars Ensures that Rape Cannot Be Eradicated," *Psychology of Women Quarterly* 34, no. 4 (2010): 542, 544, https://doi.org/10.1111 /j.1471-6402.2010.01603.x

8. Sexual violence and military violence correspond not only in combat zones in which enemy women are raped, but off the battlefield as well. Researchers have established significant correlation between military service and domestic violence perpetration for both active-duty service members and veterans. This correlation is mediated by the role of Post-Traumatic Stress Disorder among veterans, but it is worth noting that we see similarly inflated rates of domestic violence perpetration in domestic police forces. Resul Cesur and Joseph J. Sabia, "When War

Comes Home: The Effect of Combat Service on Domestic Violence," *Review of Economics and Statistics* 98, no. 2 (2016): 209–25, https://doi.org/10.1162/REST_a_00541; Jennifer M. Gierisch, et al., "Intimate Partner Violence: Prevalence Among U.S. Military Veterans and Active Duty Servicemembers and a Review of Intervention Approaches," Evidence-Based Synthesis Program Center, report prepared for the Department of Veterans Affairs (Durham, NC: Durham Veterans Affairs Healthcare System, 2013); Holly G. Prigerson, Paul K. Maciejewski, and Robert A. Rosenheck, "Population Attributable Fractions of Psychiatric Disorders and Behavioral Outcomes Associated with Combat Exposure Among US Men," *American Journal of Public Health* 92, no. 1 (2002): 59–63; Leanor Boulin Johnson, "On the Front Lines: Police Stress and Family Well-Being. Hearing Before the Select Committee on Children, Youth, and Families House of Representatives," 102 Congress First Session, May 20 (Washington, DC: US Government Printing Office, 1991), 32–48; Peter H. Neidig, Harold E. Russell, and Albert F. Seng, "Interspousal Aggression in Law Enforcement Families: A Preliminary Investigation," *Police Studies* 15, no. 1 (1991): 30–38.

9. Amnesty International's fact sheet about violence against women in armed conflict reads that women "experience armed conflicts as sexual objects, as presumed emblems of national and ethnic identity, and as female members of ethnic, racial, religious, or national groups." "Violence Against Women in Armed Conflict: A Fact Sheet," *Amnesty International* (25 August 2015), https://docgo.net/vaw-in-armed-conflict-fact-sheet

10. Brownmiller argues that rape is a part of a conscious effort to destroy the enemy and mark the men as impotent when they can no longer do their masculine duty to protect "their" women. Brownmiller, *Against Our Will*, 31. For an excellent gloss of Brownmiller's larger argument on war rape, see Cahill, *Rethinking Rape*, 18–19.

11. This production uses the Swedish character names from Verdi's original version of the opera. I have included the character names from the more familiar later version, set in Boston, in parentheses.

12. Inger Skjelsbæk, *The Political Psychology of War Rape: Studies from Bosnia and Herzegovina* (New York: Routledge, 2012), 140.

13. Brownmiller, *Against Our Will*, 285.

14. Cahill problematizes Brownmiller's claim that rape is not a sexual act in *Rethinking Rape*, though she also fails to consider sexual violence against trans people.

15. Cahill, *Rethinking Rape*, 13.

16. Brownmiller, *Against Our Will*, 31.

17. Tilman Knabe, "Ein Gespräch mit dem Produktionsteam," 9. "Vielleicht findet Kalaf Turandot attraktiv, vielleicht nicht. Sicher ist: Sie ist wichtig für ihn, weil sie das verkörpert, was er braucht. . . . Kalaf fist kein Dummkopf und schmachtender Liebhaber, ganz im Gegenteil: Er ist ein raffinierter, hochstrategischer Politiker." All translations are mine.

18. "Non profanarmi!," "mai nessun m'avrà!," "Non mi toccar, straniero!" The

Italian word "straniero" literally translates to "stranger" or "foreigner," and it has connotations of "enemy."

19. "Onta su me!" I discuss the cut in more detail later.

20. Tilman Knabe and Stefan Soltesz, "Ein Gespräch mit dem Produktionssteam," 7, 11. Knabe: "Liebe ist immer nur ein Vehikel für etwas. Wenn Liebe gesagt wird, ist immer Überleben oder Politik und Macht gemeint." Soltesz: "Sie sind nur Vehikel, damit Kalaf an die Macht kommen kann."

21. Siobhán K. Fisher, "Occupation of the Womb: Forced Impregnation as Genocide," *Duke Law Journal* 46, no. 1 (1996): 92, https://doi.org/10.2307/137 2967

22. Cahill, *Rethinking Rape*, 9.

23. Brownmiller, *Against Our Will*, 5.

24. This element of group sexual assault exists outside of war as well. One real-world example is the 2019 case of two men who filmed themselves high fiving after raping a woman in a London nightclub. Samuel Osborne, "Men Who Filmed Themselves Raping Woman in Nightclub then Ran Off High-Fiving Each Other Both Jailed for 7 Years," *Independent*, November 22, 2019.

25. This production is of the original 1862 version of *Forza* rather than the popular 1869 revision. For the purposes of my analysis, the differences are not significant; the order of events is different in Act 3 scene 3, but the content is largely unchanged.

26. "Viva, viva la pazzia che qui sola ha da regnar!"

27. Catharine A. MacKinnon, "Turning Rape into Pornography: Postmodern Genocide," in Stiglmayer, *Mass Rape*, 78–79.

28. Reviews of Michieletto's *Tell* frequently identified the setting as the Balkan Conflict, despite the ambiguous pan-military uniforms the soldiers wear. The publicity of the rape camps in Bosnia and Herzegovina led to important and overdue reforms in the way we think about wartime rape, but it has also resulted in a tendency among the general population to think that war rape, and especially systemic rape as a weapon of war, are unique to the Serbian occupation of Bosnia and Herzegovina.

29. Risi, *Oper in Performance*, 34.

30. Jürgen Kühnel, "Regietheater. Konzeption und Praxis am Beispiel Mozarts. Versuch einter Typologie," in *Regietheater. Konzeption und Praxis am Beispiel der Bühnenwerke Mozarts*, essays from the Salzburg Symposion 2005 by Jürgen Kühnel, Ulrich Müller, and Oswald Panagl (Salzburg: Verlag Mueller-Speiser, 2007), 23.

31. Joy Calico, *Brecht at the Opera* (Berkeley: University of California Press, 2008), 140–63.

32. Calico, *Brecht at the Opera*, 142.

33. Brecht writes that in epic theater, "the object of this 'effect' is to allow the spectator to criticize constructively from a social point of view." It constitutes a "changeover from representation to commentary." Berthold Brecht, *Brecht on Theatre*, ed. and trans. John Willett (New York: Hill and Wang, 1964), 125–26.

34. "Le gloriose ferite col trionfo il destin coronò. . . . La vittoria più rifulge de' figli al valor!" The text of this scene, including the "Rataplan" chorus, comes from Schiller's *Wallensteins Lager* and was added to *Forza*'s libretto to introduce more comedy to the generally somber opera. Kratzer's production does not benefit from this infusion of comedy; he reimagines this scene as a display of vicious cruelty.

35. In the written text of *Turandot*, the chorus addresses the old Chinese emperor. In Knabe's staging, they address Calaf, the foreign prince who seeks the throne.

36. The chorus in these productions evoke ideas about the crowd formulated by Gustave Le Bon in 1895. He argues that crowds are violent, ferocious, and suggestible. Gustave Le Bon, *The Crowd* (1895; repr. London: Routledge, 1995).

37. In the program notes for *Turandot*, Knabe argues that he already hears fascism in the opera, especially in the crowd scenes. Tilman Knabe, "Ein Gespräch mit dem Produktionsteam," in program for Puccini's *Turandot* (Essen: Aalto-Musiktheater, 2007), 7.

38. Knabe, "Ein Gespräch mit dem Produktionsteam," 7.

39. The sopranos in 2007 and 2018 both wear long blond wigs, whereas the tenors wear their natural hair: one is bald and one has dark curly hair. My interpretation of this is that Turandot's hair matters to the production whereas Calaf's does not necessarily.

40. Angela Y. Davis, Gina Dent, Erica R. Meiners, and Beth E. Richie, *Abolition. Feminism. Now.* (Chicago: Haymarket Books, 2022), especially 96, 110.

41. Alexandra Coghlan, "The Gang Rape Was the Least Offensive Thing about Royal Opera's New William Tell," *Spectator*, June 29, 2015, https://www.spectator.com.au/2015/07/the-gang-rape-was-the-least-offensive-thing-about-royal-operas-new-william-tell

42. Rupert Christiansen, "Guillaume Tell, Royal Opera House, Review: 'Lame and Pretentious,'" *Telegraph*, June 30, 2015, https://www.telegraph.co.uk/culture/music/opera/11708131/Guillaume-Tell-Royal-Opera-House-review-lame-and-pretentious.html

43. Mark Valencia, "Guillaume Tell (Royal Opera House)," *WhatsOnStage*, 30 June 2015, https://www.whatsonstage.com/london-theatre/reviews/guillaume-tell-royal-opera-house_38171.html

44. Friedrich Schiller, *Wilhelm Tell*, trans. William F. Mainland (Chicago: University of Chicago Press, 1972), 9.

45. This production is explicitly critical of the heroic narrative of William Tell the legendary figure. One of the defining features of this production is the presence of an actor representing an idealized comic-book image of Tell, who highlights the contrast between the real Tell and the legend, between the reality of war and the fantasy.

46. Kasper Holten, "Small Adjustments Made to Production of *Guillaume Tell*," *Royal Opera House News*, July 5, 2015; archived at *Wayback Machine*, capture dated 5 September 2015, https://web.archive.org/web/20150905204706/roh.org.uk/news/small-adjustments-made-to-production-of-guillaume-tell

47. "Trascinata da un uomo, come te, come te, straniero, là nella notte atroce, dove si spense la sua fresca voce!"

48. The synopsis in the program for Knabe's *Turandot* reads, "she wants to escape the fate of her ancestor Lo-u-Ling, who was raped and murdered." "Handlung," in program for Puccini's *Turandot*, 2. Similar language appears in many synopses of *Turandot* online.

49. "Dell'ava lo strazio non si rinnoverà!"

50. The music for this scene was composed by Franco Alfano after Puccini's death.

51. Roger Parker, *Remaking the Song: Operatic Visions and Revisions from Handel to Berio* (Berkeley: University of California Press, 2006), 98.

52. Englund sees this directorial approach as fulfilling what Catherine Clément asks for when she imagines a staging of *The Magic Flute* in which Sarastro's priests perform the violence against Pamina and the Queen that is implied by their misogynistic worldview. Englund, *Deviant Opera*, 37; Clément, *Opera, or the Undoing of Women*, 75–76.

53. Englund, *Deviant Opera*, 41.

54. Englund, *Deviant Opera*, 42.

55. Micaela Baranello, "Staging Opera Ballet," in Cusick et al., "Colloquy: Sexual Violence in Opera," 226.

56. I suspect the fact that the music lost to this cut was composed by Franco Alfano and not Puccini made it an easier sell. Music director Stefan Soltesz explains that they play the Toscanini version with an additional cut, "because we think Puccini wanted to get to the end quickly" ("da Puccini unserer Ansicht nach zügig zum Ende finden wollte"). Soltesz, "Ein Gespräch mit dem Produktionsteam," 10.

57. "Il suo nome è Amor!"

58. "Violence Against Women in Armed Conflict: A Fact Sheet," *Amnesty International*, 25 August 2015, https://docgo.net/vaw-in-armed-conflict-fact-sheet

59. Article 2 of the Convention on the Prevention and Punishment of the Crime of Genocide, ratified by the General Assembly of the United Nations 12 January 1951.

60. Rhonda Copelon, "Surfacing Gender: Reconceptualizing Crimes Against Women in Times of War," in Stiglmayer, *Mass Rape*, 208.

61. Kate Manne argues that the status of women as interchangeable and representative of a certain type of woman (if not all women) is an element of misogyny. Manne, *Down Girl*, 58. See also Martha Nussbaum, "Objectification," *Philosophy and Public Affairs* 24, no. 4 (1995): 257, https://www.jstor.org/stable/2961930; Rae Langton, *Sexual Solipsism: Philosophical Essays on Pornography and Objectification* (Oxford: Oxford University Press, 2009), 226.

62. Airey, *The Politics of Rape*, 12.

63. Airey, *The Politics of Rape*, 26.

64. Fitzpatrick, *Rape on the Contemporary Stage*, 138.

65. Sabine Sielke, *Reading Rape: The Rhetoric of Sexual Violence in American Literature and Culture, 1790–1990* (Princeton: Princeton University Press, 2002), 183.

Similarly, Anikó Imre traces feminist analyses of post-colonial texts that problematize the use of the violation of women as a metaphor for the suffering of the nation. Imre, "Hungarian Poetic Nationalism or National Pornography? Eastern Europe and Feminism—With a Difference," in *Violence and the Body: Race, Gender, and the State*, ed. Arturo J. Aldama (Bloomington: Indiana University Press, 2003), 43–44.

66. Jean-Charles is writing here about the 1968 novella by Marie Vieux-Chauvet, *Amour, colère, folie*. Régine Michelle Jean-Charles, *Conflict Bodies: The Politics of Rape Representation in the Francophone Imaginary* (Columbus: Ohio State University Press, 2014), 60.

67. Catharine Woodward, "A Follow-Up," blog post on *Opera Div*, July 1, 2015, https://operacat.tumblr.com/post/122933791828/a-follow-up; emphasis in the original.

68. Cahill, *Rethinking Rape*, 143.

69. "Die Männerphantasie, welche der Komponist und seine Autoren in dem Stück verwirklichen, ist schon starker Tobak. Da sind drei Machos am Werk, die die einzigen Frauen in der Oper auf brutalste Weise vernichten: Die eine bringt sich um und die andere wird missbraucht. Zynisch formuliert: Es lebe das Patriarchat." Knabe, "Ein Gespräch mit dem Produktionsteam," 11.

Conclusion

1. On the Met's decision to stop using blackface makeup in productions of *Otello* in 2015: Michael Cooper, "An 'Otello' without Blackface Highlights an Enduring Tradition in Opera," *New York Times*, September 17, 2015, https://www.nytimes.com/2015/09/20/arts/music/an-otello-without-the-blackface-nods-to-modern-tastes.html. On the Paris Opera's efforts to deal with racial stereotypes: Alex Marshall, "Paris Opera to Act on Racist Stereotypes in Ballet," *New York Times*, February 8, 2021, https://www.nytimes.com/2021/02/08/arts/dance/paris-ballet-diversity.html. See also André, *Black Opera*, especially 2, 13–14.

2. Dylan Robinson, "Decolonial Regietheater," on the panel "On 'Music Colonialism': Intersectional and Interdisciplinary Methodologies in New Critical Studies of Western Art Musics" (paper, Joint Annual Meeting of the American Musicological Society, the Society for Ethnomusicology, and the Society for Music Theory, New Orleans, LA, November 11, 2022).

3. Steve Paulson, "Critical Intimacy: An Interview with Gayatri Chakravorty Spivak," *LA Review of Books*, July 29, 2016, https://lareviewofbooks.org/article/critical-intimacy-interview-gayatri-chakravorty-spivak

4. Susan McClary argues that *Regietheater* gives audience members an "arch way of relating to our shared cultural legacy, reveling in the guilty pleasures of favorite arias while maintaining ironic distance." Susan McClary, *The Passions of Peter Sellars: Staging the Music* (Ann Arbor: University of Michigan Press, 2019).

5. Carolyn Abbate, Richard Taruskin, and James Hepokoski have all pointed out a tendency among musicologists to perceive a moral urgency or ethical debt owed to anthropomorphized works. Carolyn Abbate, "Music—Drastic or Gnos-

tic?" *Critical Inquiry* 30, no. 3 (2004), 517, https://doi.org/10.1086/421160; Richard Taruskin, *Text and Act: Essays on Music and Performance* (New York: Oxford University Press, 1995), 24; James Hepokoski, "Operatic Stagings: Positions and Paradoxes: Response to David J. Levin," in *Verdi 2001: Proceedings of the International Conference, Parma, New York, New Haven,* ed. Fabrizio Della Seta, Roberta Montemorra Marvin, Marco Marica (Florence: L.S. Olschki, 2003), 2:479.

6. In 2016, Tonia Sina, Siobhan Richardson, and Alicia Rodis founded Intimacy Directors International, based in part on Sina's 2006 Master's thesis. Tonia Sina Campanella, "Intimate Encounters; Staging Intimacy and Sensuality" (Master's thesis, Virginia Commonwealth University, 2006).

7. Tonia Sina, Siobhan Richardson, and Alicia Rodis, "Pillars of Safe Intimacy: Rehearsal and Performance Practice," Intimacy Directors International, teamidi.org, https://docs.wixstatic.com/ugd/924101_1620d7333f6a4809a2765257e750e255.pdf

8. William Cheng, *Loving Music Till It Hurts* (Oxford: Oxford University Press, 2019), 5.

Bibliography

Abbate, Carolyn. "Music—Drastic or Gnostic?" *Critical Inquiry* 30, no. 3 (2004): 505–36. https://doi.org/10.1086/421160

Abbate, Carolyn. "Opera; or, the Envoicing of Women." In *Musicology and Difference: Gender and Sexuality in Music Scholarship*, edited by Ruth A. Solie, 225–58. Berkeley: University of California Press, 1993.

Abbate, Carolyn. *Unsung Voices: Opera and Musical Narrative in the Nineteenth Century*. Princeton: Princeton University Press, 1996.

Abbey, Antonia, Tina Zawacki, Philip O. Buck, A. Monique Clinton, and Pam McAuslan. "Alcohol and Sexual Assault." *Alcohol Research & Health* 25, no. 1 (2001): 43–51.

Ahmed, Sara. *Living a Feminist Life*. Durham: Duke University Press, 2017.

Airey, Jennifer L. *The Politics of Rape: Sexual Atrocity, Propaganda Wars, and the Restoration Stage*. Newark: University of Delaware, 2012.

Allanbrook, Wye Jamison. *Rhythmic Gesture in Mozart: Le nozze di Figaro & Don Giovanni*. Chicago: University of Chicago Press, 1983.

Anderson, Irina, and Kathy Doherty. *Accounting for Rape: Psychology, Feminism and Discourse Analysis in the Study of Sexual Violence*. London: Routledge, 2008.

Anderson, Scott A. "Conceptualizing Rape as Coerced Sex." *Ethics: An International Journal of Social, Political, and Legal Philosophy* 127, no. 1 (2016): 50–87. https://doi.org/10.1086/687332

André, Naomi. *Black Opera: History, Power, Engagement*. Urbana: University of Illinois Press, 2018.

Andrijasevic, Rutvica. "The Figure of the Trafficked Victim: Gender, Rights and Representation." In *SAGE Handbook of Feminist Theory*, edited by Mary Evans, Clare Hemmings, Marsha Henry, Hazel Johnstone, Sumi Madhok, Ania Plomien, and Sadie Wearing, 359–73. London: SAGE Publications, 2014.

Armatage, Kay, and Caryl Clark. "Seeing and Hearing Atom Egoyan's *Salome*." In *Image and Territory: Essays on Atom Egoyan*, edited by Monique Tschofen and Jennifer Burwell, 307–28. Waterloo: Wilfred Laurier University Press, 2007.

Aston, Elaine. *An Introduction to Feminism and Theatre*. London: Routledge, 1994.

Baker, Evan. *From the Score to the Stage: An Illustrated History of Continental Opera Production and Staging*. Chicago: University of Chicago Press, 2013.

Barry, Kathleen. *The Prostitution of Sexuality*. New York: New York University Press, 1995.

Barthes, Roland. "From Work to Text." In *Image, Music, Text*, translated by Stephen Heath, 155–64. New York: Fontana Press, 1977.

Berlo, Willy van, and Bernardine Ensink. "Problems with Sexuality after Sexual Assault," *Annual Review of Sex Research* 11, no. 1 (2000): 235–57. http://dx.doi.org/10.1080/10532528.2000.10559789

Boyd, Melanie. "To Blame Her Sadness: Representing Incest in Atom Egoyan's *The Sweet Hereafter*." In *Image and Territory: Essays on Atom Egoyan*, edited by Monique Tschofen and Jennifer Burwell, 275–94. Waterloo: Wilfrid Laurier University Press, 2007.

Brecht, Berthold. *Brecht on Theatre*. Edited and translated by John Willett. New York: Hill and Wang, 1964.

Brownmiller, Susan. *Against Our Will: Men, Women and Rape*. New York: Bantam, 1976. Originally published by Simon and Schuster 1975.

Brown-Montesano, Kristi. *Understanding the Women of Mozart's Operas*. Berkeley: University of California Press, 2007.

Burgess, Ann Wolbert, and Lynda Lytle Holmstrom. "Coping Behavior of the Rape Victim." *American Journal of Psychiatry* 133, no. 4 (1976): 413–18. https://doi.org/10.1176/ajp.133.4.413

Burt, Martha R. "Cultural Myths and Supports for Rape." *Journal of Personality and Social Psychology* 38, no. 2 (1980): 217–30. https://psycnet.apa.org/doi/10.1037/0022-3514.38.2.217

Caddy, Davinia. "Variations on the Dance of the Seven Veils." *Cambridge Opera Journal* 17, no. 1 (2005): 37–58. https://doi.org/10.1017/S095458670500193X

Cahill, Ann J. *Rethinking Rape*. Ithaca: Cornell University Press, 2001.

Calico, Joy H. *Brecht at the Opera*. Berkeley: University of California Press, 2008.

Campanella, Tonia Sina. "Intimate Encounters; Staging Intimacy and Sensuality." Master's thesis, Virginia Commonwealth University, 2006.

Canning, Charlotte. *Feminist Theaters in the U.S.A.: Staging Women's Experience*. London: Routledge, 1996.

Cannon, Katie G. *Black Womanist Ethics*. Atlanta: Scholar's Press, 1988.

Caruth, Cathy, ed. *Trauma: Explorations in Memory*. Baltimore: Johns Hopkins University Press, 1995.

Cesur, Resul, and Joseph J. Sabia. "When War Comes Home: The Effect of Combat Service on Domestic Violence." *Review of Economics and Statistics* 98, no. 2 (2016): 209–25. https://doi.org/10.1162/REST_a_00541

Cheng, William. *Loving Music Till It Hurts*. Oxford: Oxford University Press, 2019.

Clark, Caryl. "The Dirt on Salome." In *Performing Salome, Revealing Stories*, edited by Clair Rowden, 155–70. Farnham, UK: Ashgate, 2013.

Clément, Catherine. *Opera, or the Undoing of Women*. Translated by Betsy Wing. Minneapolis: University of Minnesota Press, 1988.

Collins, Patricia Hill. *Black Feminist Thought: Knowledge, Consciousness, and the Politics of Empowerment.* Boston: Unwin Hyman, 1990.

Collins, Patricia Hill. "The Social Construction of Black Feminist Thought." *SIGNS: A Journal of Women in History and Culture* 14, no. 4, Common Grounds and Crossroads: Race, Ethnicity, and Class in Women's Lives (Summer 1989): 745–73. https://www.jstor.org/stable/3174683

Cusick, Suzanne G., Monica A. Hershberger, Richard Will, Micaela Baranello, Bonnie Gordon, and Ellie M. Hisama. "Colloquy: Sexual Violence in Opera: Scholarship, Pedagogy, and Production as Resistance." *Journal of the American Musicological Society* 71, no. 1 (Spring 2018): 213–53. https://doi.org/10.1525/jams.2018.71.1.213

Davis, Angela Y., Gina Dent, Erica R. Meiners, and Beth E. Richie. *Abolition. Feminism. Now.* Chicago: Haymarket Books, 2022.

De Lauretis, Teresa. *Alice Doesn't: Feminism, Semiotics, Cinema.* Bloomington: Indiana University Press, 1984.

Diamond, Elin. *Unmaking Mimesis.* London: Routledge, 1997.

Dierkes-Thrun, Petra. *Salome's Modernity: Oscar Wilde and the Aesthetics of Transgression.* Ann Arbor: University of Michigan Press, 2011.

Doane, Mary Ann. *Femmes Fatales: Feminism, Film Theory, Psychoanalysis.* New York: Routledge, 1991.

Dominelli, Lena. "Betrayal of Trust: A Feminist Analysis of Power Relationships in Incest Abuse and its Relevance for Social Work Practice." *British Journal of Social Work* 19, no. 4 (1989): 291–307. https://doi.org/10.1093/oxfordjournals.bjsw.a055541

Dworkin, Andrea. *Life and Death: Unapologetic Writings on the Continuing War Against Women.* New York: Free Press, 1997.

Englund, Axel. *Deviant Opera: Sex, Power, and Perversion on Stage.* Berkeley: University of California Press, 2020.

Ewing, Katherine Pratt. "Living Islam in the Diaspora: Between Turkey and Germany." *South Atlantic Quarterly* 102, no. 2–3 (2003): 405–31. https://doi.org/10.1215/00382876-102-2-3-405

Farley, Melissa, and Vanessa Kelly. "Prostitution: A Critical Review of the Medical and Social Sciences Literature." *Women & Criminal Justice* 11, no. 4 (2000): 29–64. https://doi.org/10.1300/J012v11n04_04

Finch, Emily, and Vanessa E. Munro. "Juror Stereotypes and Blame Attribution in Rape Cases Involving Intoxicants: *The Findings of a Pilot Study.*" *British Journal of Criminology* 45, no. 1 (2005): 25–38. https://doi.org/10.1093/bjc/azh055

Fisher, Siobhán K. "Occupation of the Womb: Forced Impregnation as Genocide." *Duke Law Journal* 46, no. 1 (1996): 91–133. https://doi.org/10.2307/1372967

Fitzpatrick, Lisa. *Rape on the Contemporary Stage.* London: Palgrave Macmillan, 2018.

Gierisch, Jennifer M., Abigail Shapiro, Nicole N. Grant, Heather A. King, Jennifer R. McDuffie, John W. Williams Jr., Avishek Nagi, and Liz Wing. "Intimate Partner Violence: Prevalence Among U.S. Military Veterans and Active Duty

Servicemembers and a Review of Intervention Approaches." Evidence-Based Synthesis Program Center. Report prepared for the Department of Veterans Affairs. Durham, NC: Durham Veterans Affairs Healthcare System, 2013.

Gill, Rosalind. *Gender and the Media*. Cambridge: Polity Press, 2007.

Gilligan, Carol. *In a Different Voice: Psychological Theory and Women's Development*. Cambridge, MA: Harvard University Press, 2016. Originally published 1982.

Gilman, Sander L. *Disease and Representation: Images of Illness from Madness to AIDS*. Ithaca: Cornell University Press, 1988.

Glenn, Susan Anita. *Female Spectacle: The Theatrical Roots of Modern Feminism*. Cambridge, MA: Harvard University Press, 2000.

Gravelin, Claire R., Monica Biernat, and Caroline E. Bucher. "Blaming the Victim of Acquaintance Rape: Individual, Situational, and Sociocultural Factors." *Frontiers in Psychology* 9 (2019): 2422–50. http://doi.org/10.3389/fpsyg.2018.02422

Habermas, Jürgen. *Moral Consciousness and Communicative Action*. Cambridge, MA: MIT Press, 1990.

Hahl-Koch, Jelena, ed. *Arnold Schoenberg/Wassily Kandinsky: Letters, Pictures and Documents*. New York: Faber, 1984.

Hartsock, Nancy. "The Feminist Standpoint: Developing the Ground for a Specifically Feminist Historical Materialism." In *The Feminist Standpoint Theory Reader: Intellectual and Political Controversies*, edited by Sandra Harding, 35–54. New York: Routledge, 2004.

Haskell, Lori, and Melanie Randall. "How Trauma Affects Memory and Recall." In *The Impact of Trauma on Adult Sexual Assault Victims*. Submitted to Research and Statistics Division, Justice Canada (2019). https://www.justice.gc.ca/eng/rp-pr/jr/trauma/p4.html

Head, Matthew. *Orientalism, Masquerade and Mozart's Turkish Music*. London: Royal Musical Association, 2000.

Hepokoski, James. "Operatic Stagings: Positions and Paradoxes: A Reply to David J. Levin." In *Verdi 2001: Proceedings of the International Conference, Parma, New York, New Haven*, edited by Fabrizio Della Seta, Roberta Montemorra Marvin, Marco Marica, 2: 477–84. Florence: L.S. Olschki, 2003.

Herman, Judith. *Trauma and Recovery: The Aftermath of Violence—From Domestic Abuse to Political Terror*. New York: Basic Books, 1997. Originally published 1992.

Herman, Judith, and Lisa Hirschman. "Father-Daughter Incest." *Signs* 2, no. 4 (Summer 1977): 735–56.

Higgins, Lynn A., and Brenda R. Silver, eds. *Rape and Representation*. New York: Columbia University Press, 1991.

Hisama, Ellie. "John Zorn and the Postmodern Condition." In *Locating East Asia in Western Art Music*, edited by Yayoi Uno Everett and Frederick Lau, 72–84. Middletown, CT: Wesleyan University Press, 2004.

Hoffmann, E. T. A. "Don Juan: A Fabulous Incident which Befell a Travelling Enthusiast." In *E. T. A. Hoffmann and Music*, edited and translated by R. Murray Schafer, 63–73. Toronto: University of Toronto Press, 1975.

hooks, bell. "The Oppositional Gaze: Black Female Spectators." In *Black Looks: Race and Representation*, 115–32. New York: Routledge, 2015. Originally published 1992.

Howe, Elizabeth. *The First English Actresses: Women and Drama 1660–1700*. Cambridge: Cambridge University Press, 1992.

Hudson, Elizabeth. "Gilda Seduced: A Tale Untold." *Cambridge Opera Journal* 4, no. 3 (1992): 229–51. http://www.jstor.org/stable/823693

Hughes, Donna M. *The Demand for Victims of Sex Trafficking*. Kingston: University of Rhode Island, 2005.

Humphreys, Terry. "Perceptions of Sexual Consent: The Impact of Relationship History and Gender." *Journal of Sex Research* 44, no. 4 (2007): 307–15. https://doi.org/10.1080/00224490701586706

Hunter, Mary. "Some Representations of *Opera Seria* in *Opera Buffa*." *Cambridge Opera Journal* 3, no. 2 (1991): 89–108. https://doi.org/10.1017/S0954586700003426

Hutcheon, Linda, and Michael Hutcheon. "Adaptation and Opera." In *The Oxford Handbook of Adaptation Studies*, edited by Thomas Leitch, 305–23. Oxford: Oxford University Press, 2017.

Hutcheon, Linda, and Michael Hutcheon. "'Here's Lookin' at You, Kid:' The Empowering Gaze in 'Salome.'" *Profession* (1998): 11–22. https://www.jstor.org/stable/25595633

Hutcheon, Linda, and Michael Hutcheon. "Opera: Forever and Always Multimodal." In *New Perspectives on Narrative and Multimodality*, edited by Ruth Page, 65–77. London: Routledge, 2009.

Imre, Anikó. "Hungarian Poetic Nationalism or National Pornography? Eastern Europe and Feminism—With a Difference." In *Violence and the Body: Race, Gender, and the State*, edited by Arturo J. Aldama, 39–58. Bloomington: Indiana University Press, 2003.

Jean-Charles, Régine Michelle. *Conflict Bodies: The Politics of Rape Representation in the Francophone Imaginary*. Columbus: Ohio State University Press, 2014.

Jeffreys, Sheila. *The Idea of Prostitution*. Melbourne: Spinifex, 1997.

Johnson, James H. "Antisemitism and Music in Nineteenth-Century France." *Musica Judaica* 5, no. 1 (1982–83): 79–96. https://www.jstor.org/stable/23687595

Joncus, Berta. "'Ich bin eine Engländerin, zur Freyheit geboren': Blonde and the Enlightened Female in Mozart's *Die Entführung aus dem Serail*." *Opera Quarterly* 26, no. 4 (2010): 552–87. https://doi.org/10.1093/oq/kbq050

Jozkowski, Kristen N., Zoë D. Peterson, Stephanie A. Sanders, Barbara Dennis, and Michael Reece. "Gender Difference in Heterosexual College Students' Conceptualizations and Indicators of Sexual Consent: Implications for Contemporary Sexual Assault Prevention Education." *Journal of Sex Research* 51, no. 8 (2014): 909–10, 913. https://doi.org/10.1080/00224499.2013.792326

Kerman, Joseph. "Verdi and the Undoing of Women." *Cambridge Opera Journal* 18, no. 1 (2006): 21–31. https://doi.org/10.1017/S0954586706002072

Kessler, Ronald C., Sergio Aguilar-Gaxiola, Jordi Alonso, Corina Benjet, Evelyn J.

Bromet, Graça Cardoso, Louisa Degenhardt, et al. "Trauma and PTSD in the WHO World Mental Health Surveys." *European Journal of Psychotraumatology* 8, no. 5 (2017), section 3.3. https://doi.org/10.1080/20008198.2017.1353383

Kohlberg, Lawrence. "The Current Formulation of the Theory." In *Essays on Moral Development*, Vol. 2. San Francisco: Harper & Row, 1984.

Kolk, Bessel A. van der, and Jose Saporta. "The Biological Response to Psychic Trauma: Mechanisms and Treatment of Intrusion and Numbing." *Anxiety Research* 4 (1991): 199–212. https://doi.org/10.1080/08917779108248774

Kramer, Lawrence. "One Coughs, the Other Dances: Freud, Strauss, and the Perversity of Modern Life." *Muzikološki Zbornik* 45, no. 2 (2009): 33–44. https://doi.org/10.4312/mz.45.2.33-44

Kramer, Lawrence. *Opera and Modern Culture: Wagner and Strauss*. Berkeley: University of California Press, 2004.

Kühnel, Jürgen. "Regietheater. Konzeption und Praxis am Beispiel Mozarts. Versuch einter Typologie." In *Regietheater. Konzeption und Praxis am Beispiel der Bühnenwerke Mozarts*, essays from the Salzburg Symposion 2005 by Jürgen Kühnel, Ulrich Müller, and Oswald Panagl, 13–30. Salzburg: Verlag Mueller-Speiser, 2007.

Langton, Rae. *Sexual Solipsism: Philosophical Essays on Pornography and Objectification*. Oxford: Oxford University Press, 2009.

LeBeau, Marc, and Ashraf Mozayani. *Drug-Facilitated Sexual Assault: A Forensic Handbook*. London: Academic Press, 2001.

Le Bon, Gustave. *The Crowd: A Study of the Popular Mind*. London: Routledge, 1995. Originally published in French 1895.

Levin, David. "Operatic School for Scandal." In *Operatic Migrations: Transforming Works and Crossing Boundaries*, edited by Roberta Montemorra Marvin and Downing A. Thomas, 241–52. Burlington: Ashgate, 2006.

Levin, David. *Unsettling Opera: Staging Mozart, Verdi, Wagner, and Zemlinsky*. Chicago: University of Chicago Press, 2007.

Locke, Ralph P. "Constructing the Oriental 'Other': Saint-Saëns's 'Samson et Dalila.'" *Cambridge Opera Journal* 3, no. 3 (1991): 261–302. http://www.jstor.org/stable/823619

Locke, Ralph P. "What Are These Women Doing in Opera?" In *En travesti: Women, Gender Subversion, Opera*, edited by Corinne E. Blackmer and Patricia Juliana Smith, 59–98. New York: Columbia University Press, 1995.

MacKinnon, Catharine A. "Rape: On Coercion and Consent." In *Applications of Feminist Legal Theory*, edited by D. Kelly Weisberg, 471–83. Philadelphia: Temple University Press, 1996.

MacKinnon, Catharine A. *Toward a Feminist Theory of the State*. Cambridge, MA: Harvard University Press, 1989.

Manne, Kate. *Down Girl: The Logic of Misogyny*. New York: Oxford University Press, 2018.

McClary, Susan. *Feminine Endings: Music, Gender, and Sexuality*. Minneapolis: University of Minnesota Press, 1991.

McClary, Susan. *The Passions of Peter Sellars: Staging the Music*. Ann Arbor: University of Michigan Press, 2019.

Millett, Kate. *Sexual Politics*. Garden City, NY: Doubleday, 1970.

Mozart, W. A. *Il dissoluto punito ossia il Don Giovanni, Dramma giocoso in zwei Akten*. Libretto by Lorenzo Da Ponte. Vocal Score. Kassel: Bärenreiter, 2005.

Mozart, W. A. *Die Entführung aus dem Serail*. Libretto by Gottlieb Stephanie. Vocal Score. Kassel: Bärenreiter, 1996.

Neidig, Peter H., Harold E. Russell, and Albert F. Seng. "Interspousal Aggression in Law Enforcement Families: A Preliminary Investigation." *Police Studies* 15, no. 1 (1991): 30–38.

Nevitt, Lucy. *Theatre & Violence*. New York: Palgrave Macmillan, 2013.

Norton, Russell, and Tim Grant. "Rape Myth in True and False Rape Allegations." *Psychology, Crime & Law* 14, no. 4 (2008): 275–85. https://doi.org/10.1080/106 83160701770286

Nussbaum, Martha C. "Objectification," *Philosophy & Public Affairs* 24, no. 4 (1995): 249–91. https://www.jstor.org/stable/2961930

O'Callaghan, Erin, Veronica Shepp, Sarah E. Ullman, and Anne Kirkner. "Navigating Sex and Sexuality after Sexual Assault: A Qualitative Study of Survivors and Informal Support Providers," *Journal of Sex Research* 56, no. 8 (2019): 1045–57. https://doi.org/10.1080/00224499.2018.1506731

Parker, Roger. "Reading the *livrets*, or the Chimera of 'Authentic' Staging." In *Leonora's Last Act: Essays in Verdian Discourse*, 126–48. Princeton: Princeton University Press, 2014.

Parker, Roger. *Remaking the Song: Operatic Visions and Revisions from Handel to Berio*. Berkeley: University of California Press, 2006.

Paulson, Steve. "Critical Intimacy: An Interview with Gayatri Chakravorty Spivak." *LA Review of Books*, July 29, 2016, https://lareviewofbooks.org/article/criti cal-intimacy-interview-gayatri-chakravorty-spivak

Penner, Nina. *Storytelling in Opera and Musical Theater*. Bloomington: University of Indiana Press, 2020.

Pollock, Griselda. *Vision and Difference: Femininity, Feminism, and the Histories of Art*. New York: Routledge, 1988.

Prigerson, Holly G., Paul K. Maciejewski, and Robert A. Rosenheck. "Population Attributable Fractions of Psychiatric Disorders and Behavioral Outcomes Associated with Combat Exposure Among US Men." *American Journal of Public Health* 92, no. 1 (2002): 59–63.

Puccini, Giacomo. *Turandot*. Libretto by Giuseppe Adami and Renato Simoni. Full score. Milan: Ricordi, 1977.

Puffett, Derrick, ed. *Richard Strauss: Salome*. Cambridge: Cambridge University Press, 1989.

Puka, Bill. "The Liberation of Caring; A Different Voice for Gilligan's 'Different Voice.'" *Hypatia* 55, no. 1 (1990): 59. https://doi.org/10.1111/j.1527-2001.1990 .tb00390.x

Pundik, Amit. "Coercion and Deception in Sexual Relations." *Canadian Journal of*

Law and Jurisprudence 28, no. 1 (2015): 97–127. https://doi.org/10.1017/cjlj.2015.19

Raymond, Janice G. "Ten Reasons for *Not* Legalizing Prostitution and a Legal Response to the Demand for Prostitution." *Journal of Trauma Practice* 2, no. 3–4 (2004): 315–32.

Risi, Clemens. *Oper in Performance: Analysen zur Aufführungsdimension von Operninszenierungen*. Berlin: Theater der Zeit, 2017.

Robinson, Dylan. "Decolonial Regietheater." Paper presented on the panel "On 'Music Colonialism': Intersectional and Interdisciplinary Methodologies in New Critical Studies of Western Art Musics" at the Joint Annual Meeting of the American Musicological Society, the Society for Ethnomusicology, and the Society for Music Theory, New Orleans, LA, November 11, 2022.

Robinson, Dylan. *Hungry Listening: Resonant Theory for Indigenous Sound Studies*. Minneapolis: University of Minnesota Press, 2020.

Robinson, Paul. "It's Not Over Until the Soprano Dies." *New York Times Book Review*, January 1, 1989. https://www.nytimes.com/1989/01/01/books/it-s-not-over-until-the-soprano-dies.html

Rossini, Gioacchino. *Guillaume Tell*. Libretto by Étienne de Jouy and Hippolyte Bis. London: Boosey & Co., n.d.

Rubenfeld, Jed. "The Riddle of Rape-by-Deception and the Myth of Sexual Autonomy." *Yale Law Journal* 122, no. 6 (2012–2013): 1372–669. http://hdl.handle.net/20.500.13051/4879

Said, Edward. *Covering Islam: How the Media and the Experts Determine How We See the Rest of the World*. New York: Vintage, 1997. Originally published 1981.

Saunders, Candida L. "The Truth, the Half-Truth, and Nothing Like the Truth: Reconceptualizing False Allegations of Rape." *British Journal of Criminology* 52, no. 6 (2012): 1152–71. https://doi.org/10.1093/bjc/azs036

Schiller, Friedrich. *Wilhelm Tell*. Translated by William F. Mainland. Chicago: University of Chicago Press, 1972. Originally published in German 1804.

Schmidgall, Gary. "Richard Strauss: Salome." In *Literature as Opera*, 247–86. New York: Oxford University Press, 1977.

Schneider, Magnus Tessing. *The Original Portrayal of Mozart's Don Giovanni*. London: Routledge, 2022.

Schroeder, Patricia R. *The Feminist Possibilities of Dramatic Realism*. Madison, NJ: Fairleigh Dickinson University Press, 1996.

Showalter, Elaine. "The Veiled Woman." In *Sexual Anarchy: Gender and Culture at the Fin de Siècle*, 144–68. New York: Viking, 1990.

Sielke, Sabine. *Reading Rape: The Rhetoric of Sexual Violence in American Literature and Culture, 1790–1990*. Princeton: Princeton University Press, 2002.

Simonson, Mary. "Choreographing Salome: Re-creating the Female Body." In *Body Knowledge: Performance, Intermediality, and American Entertainment at the Turn of the Twentieth Century*, 27–47. New York: Oxford University Press, 2013.

Sina, Tonia, Siobhan Richardson, and Alicia Rodis. "Pillars of Safe Intimacy: Rehearsal and Performance Practice," Intimacy Directors International. *team-*

idi.org. https://docs.wixstatic.com/ugd/924101_1620d7333f6a4809a2765257e
750e255.pdf

Skjelsbæk, Inger. *The Political Psychology of War Rape: Studies from Bosnia and Herzegovina*. New York: Routledge, 2012.

Smart, Mary Ann, ed. *Siren Songs*. Princeton: Princeton University Press, 2014.

Solga, Kim. *Violence Against Women in Early Modern Performance: Invisible Acts*.
Basingstoke: Palgrave Macmillan, 2009.

Spivak, Gayatri Chakravorty. "Can the Subaltern Speak?" In *Marxism and the
Interpretation of Culture*, edited by Cary Nelson and Lawrence Grossberg, 271–
316. Urbana: University of Illinois Press, 1988.

Spivak, Gayatri Chakravorty. "The Rani of Sirmu." In *Europe and Its Others*, edited
by Francis Barker, 146–58. Colchester: University of Essex Press, 1985.

Stiglmayer, Alexandra, ed. *Mass Rape*. Lincoln: University of Nebraska Press, 1992.

Strauss, Richard. *Salome*. Libretto by Oscar Wilde, German translation by Hedwig
Lachmann. Full score. London: Boosey & Hawkes, 1943.

Taruskin, Richard. *Text and Act: Essays on Music and Performance*. Oxford: Oxford
University Press, 1995.

Temkin, Jennifer. "'And Always Keep A-Hold of Nurse, for Fear of Finding Something Worse': Challenging Rape Myths in the Courtroom." *New Criminal Law
Review* 13, no. 4 (2010): 710–34. https://doi.org/10.1525/nclr.2010.13.4.710

Thompson, James. "Towards an Aesthetics of Care." In *Performing Care: New Perspectives on Socially Engaged Performance*, edited by Amanda Stuart Fisher and
James Thompson, 36–48. Manchester: Manchester University Press, 2020.

Tronto, Joan. *Moral Boundaries: A Political Argument for an Ethic of Care*. New York:
Routledge, 1993.

Turvey, Brent E. *False Allegations: Investigative and Forensic Issues in Fraudulent
Reports of Crime*. London: Academic Press, 2018.

Unseld, Melanie. *"Man töte dieses Weib!": Weiblichkeit und Tod in der Musik der Jahrhundertwende*. Stuttgart: Metzler, 2001.

Verdi, Giuseppe. *Un ballo in maschera*. Libretto by Antonio Somma. Full score.
Mineloa, NY: Dover, 1996.

Verdi, Giuseppe. *La forza del destino*. Libretto by Francesco Maria Piave. Full score.
Mineola, NY: Dover, 1991.

Wilde, Oscar. *Salomé*. In *The Plays of Oscar Wilde*, 83–124. New York: Vintage Books,
1988.

Wolff, Larry. *The Singing Turk: Ottoman Power and Operatic Emotions on the European Stage from the Siege of Vienna to the Age of Napoleon*. Stanford: Stanford
University Press, 2016.

Wolkowitz, Carol. *Bodies at Work*. London: SAGE Publications, 2006.

Zurbriggen, Eileen L. "Rape, War, and the Socialization of Masculinity: Why Our
Refusal to Give Up Wars Ensures that Rape Cannot Be Eradicated." *Psychology
of Women Quarterly* 34, no. 4 (2010): 538–49. https://doi.org/10.1111/j.1471-64
02.2010.01603.x

Index

#MeToo movement, 3, 44, 46

Metropolitan Opera, 43; *Entführung* (2019), 80; Levine dismissed by, 3; *Salome* (1907 performance), 48

Metzger, Kay, 61, 74

Michael, Nadja, 59

Michieletto, Damiano, 8, 11, 15, 84, 116; changes to *Guillaume Tell* made by, 132–33, 139, 146; criticisms of, 131. *See also Guillaume Tell* (Rossini, Michieletto production)

The Mikado: Reclaimed (GenEnCo), 111

Millett, Kate, 163–64n72

Minaker, Clea, 69–70, 73, 164n77

misogyny, 154n1; criticism of by Bieito, 44–45, 83; excused by humanization, 105; #MeToo movement highlighting of, 3, 44, 46; neglected in *Turandot*, 141; in opera canon, 142–47; wartime rape and structures of, 116–17, 139–41; Western European pointed out by Mouawad, 105–6, 109; women said to be childlike, 59; women said to be irrational, 37–38; in written texts, 6, 101, 141

Moneka, Ahmed, 109

Mouawad, Wajdi, 14, 80, 101–14

Mozart, Wolfgang Amadeus: *Così fan tutte*, 87; and current ethical standards, 46; failure to produce commentary on, 81; musical and scenic correlation, 96–97, 106, 158n43; *Le nozze di Figaro*, 4, 87; opera seria style in comic operas, 24, 25, 38, 90; scatological humor in letters of, 84. *See also Don Giovanni* (Mozart); Die Entführung aus dem Serail

musical correlation with characters and staging, 70–71, 96–97, 106, 136, 158n43

Narraboth (*Salome*), 50, 54, 59

Neef, Alexander, 104

Negrin, Francisco, 62, 68

Nevitt, Lucy, 69, 71–72, 77

Norris, Rufus, *Don Giovanni* production, 17, 28–29, 32–34, 33, 38–39, 43

Le nozze di Figaro (Mozart), 4, 87

nudity, 5; in Bieito's *Entführung*, 81, 83–85, 92–94, 100; in Egoyan's *Salome*, 72, 75, 77; not made visible, 132–33, 135; reduction of, 139–40

objectification of women's bodies, 14; in *Entführung* productions, 83, 88, 101, 112; in *Salome* productions, 56, 72, 74; during wartime, 120, 136–37

Oedipus complex, 60

offstage: as location for rape, 4, 19–20, 32–36, 42–43, 56, 64, 68; as locus of pathology, 51–52

Opera, or the Undoing of Women (Clément), 8

opera buffa, 41, 156n17

opera canon, 2, 12, 15; as collection of problems, 142; cultural anxieties about, 116; male violence as norm in, 134; multiple problems with, 146–47; nonliteral stagings and estrangement effect, 128; wartime operas, 115–16, 132

opera industry: abuse and sexual violence in, 2–3, 145; whiteness of, 129–30, 143

operas, as texts, 6–7

opera seria style, 24, 25, 38, 90

Oper Frankfurt, 115–16, 123

Orientalism, 168n56; *alla turca* style, 79, 96, 143; East/West binary, 104–6, 110; Enlightenment thought as counter to, 79, 86, 88; linked with Salome, 70, 75, 164n73; monolithic other created by, 110; and reparation, 109–11; in score of Dance of the Seven Veils, 75, 7076; and whitewashing, 81, 98–99, 143; in Wilde's *Salomé*, 48. *See also* Islam

Osmin (*Die Entführung aus dem Serail*), 79, 82, 87; as gangster in Bieito production, 81–82, 99; Mozart's musical